OXFORD WORLD'S CLASSICS

THE OXFORD SHAKESPEARE

General Editor · Stanley Wells

The Oxford Shakespeare offers new and authoritative editions of Shakespeare's plays in which the early printings have been scrupulously re-examined and interpreted. An introductory essay provides all relevant background information together with an appraisal of critical views and of the play's effects in performance. The detailed commentaries pay particular attention to language and staging. Reprints of sources, music for songs, genealogical tables, maps, etc. are included where necessary; many of the volumes are illustrated, and all contain an index.

ARTHUR HUMPHREYS, the editor of *Julius Caesar* in the Oxford Shakespeare, is Emeritus Professor of English in the University of Leicester. He has also edited Parts One and Two of *Henry IV* and *Much Ado About Nothing* for the Arden Shakespeare and *Henry V* and *Henry VIII* for the New Penguin Shakespeare.

D0036479

THE OXFORD SHAKESPEARE

Currently available in paperback

The rest of the plays are forthcoming

OXFORD WORLD'S CLASSICS

WILLIAM SHAKESPEARE

Julius Caesar

Edited by
ARTHUR HUMPHREYS

OXFORD
UNIVERSITY PRESS

OXFORD
UNIVERSITY PRESS

Great Clarendon Street, Oxford OX2 6DP

Oxford University Press is a department of the University of Oxford.
It furthers the University's objective of excellence in research, scholarship,
and education by publishing worldwide in

Oxford New York

Athens Auckland Bangkok Bogotá Buenos Aires Cape Town
Chennai Dar es Salaam Delhi Florence Hong Kong Istanbul Karachi
Kolkata Kuala Lumpur Madrid Melbourne Mexico City Mumbai Nairobi
Paris São Paulo Shanghai Singapore Taipei Tokyo Toronto Warsaw

with associated companies in Berlin Ibadan

Oxford is a registered trade mark of Oxford University Press
in the UK and in certain other countries

Published in the United States
by Oxford University Press Inc., New York

First published by the Clarendon Press 1984
First published as a World's Classic paperback 1994
Reissued as an Oxford World's Classics paperback 1998
Reissued 2008

British Library Cataloguing in Publication Data

Data available

Library of Congress Cataloging in Publication Data

Shakespeare, William, 1564–1616.
Julius Caesar
(The Oxford Shakespeare) (Oxford paperbacks)
Bibliography: p.
Includes index.
1. Caesar, Julius—Drama. I. Humphreys, A. R. (Arthur
Raleigh), 1911– . II. Title. III. Series:
Shakespeare, William, 1564–1616. Works. 1982.
[PR2808.A2H87 1984] 822.3'3 83–19330

ISBN 978-0-19-953612-2

1

Printed in Great Britain by
Clays Ltd, St Ives plc

PREFACE

EDITING a Shakespeare play is like climbing a high peak solo, at altitudes where critical winds bite shrewdly. The climber is alone, but his goal would defeat him were he not amply aided by others. This edition has been worked out freshly and independently, yet inevitably, and gratefully, it owes much to precursors, particularly to the New Variorum by H. H. Furness, Jr., the New Cambridge by John Dover Wilson, and the new Arden by T. S. Dorsch, as it does also to the critics whose works the Notes and Commentary acknowledge, particularly Geoffrey Bullough's *Narrative and Dramatic Sources of Shakespeare*, volume 5 (1964) and, in the account of the play in performance, John Ripley's *'Julius Caesar' on Stage in England and America, 1599–1973* (Cambridge, 1980).

The help and encouragement afforded by the General Editor, Dr Stanley Wells, and his associates, particularly Mr Gary Taylor, Dr John Jowett, and Miss Christine Avern-Carr, has far surpassed any normal course of their duties. Their guidance has been searching, generous, and wholly constructive. They have scrutinized every detail of what I put before them, and shared with me the investigations which they have in progress. They have, moreover, been virtually research assistants in checking details with which, through long absences in the Near and Far East, I could not myself deal.

For guidance with illustrations, as for friendship and help over the years, I owe much to Dr Levi Fox of the Shakespeare Centre, Stratford-upon-Avon; his assistant, Miss Shirley Watkins, has been very helpful, as also have Dr Lois Potter of the University of Leicester and Professor Edwin Thumboo of the University of Singapore. My colleagues and friends at the University of the Bosphorus, Turkey, arranged my teaching programme there to give me every chance of furthering my work on the play, and my wife's interest and encouragement have throughout heartened me on the long ascent. My gratitude to them all is very deep. Were a dedication in order, it should go to Philip and Joyce Collins of the University of Leicester; since it is not, I wish at least to acknowledge how much their intelligence, vivacity, generosity, and warmth of friendship have meant to my wife and me in personal and academic life.

ARTHUR HUMPHREYS

CONTENTS

LIST OF ILLUSTRATIONS

INTRODUCTION

The Play's Date and Place in the Shakespeare Canon

IN the autumn of 1599 a Swiss doctor from Basle, Thomas Platter, saw what in all likelihood was *Julius Caesar* played by the Lord Chamberlain's Men at the newly-built Globe Theatre, finished in the late summer of that year and, as Dover Wilson observes in the New Cambridge edition of the play, conspicuous as its bright yellow thatch rose above the dark older roofs of Bankside.[1] In his travel notes Platter recorded (in German):

> On the 21st of September, after dinner, at about two o'clock, I went with my party across the water; in the straw-thatched house we saw the tragedy of the first Emperor Julius Caesar, very pleasingly performed, with approximately fifteen characters; at the end of the play they danced together admirably and exceedingly gracefully, according to their custom, two in each group dressed in men's and two in women's apparel.[2]

The play was one of the new theatre's first productions, perhaps composed for its opening. It was printed in the First Folio, 1623.

Contemporary references confirm 1599 as its date. *Henry V*'s fifth-act prologue, completed by the summer of that year, shows that Shakespeare was then investigating Plutarch's *Lives* (in Sir Thomas North's translation of 1579, or its 1595 reprint). The prologue's lines telling how

> the senators of th'antique Rome
> With the plebeians swarming at their heels,
> Go forth and fetch their conqu'ring Caesar in,

[1] Ernest Schanzer, in 'Thomas Platter's Observations on the Elizabethan Stage' (*N. & Q.*, 201 (1956), 465–7), suggests that what Platter saw might have been some other play, by the rival company the Admiral's Men, at their theatre The Rose (also thatched), but the pretty full dramatic records by Philip Henslowe for the company in 1599 mention no *Caesar* play.

[2] The German text, first printed in *Anglia*, 22 (1899), p. 456, is reprinted in E. K. Chambers's *The Elizabethan Stage* (4 vols., Oxford, 1923), ii. 364–5. The translation here given is by Ernest Schanzer (see note 1, above). Though *Julius Caesar* has about fifty distinguishable roles it can be played by a company of sixteen (Ringler, p. 121), and since actors normally appeared together when the play ended (W. J. Lawrence, *Pre-Restoration Stage Studies* (Cambridge, Mass., and Oxford, 1927), p. 49) Platter could have counted them. Platter's last sentence refers to the usual jig danced after the main play.

draw on Plutarch's observation that 'when Caesar was returned from ... Spain, all the chiefest nobility of the city rode many days' journey from Rome to meet him' (*Antonius*, p. 185).[1] Shakespeare's addition of the plebeians suggests that he was already devising *Julius Caesar*'s opening scene.[2] Moreover, echoes in *Julius Caesar* of works recorded during 1599 in the registers of the Stationers' Company seem clear. Sir John Davies's *Nosce Teipsum*, registered on 14 April, probably suggested Cassius' lines on how the eye sees other things but not itself (1.2.51–8; see the Commentary); the idea was semi-proverbial but it is so elaborated in the play that indebtedness seems likely. Samuel Daniel's *Musophilus*, registered as *Poetical Essays* on 9 January and published the same year, may well lie behind Cassius' prophecy that 'many ages hence' Caesar's assassination will be enacted 'In states unborn and accents yet unknown' (see the Commentary to 3.1.111–16). The anonymous *A Warning for Fair Women*, printed in 1599, includes lines about wounds like accusing mouths from which bloody tongues will speak,[3] and these find parallels in *Julius Caesar* (3.1.259–61, 3.2.218–22); but the simile was not uncommon and its occurrence in both plays may be mere coincidence.

That *Julius Caesar* was not extant before 1599 is suggested by its absence from *Palladis Tamia*, Francis Meres's list of notable works, registered on 7 September 1598 and sufficiently up-to-date to include Everard Guilpin's *Skialethia*, registered on 15 September. Meres names six comedies and six tragedies (four of them, in fact, histories) to prove Shakespeare 'the most excellent in both kinds for the stage', and one would expect so noteworthy a work as *Julius Caesar* to be included had it already appeared. 1599, then, seems the earliest likely date for its completion.

[1] References to Plutarch, except where otherwise attributed, are to T. J. B. Spencer's selection, in modernized spelling, from North's translation: *Shakespeare's Plutarch* (Harmondsworth, 1964).

[2] In *Henry V*, too, Fluellen draws a (comical) 'parallel lives' comparison between the King and Alexander the Great (4.7.12–48); possibly Shakespeare was parodying Plutarch's convention.

[3] *A Warning for Fair Women*, ed. Charles D. Cannon (The Hague, 1975), ll. 1995–8: 'I gave him fifteen wounds, | Which now be fifteen mouths that do accuse me; | In ev'ry wound there is a bloody tongue, | Which will all speak.' In his article '*Musophilus, Nosce Teipsum*, and *Julius Caesar*' (*N. & Q.*, forthcoming), Gary Taylor suggests other possible echoes from Daniel and Davies; none seems individually clear enough to carry conviction, yet the concurrence of several loose resemblances suggests – as must surely have been the case – that many traces of his current reading lodged themselves subconsciously in Shakespeare's mind.

Since allusions to it sprang up without delay, 1599 is also the latest likely date.[1] Jonson's *Every Man Out Of His Humour*, registered on 8 April 1600, jests that 'reason long since is fled to animals, you know' (3.4.28–9), a clear take-off of 'O judgement, thou art fled to brutish beasts, | And men have lost their reason' (*Julius Caesar* 3.2.104–5), as also is 'Then reason's fled to animals, I see' of the anonymous *The Wisdom of Doctor Dodypoll*, registered on 7 October 1600 (Malone Society reprint, 1965, line 907). '*Et tu, Brute*' (*Julius Caesar* 3.1.77) occurs, humorously, in *Every Man Out Of His Humour* (5.6.70) and again in Samuel Nicholson's *Acolastus His Afterwit*, 1600 (sig. E3ʳ, line 7) – though there the whole line ('Et tu, Brute, wilt thou stab Caesar too?') is verbatim from *The True Tragedy of Richard Duke of York* (1595), the 'bad quarto' version of *3 Henry VI* (in the First Folio *3 Henry VI* the line does not occur). The phrase, the origins of which are discussed below (pp. 24–5), was seemingly a stage tag, but Jonson and Nicholson presumably brought it in because of its impressive effect in *Julius Caesar*.

A notable contemporary allusion, in John Weever's *The Mirror of Martyrs*, consists of the lines in stanza 4:

> The many-headed multitude were drawn
> By Brutus' speech, that Caesar was ambitious.
> When eloquent Mark Antony had shown
> His virtues, who but Brutus then was vicious?

Printed in 1601, *The Mirror*, according to its dedication, had been 'some two years ago ... made fit for the print', but it contains echoes of Edward Fairfax's *Godfrey of Bulloigne* of 1600, so either Weever saw that work in manuscript or he was still writing his poem after 1599; his allusion does not precisely clarify *Julius Caesar*'s date. But that around the turn of the century the play was widely noted is evident, and this at a time, two decades before it was published, when it could be known only from stage performance or (less probably) from access to a manuscript. Jonson's *Cynthia's Revels* (acted in 1600) and Drayton's *The Barons' Wars* (revised in 1602 from the *Mortimeriados* of 1596 and printed in 1603) have

---

[1] The most piquant allusion is Shakespeare's own. In *Hamlet*, written a year or two after *Julius Caesar*, Polonius discloses that he has been a university actor – 'I did enact Julius Caesar; I was killed i'th' Capitol; Brutus killed me' (3.2.100–1). Shakespeare amusedly reminds his audience of his own play.

what seem clear echoes of Antony's eulogy over the dead Brutus:
these are pointed out in the Commentary to 5.5.74–6.

Two other allusions call for a word. The first consists of lines by
Leonard Digges prefixed to the 1623 Folio, 'To the Memory of the
Deceased Author Master W. Shakespeare', lines which among
more general praises commend *Romeo and Juliet* and *Julius Caesar*.
Digges avers that he will not believe Shakespeare dead until some
other author surpasses the passion of the two lovers,

> Or till I hear a scene more nobly take
> Than when thy half-sword parleying Romans spake.

That the great scene of the quarrel between Brutus and Cassius
was in his mind is clear from his later verses, prefixed to the 1640
edition of Shakespeare's poems and probably written for the 1632
Second Folio but held over because they denigrated Ben Jonson,
alive until 1637:

> So have I seen, when Caesar would appear,
> And on the stage at half-sword parley were
> Brutus and Cassius: oh, how the audience
> Were ravished, with what wonder they went thence,
> When some new day they would not brook a line
> Of tedious though well-laboured *Catiline*:
> *Sejanus* too was irksome . . .

The fame of this scene is further illustrated in the discussion of the
play's stage history (p. 49); it captivated its audiences from the
first.

The other most striking early allusion is by Ben Jonson himself.
Timber; or Discoveries upon Men and Matter (published 1640) contains jottings made between 1623 and his death in 1637.[1] In it he
penned his famous praise of Shakespeare ('I loved the man, and do
honour his memory (on this side idolatry) as much as any') and
then, reflecting on his friend's facility, he mocked – it would seem
– a solecism in *Julius Caesar* (3.1.47–8): 'Many times he fell into
those things, could not escape laughter: as when he said in the
person of *Caesar*, one speaking to him; *Caesar, thou dost me wrong.*
He replied: *Caesar did never wrong, but with just cause* and such like:
which were ridiculous.' Then Jonson redressed his stricture with

---

[1] Chambers, ii. 210. For full references for works cited repeatedly in the Commentary and Introduction, see pp. 87–91.

4

judicious praise: 'But he redeemed his vices with his virtues. There was ever more in him to be praised than to be pardoned.' The same jibe occurs, however, in the Induction (ll. 35–7) to *The Staple of News* (1626): Gossip Expectation says that she can prompt her mates to expect surpassing things of the play '*if I have cause*'. The Prologue replies, '*Cry you mercy*, you never did wrong but with just cause', the italic type giving way to roman to make clear that this is quotation.

Since the existing text contains neither 'Caesar, thou dost me wrong' nor the alleged solecism, what may have happened has been much discussed and is considered below (p. 82). Jonson was known for a good verbal memory and was unlikely so long to relish a mere figment of his imagination. What is teasing is not that Shakespeare may have written a questionable phrase but that as late as 1626, twenty-seven years after *Julius Caesar* first saw the stage, and three years after it first was printed in the 1623 Folio, the audience at *The Staple of News* was apparently expected, unprompted, to rise to the joke.

As for the play's place in Shakespeare's canon, he had already tried one Roman subject in the Senecan *Titus Andronicus* (printed in 1594). Though high notions of Roman role-playing are common to both, this is worlds away from the spirit of *Julius Caesar*, and far closer to the standard Renaissance view that Rome's story was spasmodic and violent than is its successor's portrayal of noble contestants moved, in general, by high public spirit and expressing themselves with distinction.[1] Shakespeare's sense of Roman history had considerably altered under the influence of Plutarch, who in his great sequence of *Parallel Lives* deals less with the turbulence of Rome's history than with the greatness of her great men; the title that North (following Amyot's *Les Vies des Hommes Illustres Grecs et Romains*) gave to his translation was *The Lives of the Noble Grecians and Romans* (1579). In other plays of the 1590s Shakespeare repeatedly celebrated Caesar's greatness – which indeed was axiomatic – though his references to Brutus (whom Plutarch presents most admiringly) had been censorious, drawn from non-Plutarchan traditions. In *1 Henry VI*, Caesar's soul is the only one in history outshone by the 'far more glorious star' of Henry V (1.1.55–6); in *2 Henry VI*, Suffolk proclaims that 'Great men oft die

---

[1] Spencer, p. 32.

by vile bezonians: | . . . Brutus' bastard hand | Stabbed Julius Caesar' (4.1.134–7; 'bastard' hints at the story, unmentioned in *Julius Caesar*, that Caesar had in fact fathered him); in *3 Henry VI* Queen Margaret compares the slaying of her son Prince Edward at Tewkesbury with the foulest precedent she can call to mind, Caesar's murder (5.5.52–5); in *Richard III* young Prince Edward hails Caesar's immortal fame (3.1.84–8); in *2 Henry IV* the rumoured victory of Hotspur is received by his friends as un- paralleled 'Since Caesar's fortunes' (1.1.20–3). But that Caesar's greatness might become grandiose Shakespeare recognized too, parodying the famous '*Veni, vidi, vici*' with Armado's bombast in *Love's Labour's Lost* (4.1.68 ff.), and having Falstaff, as he captures Colevile in *2 Henry IV*, echo it as from 'the hook-nosed fellow of Rome' (4.3.40–1), Rosalind in *As You Like It* mock 'Caesar's thrasonical brag' (5.2.29–30), and, later, the Queen in *Cymbeline* likewise scoff at 'his brag' (3.1.22–4).

These two facets of the great man suggest, though only semin- ally, the dilemma: does Caesar present real greatness or only the pose of greatness? That, taking all in all, Shakespeare held the former view is suggested in the immediately following tragedy, *Hamlet*: there, recalling the prodigies before Caesar's death, Horatio signals the days before 'the mightiest Julius fell' as 'the most high and palmy state of Rome' (1.1.113–14). Brutus and his allies struck down the greatest figure of the Roman world – indeed, it seemed, of all secular history. Yet so persuasive is Plutarch's influence that Brutus, with whatever imperfections on his head, emerges from the play as movingly virtuous, and his confederates, though less admirable, still as men of notable distinction.

Julius Caesar is a crucial play in various ways. As Granville- Barker observed, the problem of the virtuous murderer is peculiarly taxing; 'Brutus best interprets the play's theme: Do evil that good may come, and see what does come!'[1] *Julius Caesar* points towards the dilemmas, the 'purposes mistook, | Fall'n on th'inventors' heads', of *Hamlet*, indeed of *Othello*. It offers the poignant spectacle of a good man creating tragic harm – 'a new path opened out for the development of the tragic art'.[2] It is the first of Shakespeare's tragedies in which moral bewilderments become fundamentally important (though some of the English histories – notably the three

[1] Granville-Barker, ii. 351.
[2] W. Warde Fowler, *Roman Essays and Interpretations* (Oxford, 1920), p. 279.

parts of *Henry VI, Richard II*, and the two parts of *Henry IV* – had dealt movingly with these in the context of rule). Moreover, though the English histories had been shaded by the ironies of history, and *Romeo and Juliet* by the ironies of fate, a more complex sense develops in *Julius Caesar* of how consequences defeat intentions. Here 'The two elements which Aristotle thought necessary for the profoundest tragedy, *peripeteia* and *anagnorisis*, the ironic turn of events which makes an action have the very opposite effect of that intended, and the realization of this by the agent, are thus seen to be fundamental.'[1] With this deepened awareness of the human predicament the play points towards the profound questionings of the tragedies which follow.

Yet along with the later Roman plays, *Antony and Cleopatra* and *Coriolanus*, it belongs to the Hegelian category of tragedy, balancing conflicting goods rather than contrasting good and evil. It has evident interminglings of virtues and vices but not those metaphysical oppositions which, in *Hamlet, Othello, Macbeth*, and *King Lear*, suggest so deep a religious – even if an agnostic – dimension. It has even been argued that *Julius Caesar* is less a tragedy in the full sense than, following on the English histories, a dramatized chronicle grounded not in individual afflictions but in the fate of a society.[2] Such a contention, though, goes too far. The play does very much concern itself with individual afflictions, with the mysteries of individual self-direction leading to fatality; so it is indeed tragic. Yet, like its Roman successors, it is so in a special way, as 'a play of overt challenge and debate linked to clear action, whose dilemmas are set out with Roman clarity, Roman simplicity'.[3] Appropriately to a subject disciplined by Roman decorum, its characters, if not always masters of their fates, try at least to be masters of their roles and attitudes. (These themes, and those mentioned in the following sentences, are developed in the sections below on 'Roman Values' and 'Politics and Morality'.) They have codes of resolution to live up to and these preserve them from the fundamental tragic sense of chaos. They move in the secular world of social and political relationships and within that world we lean this way and that alternately in our attitudes to them, assessing,

[1] Schanzer, p. 56.
[2] H. B. Charlton, *Shakespearian Tragedy* (Cambridge, 1948), p. 70.
[3] M. C. Bradbrook, *Shakespeare the Craftsman* (New York and London, 1969), p. 101.

as befits 'overt challenge and debate', whether this action or that is commendable or not. The pendulum of sympathy swings disconcertingly, and even with so seemingly clear-headed a play the inclination to include it among Shakespeare's 'problem plays' is understandable, though it is by no means as problematical as, say, *Hamlet* or *Troilus and Cressida* or *Measure for Measure*. The fact is simply that, as Dover Wilson observed of *Richard II*, Shakespeare 'develops the political issue in all its complexity, and leaves judgment upon it to the spectator' (New Cambridge edition, p. xxxv), or, as Coleridge observed of *Coriolanus*, it 'illustrates the wonderful philosophic impartiality of Shakespeare's politics'. Hence the varied views held about Caesar, Brutus, Cassius, and Antony. Attitudes to each fluctuate in a humanly moving alternation.

Tuning his play to Plutarch's key of noble intentions undercut by human failings, Shakespeare produces a drama of human nature poignantly balanced in its gravity and considerate tenderness. In his canon it stands with a humane, searching thoughtfulness to end a decade filled with histories of England's turbulent story, with comedies of amiable follies and generous affections, and with tragedies of exciting fervour. If not painfully disturbing like *Othello* and *King Lear*, or charged with 'thoughts beyond the reaches of our souls' like *Hamlet* and *Macbeth*, yet in the deeply-felt and responsible realism with which Shakespeare commemorates high distinction it fittingly foreshadows the works immediately to follow.

Shakespeare's Sources and his Shaping of Them

Nearly all the significant components of the play derive from *The Lives of the Noble Grecians and Romans ... Translated out of Greek into French by James Amyot: and out of French into English by Thomas North* (1579; reprinted 1595). This, North's Plutarch, is a cumbrous volume, the reading of which, for a busy man of the theatre, 'was probably the most serious experience that Shakespeare had of the bookish kind'.[1] Shakespeare drew also on general traditions about Roman life and history, but Plutarch gave him almost all his specific material, along with the sense of Roman distinction – these are indeed 'noble' Romans. Plutarch wrote about 150 years after

[1] Spencer, p. 33.

Caesar's death: that lapse of time, and, more evidently, his leaning towards ethical analysis, led him away from the ruthlessness of politics towards the sense of human distinction.

What Plutarch offered (and, via Amyot, North spiritedly translated) was good narrative and biographies vividly set within their times, their subjects shrewdly analysed as to qualities and motives, and seen to be controlled by a shaping destiny – ideal material for drama even though each Life still needed much modelling and selection. Plutarch gave, it has been said,

> whatever seemed appropriate for explanation and interpretation of his hero. The little homely citations of mere gossip, the accounts of venturesome exploits stirring to the reader's imagination, the frequent parentheses, the constant bias towards ethical judgments, have their own integrity as parts of a method of portraiture which has delighted students of human motives, reasonings, and deeds.[1]

He perhaps drew from Greek drama his biographical form, his sense of great persons confidently self-directed yet vulnerable through their failings (even noble failings), and shadowed by the implicit ironies which observers aware of tragic outcomes can perceive.[2] The Lives of Julius Caesar, Marcus Brutus, and Marcus Antonius amply furnished the formidable story of Caesar's fall and its consequences, a story offering drastic reversals of fortune in the killing of the great leader and then in the retribution which Caesar's spirit, working through Mark Antony and the crisis of the Roman state, brought down upon his killers. In addition to these three Lives, Shakespeare would almost certainly scan that of Cicero; if so, he took little if anything from it.[3]

Already, basing his English histories on Holinshed's *Chronicles*, Shakespeare had shown with what creative modification he could select from long, miscellaneous compilations the components of gripping plots. Plutarch's narrative was much better shaped than Holinshed's, yet it too needed condensing. So, from the first three-quarters of the very full Life of Caesar, Shakespeare picked merely a few details and traits. The details include Caesar's forgiveness of Brutus (and others) for siding with Pompey, his opponents'

---

[1] M. H. Shackford, *Plutarch in Renaissance England* (Wellesley, Mass., 1929), p. 9.

[2] Thomson, p. 247.

[3] Cicero's is a very minor part in the play. The Commentary at 1.2.276 and 2.1.150–2 indicates possible points from Plutarch.

hesitancy until 'he was grown to be of great strength' and seemed to threaten 'destruction of the whole . . . commonwealth' (as Brutus ruminates at 2.1.10–34), his famous victory over the Nervii (3.2.167–70), and the facts of his infirmities (in particular epilepsy, the 'falling sickness') – infirmities which in Plutarch Caesar heroically ignores but which in the play the jaundiced Cassius treats as contemptible (1.2.119–28). The more general traits guiding Shakespeare are numerous – Caesar's powerful oratory, outstanding generalship, ambition, and popularity; the alarm he inspired in fellow-patricians; and Rome's critical condition, requiring 'the absolute state of a monarchy and sovereign lord' (*Caesar*, p. 50).

In the fourth quarter of *Caesar* these themes are renewed and the events are close to those of the play. Plutarch notes that though Romans disliked Caesar's triumph over Pompey's sons (who were fellow-Romans, not foreigners), yet many hoped that his rule would bring peace; also that though he sought only such honours as became a man, yet supporters and opponents alike lauded him as a demigod, the former obsequiously, the latter intending to discredit him. To former foes he was merciful, and he was unmoved by dangers; when advised to have a bodyguard, he replied that it is 'better to die once than always to be afraid of death' (*Caesar*, p. 78; compare 2.2.32–7). Ambition made him seek popularity; with this went a zest for achievement, as if he were his own rival, striving always to outgo himself. Yet thus he provoked his foes – 'the chiefest cause that made him mortally hated was the covetous desire he had to be called king; which first gave . . . his secret enemies honest colour, to bear him ill will' (*Caesar*, pp. 80–1).

The analysis below offers a consecutive discussion of Shakespeare's use and remodelling of Plutarch; the Commentary on the text cites the passages to which he was verbally indebted.

To begin, Shakespeare picks up two hints barely noticeable in Plutarch about the stripping of Caesar's images by the tribunes.[1]

---

[1] In *Caesar*, the sentence introducing the Lupercalia mentions Caesar's 'shame and reproach, abusing the Tribunes of the People' (p. 82), but this remains unexplained until, after the Lupercalia, we hear of the tribunes' stripping the images, and their consequent loss of their offices (pp. 83–4; similarly *Antonius*, p. 187). The incident is treated very cursorily in both *Lives* (*Brutus* does not mention it) and Shakespeare makes much more of it than Plutarch.

Making this event so prominent he focuses sympathy on Caesar's opponents, towards whom up to the assassination we are predominantly to lean. An impulsive populace, idolizing a leader whose 'growing feathers' threaten tyranny, is chidden by seemingly right-thinking men. Preluded by the tribunes' honest egalitarianism, Cassius and Brutus can develop their plot with (save for a few dubious touches) the right ethical tone.

Shakespeare then interweaves elements from *Caesar* and *Antonius*. Both accounts present Caesar in triumphal robes presiding over the Lupercalia, but *Antonius* treats the race as sport, *Caesar* as a fertility rite. Neither, however, mentions Calpurnia's presence or Caesar's concern for an heir; Shakespeare's additions bring Calpurnia forward and imply Caesar's dynastic hopes. In *Caesar* the soothsayer's warning about the Ides of March is mentioned, later than the Lupercalia, as uttered 'long time afore': in the play, transferred to Caesar's hour of triumph, it has an electrifying effect. (Neither *Brutus* nor *Antonius* records it at all.)

In *Antonius*, as in the play (1.2.261 ff.), Caesar offers his throat for cutting when the populace applauds his third refusal of the crown. In *Caesar* he does so on quite a different occasion, after offending the Senate by disdain; yet it is from *Caesar* that Casca draws his report that he blamed this extravagant gesture on his epilepsy (1.2.267–8). Many large pages in Plutarch separate these two versions, and Shakespeare must have leafed back and forth noting the details which combine in the vivid mosaic of the scene (the phrasing is too close to be merely memorial impression).

Into the Lupercalia and crown-offering he dovetails Cassius' incitements. Plutarch provided the bases for these – Brutus' high repute for republican virtue; his disturbed spirit; and his estrangement from Cassius. Shakespeare accepts the first unqualified but the others he modifies. Plutarch's Brutus is troubled by the conspiracy's risks, Shakespeare's by its ethics. In Plutarch the estrangement results from rivalry for the praetorship; in the play, such self-seeking would be unfitting, and it arises from Brutus' troubled spirit (1.2.36 ff.). A point in Plutarch (*Brutus*, p. 139) which Shakespeare very notably discards is that Cassius would 'jest too broadly'; the play's Cassius is austere, critical, and unconvivial (1.2.71–8).

Cassius' instigations, including the Tiber swimming (1.2.100 ff.), are mostly Shakespeare's inventions though, as mentioned, *Caesar* gave him Caesar's courageously borne illness in Spain which Cassius distorts into a sign of weakness. Common to Plutarch and play are appeals to Roman liberty, and Cassius' stress on the very name of 'Brutus' (*Brutus*, p. 112; 1.2.142–7). When Caesar re-enters (1.2.177) the play strikingly alters Plutarch, for it aims at Cassius alone (1.2.194–5) Caesar's suspicion of 'pale-visaged and carrion lean people' – which in Plutarch applies to both Cassius and Brutus (*Caesar*, p. 85; similarly *Antonius*, p. 186). More than once in Plutarch Caesar has his doubts about Brutus but these Shakespeare ignores, stressing rather the bonds between the two so that Brutus' moral dilemma and eventual treachery are the more disturbing.

The facts of the crown-offering (1.2.220 ff.) are Plutarchan, but Casca's comic-coarse realism is original. One of the play's notable features is the way it keeps us, at this stage, mainly on the con-spirators' side while yet hinting at the ambivalence in their case, through Brutus' rationalizations, Casca's derision, and the bias in Cassius, so evident when he soliloquizes on his machinations (1.2.305–19).

Plutarch relates 'strange and wonderful signs that were said to be seen before Caesar's death' (*Caesar*, p. 86) – celestial fires, ominous birds in the market-place at noon, men in flames, a slave with blazing hand, a sacrificial animal without a heart, the sooth-sayer's warning, and Calpurnia's dreams. As manifestations 'per-haps worth the noting' these are retailed with a rather casual and incidental air. Shakespeare adds others,[1] and he uses them all for dramatic excitement but also for distinction of character – Cicero is unmoved, Casca agitated, Cassius exultant and defiant, taking the 'dreadful night' as proving Caesar's alleged (yet unproven) violence.

Brutus' enigmatic soliloquy (2.1.10 ff.) has no Plutarchan precedent. In both source and play his trouble distresses him and Portia, but in Plutarch he broods not on ethical dilemmas but on the risks involving 'the noblest, valiantest, and most courageous men of Rome' (*Brutus*, p. 116). The change is significant: Shake-speare is exploring the self-divided nature which had shown itself in Richard II and Henry IV and was to develop in Hamlet and Macbeth – Macbeth himself might well speak the anguished lines

---

[1] For possible sources see p. 28.

on 'the acting of a dreadful thing' or on conspiracy too shameful to show its face even by night (2.1.63–9, 77–85).

Shakespeare takes from Plutarch the conspirators' lack of any binding oath, the exclusion of Cicero, and the decision to spare Antony. But to each point he gives a special bearing, since he makes Brutus always the deciding factor. In Plutarch the conspirators never think of taking an oath: in Shakespeare it is Brutus who dissuades them from doing so. Cicero is left out not as in Plutarch for his timidity but because Brutus decides he will not be subservient (a trait ironically Brutus' own). And in Plutarch Antony is spared not only because, as in Shakespeare, Brutus urges that his murder would be 'not honest' (*Brutus*, p. 124) and that the conspiracy should avoid 'all villainy' (*Antonius*, p. 188), but also because Brutus thinks him noble, brave, and sure to admire their republican zeal (*Brutus*, p. 125). Shakespeare retains Brutus' scrupulousness but makes him disparagingly and fatally underestimate Antony (2.1.166, 182–90).

With these lofty attitudes, prevalent yet not immaculate in Plutarch's Brutus, Shakespeare colours the whole role. Plutarch says nothing about Caesar's murder as sacrifice, and in his pages the event is a bloody mêlée. Shakespeare evolves from Brutus' idealism the terrible irony by which the murder, planned on such blameless principles, becomes the butchery which Antony execrates (5.1.40–5). Yet in the orchard scene we feel the spell of Brutus' noble intentions and prestige as strongly as do the conspirators for whom he is the guarantor of spotless virtue, and the devoted intimacy between him and Portia (closely derived from *Brutus*, pp. 117–19, 122–3) touches the heart.

Decius discloses that Caesar has become superstitious and vulnerable to flattery. These traits derive from Plutarch, though in his story it is Calpurnia who succumbs to superstition. What Plutarch does not give and Shakespeare does is the contrast between Caesar's demigod poses and human vacillations. Plutarch's Caesar feels natural alarm at threatening omens and auguries; Shakespeare's strikes indomitable poses and then unstrikes them. For his grand stances Shakespeare takes points from Plutarch: for instance he combines (2.2.32–7) Caesar's declarations that 'It was better to die once than always to be afraid of death' and that the best death is 'death unlooked for' (*Caesar*, pp. 78, 88). Such items, along with inventions of his own, he uses to create that autonomous pride which Caesar's waverings so notably offset – waverings in Plutarch of pardonable uncertainty, in Shakespeare of plain inconstancy. We may approve of them as showing concern for Calpurnia, yet Decius readily reverses them (2.2.83 ff.) so that, betrayed by flattery, ambition, and his pose of indomitability, Caesar goes deluded to his death. Yet at this point, invoking our sympathies, Shakespeare adds a moving touch or two: Caesar is genial with the foes he thinks his friends (2.2.108 ff.), and Artemidorus grieves that 'virtue cannot live | Out of the teeth of emulation' (2.3.12–13). The former humanizing touch has no precedent in Plutarch; in Shakespeare, the kindly greeting which the unwitting victim offers his trusted companions is extraordinarily poignant, as the status-ridden dictator unbends to his 'friends'.

As the plot moves towards the assassination and its immediate consequences there is an inexorable sense of tragic doom. The catastrophe is inevitable yet the tension through which it is reached is riveting. First, from auguries mentioned earlier in Plutarch, Shakespeare repeats the Ides-of-March theme heard in the play's second scene. By another significant touch, what prevents Caesar from reading Artemidorus' warning (3.1.3, 6–7) – in Plutarch the throng of suitors – becomes in Shakespeare the impressive 'What touches us ourself shall be last served', a gesture by which he commands our admiration even as he signs his own death warrant.

Thereafter the details of the murder come selectively from *Caesar* and *Brutus* (many are common to both). The alarm caused by Popilius Lena, with Cassius jumpy and Brutus unmoved (3.1.13 ff.), is from *Brutus* (pp. 122–3), as is Trebonius' diverting of Antony (in *Caesar* Decius does this). Yet Metellus Cimber pleading for his brother is from *Caesar* (in *Brutus* it is Tullius Cimber). The conspirators in the play kneel to Caesar with ritual formality, but Antony later accuses them of bowing like bondmen and kissing the man they are betraying (5.1.42–3) – this is from *Brutus* (p. 123). Antony's further thrust, however, that Casca, standing behind, struck Caesar in the neck, is from *Caesar* (p. 93), as also is the number of Caesar's wounds (twenty-three in *Caesar*, p. 95; by a slip thirty-three in the play, 5.1.53). But neither Life has the famous climactic '*Et tu, Brute*'; for comment on this see pages 24–5.

Antony refers repeatedly to the violence of the murder. This

150. *Iulius Cæsar Veneris beneficio in Cometam mutatur.*

1. Julius Caesar 'turned to a blazing starre' (Golding's Ovid, xv. 839), from an edition of Ovid's *Metamorphoses* first published in Antwerp in 1606.

probably reflects *Caesar*'s gruesome account, that the victim was 'hacked and mangled' and finally horribly stabbed by Brutus 'about his privities' (*Caesar*, p. 94), though the story in *Brutus* too is savage enough to make bitterly ironic Brutus' proposal for sacrifice, not butchery (2.1.167). In the play the murder becomes weirdly ritualistic as, to witness to libertarian ideals, forearms are bathed 'in Caesar's blood | Up to the elbows' – an unPlutarchan touch showing the plotters' obsessive wish to be violent according to rule and form.

It is from *Caesar* that Shakespeare takes Pompey's statue, fatefully presiding over his conqueror's death and running with blood (*Caesar*, p. 95; compare 3.1.115, 3.2.185–6). And indeed it is mainly *Caesar* that suggests the hand of destiny prevailing over the great contestants, a theme natural to world-shaking events which must surely have their supernatural correlative. So divine interventions are propounded, 'manifest proofs that it was the ordinance of some god' which caused Caesar to die beneath Pompey's statue, the image seeming to take 'just revenge' (*Caesar*, pp. 92, 95). But as Pompey ultimately prevailed over his destroyer, so likewise did Caesar – his influence 'did continue afterwards in the revenge of his death' (*Caesar*, p. 99). 'When beggars die there are no comets seen', as Calpurnia observes, 'The heavens themselves blaze forth the death of princes' (2.2.30–1). In *Caesar* a comet shines for seven nights after the murder, the sun is dark, harvests fail, and Cassius and Brutus are doomed, Cassius to slay himself with the sword with which he slew Caesar (*Caesar*, p. 99; 5.3.45–6),[1] Brutus to be haunted by an 'ill angel' or 'evil spirit' (*Caesar*, p. 100; *Brutus*, p. 149); the play's 'evil spirit' and 'Ill spirit' catch at both phrases (4.2.332, 338) and Shakespeare naturally takes it as Caesar's ghost (5.5.17–18). Over and above the details of history it is this Plutarchan sense of retributive destiny which gives the play its unity, Caesar's death being the keystone of the great arch which brings the conspirators up to their triumph and down to their doom. Plutarch already adumbrates this controlling idea.

Between the murder and the entrance of Antony's servant (3.1.121) the play draws vividly upon *Caesar* and *Brutus*. There is widespread panic (*Caesar*, p. 96; *Brutus*, p. 124); the conspirators wave bloodstained swords and proclaim liberty (*Caesar*, p. 96; *Brutus*, p. 125); Brutus tries to calm the Senate (*Brutus*, p. 125); and Antony and Lepidus hide (*Caesar*, p. 96; *Antonius*, p. 188). So, for the moment, the conspirators ride high.

Then comes the event which precipitates the countermovement. In Shakespeare, Antony's emergence is superbly dramatic. In Plutarch it is far less so; finding himself safe, Antony treats peaceably with the conspirators, sends his son as a pledge, and asks Cassius to supper, as Lepidus does Brutus. The Senate appoints the conspirators to governorships (*Caesar*, p. 97; *Brutus*, p. 127), a gesture which probably suggested in the play Cassius' offer that Antony shall share 'In the disposing of new dignities' (3.1.178). Brutus delivers a well-received oration to the Senate and a coolly-received one to the people, who soon turn restive (*Brutus*, pp. 125–6). Antony proposes Caesar's honourable burial and the open reading of his testament and over Cassius' opposition Brutus agrees (*Brutus*, p. 127). This concession Plutarch calls his second error, the first being the sparing of Antony.

[1] This last point is emphasized in *Caesar* by a side-note to the text. It is not mentioned in *Brutus* or *Antonius*.

Much of this Shakespeare takes over. He ignores the confusing manoeuvres which in Plutarch follow the murder, and instead he caps the conspirators' brief triumph with Antony's rise to dominance as soon as his servant has tested the ground. His Antony, 'a shrewd contriver' indeed, proves a strategic virtuoso, whose bold initiative perhaps originated in a hint in *Antonius* where (p. 188), praised for stabilizing Rome, and 'hoping . . . to make himself the chiefest man if he might overcome Brutus', he takes the lead with his funeral oration. Yet mainly here it is *Brutus* which gave Shakespeare what he needed.

His dramatic intensification is again remarkable. He stresses Cassius' wariness as against Brutus' confidence (3.1.138–46); this alerts us to danger. Then he makes the confrontation tense and strong: his Antony is not Plutarch's ambitious rival of Brutus but the deeply moved lover of dead Caesar manoeuvring in perilous straits and in apparent honesty (as Brutus thinks, though not Cassius) proposing a funeral oration. Shakespeare adjusts Plutarch so that Brutus' two orations (*Brutus*, pp. 125–6), which in Plutarch are quite unrelated to Antony's, become a single address pre-empting Antony's appeal; Plutarch's sequence of unplanned events becomes a drama of strategies.

After the conspirators have left, before the orations, Shakespeare inserts Antony's monologue to the 'bleeding piece of earth' which is all that physically remains of his friend (3.1.254–75). This is wholly Shakespearian save in that it makes ringingly clear the *Caesar* theme that the dead hero will dominate the action. Then, just before the orations, Antony recognizes Octavius as an ally (3.1.287–9). Shakespeare ignores Plutarch's account of initial enmity between them (*Brutus*, p. 132; *Antonius*, p. 191) though later he shows them at odds (5.1.16–20). No such diversionary concern must impede the two sides' polarization, and its development has to wait for *Antony and Cleopatra*.

So, immediately after the murder, the play reaches a stronger crisis than Plutarch's narrative, and Antony, hitherto barely noticeable, thrusts to the front. From the moment he enters he is so strongly modelled as to make absurd Brutus' notion that 'he can do no more than Caesar's arm | When Caesar's head is off' (2.1.183–4).

For the orations Plutarch gave only bare leads. In quite other connections he mentions Brutus' terse Spartan style and Antony's florid 'Asiatic' one. The former of these surely gave Shakespeare the cue for Brutus' noble economy; Antony's style in the play, eloquent but not florid, arises rather from the challenge of the occasion, on which, to quote Plutarch, 'he mingled his oration with lamentable words, and by amplifying of matters did greatly move their hearts and affections' (*Antonius*, pp. 188–9; similarly *Brutus*, p. 129).

Plutarch relates that Brutus, 'with the noblest men of the city', mounted the pulpit to respectful attention (*Brutus*, p. 126) but he says nothing of his speech's contents. Shakespeare fits the oration admirably to Brutus' intellectual-idealist nature and to what Plutarch calls his 'gravity and constant mind' (*Brutus*, p. 107). Though so soon eclipsed by Antony's it is deeply moving despite its control, moving not by extravagance but by conviction and devotion. Sometimes thought stiff and cold it in fact gains its hearers' hearts (though not their understandings – as the unwittingly ironic 'Let him be Caesar' indicates: 3.2.50). Shakespeare may have wondered how he could make Antony outdo it.

In Plutarch Antony proposes the honourable burial of Caesar and the public reading of his testament, but this reading is done by an unnamed speaker, and only when this has won the crowd over does Antony start his eulogy. Then, 'perceiving that his words moved the common people to compassion, he framed his eloquence to make their hearts yearn the more' (*Brutus*, p. 129), showing the gashed gown and body, and stirring up 'such a rage and mutiny there was no more order kept'. His hearers pluck up forms and tables, make a funeral pyre in 'the most holy places', fire the conspirators' houses, lynch the poet Cinna, and scare the conspirators into flight (*Caesar*, pp. 97–8; *Brutus*, p. 129; *Antonius*, pp. 188–9).

Shakespeare's rehandling is faithful yet creative. To maintain Brutus' honourable principles he transfers from Antony to him the proposal for Caesar's funeral rites (3.1.240–1), and whereas in Plutarch Antony seems to have no plan for shaping events until they shape themselves, in the play, with the great revenge monologue behind him (3.1.254 ff.), Antony is clearly determined to turn them his way. It is he who reads the testament. But instead of making this his opening bid he keeps it for his trump card; the crowd is not to be bought over, it is to be swayed by Caesar's heroic life and by grief at his loss. Shakespeare ingeniously rearranged Plutarch. For Antony's nostalgic 'That day he overcame the

Nervii' (the summer evening, Antony recalls, when Caesar first donned the mantle in which he lies dead), Shakespeare cast a long way back into Plutarch, picking out from a mass of detail a victory hailed as outstandingly memorable (*Caesar*, pp. 41–2). Antony's stress on Caesar's love for Brutus, so treacherously repaid, draws on scattered Plutarchan instances of affection. Straight from Plutarch are the glimpses of Caesar covering his face as Brutus prepares to stab, his fall beneath Pompey's bloody statue (*Caesar*, p. 95; 3.2.185–6), and the details of the testament (*Brutus*, p. 128). But though Plutarch provides the bases, the brilliant strategies by which in the play Antony wins against almost impossible odds, controlling each move until he reads the will to show 'how Caesar loved you', are the inventions of Shakespeare's dramatic imagination.

With the death of Cinna, both Plutarch and Shakespeare signal the onset of anarchic violence. Plutarch follows the murder with miscellaneous anecdotes: Shakespeare cuts right through to the ruthless triumvirs, to show the results of Brutus' idealism. Much he takes closely from Plutarch – Lepidus' consent to his brother's death (4.1.2–6; *Antonius*, p. 194), the division of the spoils (4.1.14; *Brutus*, p. 137; *Antonius*, p. 194), and the bills 'condemning two hundred of the noblest men of Rome to suffer death, and among that number Cicero was one' (4.2.223–8; *Brutus*, p. 137).[1] But he drops the nasty fact that, to avenge Cicero's death, Brutus kills Antony's brother Caius (*Brutus*, p. 137; *Antonius*, p. 196) – this would gravely blot the Brutus who, in general, is honoured as Plutarch honours him, 'for his virtue and valiantness . . . wellbeloved . . . hated of no man, not so much as of his enemies; because he . . . had ever an upright mind with him, and would never yield to any wrong or injustice' (*Brutus*, p. 139).

It is the more striking, then, that in the great quarrel scene Brutus becomes so self-righteous and inconsiderate, opposing a Cassius who, sorely tried and deeply hurt, earns our sympathy. The episode amalgamates three in Plutarch. In the first, Brutus at Smyrna asks Cassius for funds, having spent 'all that he could rap and rend of his side' (which sounds pretty ruthless): Cassius' men urge him not to hand over resources saved by thrift and 'levied with great evil will', just to let Brutus gain favour with his troops

---

[1] In Shakespeare the total is variously reported as one hundred or seventy (4.2.225–7).

– nevertheless he parts with one-third (*Brutus*, pp. 140–1). The second story, told later, relates how at Sardis Brutus and Cassius quarrelled privately over mutual grievances and how their followers dared not intervene until, 'with a certain bedlam and frantic motion', an eccentric former friend of Cato the Stoic burst in quoting a tag from Homer, whereupon Cassius laughed and Brutus angrily ejected him (*Brutus*, pp. 145–6). The third story occurs next day: as at 4.2.54–5 Brutus had 'condemn[ed] and noted Lucius Pella', whom the Sardians had accused of peculation, and Cassius protested that this was uncalled for at so ticklish a time; whereon Brutus 'answered that he should remember the Ides of March, at which time they slew Julius Caesar; who neither pilled nor polled the country, but only was a favourer ... of all them that did rob and spoil by his countenance and authority' (*Brutus*, p. 147).

So strikingly does Shakespeare combine these incidents that, as Johnson observed when he annotated the play, 'the contention and reconcilement of *Brutus* and *Cassius* is universally celebrated'. He begins with the third story (about Lucius Pella's corruption), follows this with the first (to explain the quarrel's cause, but he alters it – Brutus has not had the funds which in Plutarch Cassius sends), and lightens its end with the crazy philosopher. So doing, he sharply explores the two men's natures. Cassius is the realist we know – campaigns are not won spotlessly – but what shows up newly is his emotional vulnerability which redeems him from the conspiratorial rigour he has hitherto shown. As for Brutus, he appears disconcertingly; unwilling to raise money 'by vile means' (4.2.123), he wants to share what Cassius has so raised, his rectitude hardening into insensitive obstinacy not apparent in Plutarch.

Then, having shown Brutus so unpleasingly, Shakespeare provides Cassius' grieved surrender to lead to restored affection. Why so alter Plutarch? The answer lies in another, a crucial, adjustment. This is the transference of Portia's suicide from where Plutarch records it (in the very last paragraph of *Brutus*) to precede the quarrel (though Brutus conceals it). Plutarch makes it seem a sad postscript to Brutus' own death (though if read attentively he indicates that it occurred some unspecified time earlier). Shakespeare redeploys these events to moving effect. The disclosure of Portia's death, at this crucial moment, explains Brutus' unwonted agitation, and the whole quarrel takes on a new dimension.

Brutus' rigour is seen as the intolerable overstrain of one who, however self-commanding, is 'sick of many griefs', and Cassius' 'How scaped I killing when I crossed you so?' is a measure of the strain Brutus endures. Sympathies which have swung away from the doctrinaire moralist swing back to the stricken husband, and Cassius too, revealed as vulnerably human, moves towards that dignity of nature which is to be our final impression of him.[1] Shakespeare has revised Plutarch's strong but uncoloured narrative of the quarrel to produce this justly renowned scene with its striking range of emotions, a masterpiece of transformation. Then, in a coda of strange significance, the ghost appears (Plutarch's 'evil spirit'), enhancing our sense of Brutus as the leading anti-Caesarian, even as the kindly exchanges with Lucius, Varro, and Claudius (4.2.289–322) confirm the tenderness underlying the self-command. (Plutarch has no Lucius at all.)

In Plutarch the ghost, though not specifically Caesar's, proves that 'the gods were offended', and Caesar's influence pursues his killers to their doom (*Caesar*, p. 99). The main source here, though a touch or two comes from *Caesar*,[2] is *Brutus* (p. 149), where, reading late, Brutus sees a 'monstrous shape', asks whether it be god or man, utters the precise words Shakespeare adopts ('then I shall see thee again'), and calls up his men, who have heard nothing. So the Act ends, with proof that the conspirators are doomed, yet with Brutus and Cassius restored in our esteem.

As events move towards Philippi they have in the play a somewhat episodic air, and an audience may with reason feel a sense of structural disintegration. Yet Shakespeare did much to give coherence to what in Plutarch is a long episodic story. Plutarch's two battles of Philippi, twenty days apart, resulting respectively in the deaths of Cassius and Brutus (*Brutus*, pp. 160–5), become two stages of one battle, the two friends dying almost simultaneously, with little more than a hundred lines separating Brutus' eulogy over Cassius from Antony's over Brutus. Into the warriors' defiances (5.1.1–66) Shakespeare concentrates items dispersed through earlier pages in Plutarch – tensions between Antony and Octavius, and reminders of the treacherous cruelty

---

[1] Plutarch's single account of Portia's death throws no light on why the play has two. See pp. 78–81 for discussion as to whether the first (4.2.194–208) is a later-written version meant to replace the second (4.2.231–45).

[2] In *Caesar*, p. 100, at first Brutus is 'marvellously afraid' (as at 4.2.330, where his blood runs cold). In *Brutus*, p. 149, he ' boldly' confronts his visitant.

involved in Caesar's murder, of Brutus' error in sparing Antony, of Cassius' age and Octavius' youth, and of Antony's reputation as a reveller. Incidental though these details are, they show how Shakespeare keeps actively in mind the constituents of wide-ranging significances.

Through all the battle preliminaries Plutarch is closely followed (especially *Brutus*, pp. 150–5) – the unfavourable omens, Cassius' wavering in his Epicurean scepticism, his confessing to Messala that he fights against his better judgement, and the Cassius–Brutus discussion on suicide (where an ambiguity in North's translation results in Brutus' apparent self-contradiction; see the Commentary at 5.1.111). Once the battle begins, almost every line draws on Plutarch; to list particulars would be tedious. What unifies the incidental details is the sense of an ending: Brutus and his friends have misread Rome's political destiny, and error follows upon error. Brutus attacks too early, his troops fail to relieve Cassius, and Cassius, misreading Titinius' mission, hastily kills himself. As 'in his red blood Cassius' day is set' so too 'The sun of Rome is set', the hope of a restored republic. The sword which killed Caesar kills Cassius (a symbolic point transported from *Caesar*, p. 99), and it kills Titinius too. Twice visited by the ghost, Brutus knows that Caesar is 'mighty yet' and 'turns our swords | In our own proper entrails' (5.3.94–6). And with his last words he seeks to appease with his own death the dead leader's spirit (5.5.51–2). This is all entirely Plutarchan, in detail and atmosphere.

Finally, for Antony's eulogy Shakespeare turned back several pages to where in *Brutus* (p. 140)

Antonius spake it openly divers times that he thought that of all them that had slain Caesar there was none but Brutus only that was moved to do it as thinking the act commendable of itself; but that all the other conspirators did conspire his death for some private malice.

The last touch of all, the care for Brutus' honourable burial, is credited in Plutarch to Antony (*Brutus*, p. 172; *Antonius*, p. 196). The play transfers it to Octavius, the future leader of the Roman world. So both he and Antony, elsewhere unpleasing in their opportunism, are allowed a show of generosity, to end the play with the Roman distinction it calls for.

It has been suggested that for his portrait of Brutus Shakespeare drew not only on Plutarch's Life of him but also on the parallel Life of the Greek patriot Dion, and on the Comparison Plutarch draws between the two.[1] The former possibility is unconvincing; all the traits, strong and weak, in the play's Brutus are in Plutarch's *Brutus* and there are no real signs that, amply supplied from *Caesar*, *Brutus*, and *Antonius*, Shakespeare also took from the long Life of Dion details already to hand in the others.[2] The Comparison, however, may have helped him; it is brief and compact, and it follows immediately after *Brutus*. Its resemblances to the play are found also in *Brutus* – after all, Plutarch is summarizing points he has already made – but their reiteration might focus Shakespeare's attention. The Comparison, like *Brutus*, stresses that Brutus acted solely for the general good; that his very enemies admitted this; that Cassius' instigations were precipitating causes; that Caesar's influence, even after death, prompted the 'stripling' Octavius to assert his own pre-eminence (a point lurkingly present in the play); that none of Brutus' friends failed him, since either he chose them for their honour or else, chosen by him, they became honourable; and that Antony gave him noble burial. The Comparison alone, however, shares with the play the touch by which both Antony and Octavius honour their dead antagonist. This similarity may show influence; equally, it may result from Shakespeare's own sense of dramatic propriety.

Remarkably faithful though Shakespeare is to Plutarch, his creative originality is no less striking. Plutarch furnished the play's grand strategy and many of its infillings – the main character evaluations, the sense of shaping destiny, and a lucidity of style which suited – even perhaps prompted – the play's 'classical' distinction. But Plutarch's scene is far less clarified, his sense of development far less purposeful, his characterization far less

[1] Sidney Homan, 'Dion, Alexander, and Demetrius – Plutarch's Forgotten *Parallel Lives* – as Mirrors for Shakespeare's *Julius Caesar*', *Shakespeare Studies*, 8 (1975), 195–210. This also suggests modifications of Caesar's and Antony's characters in the play, imported from the parallel lives of Alexander and Demetrius respectively, but the evidence is insubstantial and all the traits the play offers are present in their own *Lives*.

[2] That at some stage Shakespeare did scan the Life of Dion is indicated by the occurrence in *The Winter's Tale* of that name for one of the emissaries to the shrine of Apollo, and by that play's reference at 5.1.156 to Libya and Smalus. These names derive from *Dion*, which mentions a voyage from Libya to a Sicilian village under a Carthaginian governor Synalus. But *The Winter's Tale* is a dozen years later than *Julius Caesar*, and Shakespeare had been rereading Plutarch more recently, not only for *Antony and Cleopatra* and *Coriolanus* but to pick up names for several characters in the late romances, especially *The Winter's Tale*.

salient, his emotion far less deep, and his writing only now and then raised by that heartfelt nobility which is the play's special quality. Shakespeare leaves out many particulars, to create a plot comprising the conspiracy's rise and fall, and Caesar's bodily defeat and spiritual triumph. As a dramatist must, he sees history as relationships, not only as aims and strategies. Far more than in Plutarch do we sense what the conspirators meant to each other, and to Caesar, and he to them and to Antony, and Brutus to Portia (and indeed to minor figures like Lucius), and Antony to his opponents.

Shakespeare's stories, Johnson was to remark, demand Romans or kings, but he thinks only on men. Caesar himself is the sole figure more Roman or king than man; 'figure' is the apt word, for Caesar is a sequence of poses. Even so, he shows a fine imperiousness, crossed with fallibility; role and man interact in a thoroughly human predicament. As for the rest, Shakespeare vividly filled out what Plutarch drew. Energetic and impassioned, the historical figures of long ago are brought near by speech of assured distinction, the very idiom of noble Romans made flesh and blood. Plutarch, delivered through North, is an able recorder: Shakespeare brings the record to finer and fuller life than one would have thought possible.

Compared with Plutarch other sources are barely perceptible. But certain items would in the nature of things register in Shakespeare's literary and dramatic experience.[1] Caesar's cry, '*Et tu, Brute*', a Latin intrusion into the English text, was probably a stage tag. It is not found in any classical writer but Caesar's last words in Suetonius' *De vita Caesarum* are similar – 'kai su teknon' ('you also, my son'); they allude to the rumour that Caesar was in fact Brutus' father.[2] The *Caius Julius Caesar* added in 1587 to *The Mirror for Magistrates* draws upon Suetonius and Plutarch; it renders the phrase, 'And *Brutus* thou my sonne' (l. 383). The anonymous *Caesar's Revenge* (*c.*1594; printed 1607) has it as 'What *Brutus* to[o]' (line 1727). Some such lost play as Richard Eedes's *Caesar Interfectus*, acted at Christ Church, Oxford, in 1582

---

[1] For possible minor echoes of the 1587 *Mirror for Magistrates* see the Commentary at 2.3.0.1, 3.1.1–2, 3.1.6–10, 3.1.149.

[2] Suetonius, *De vita Caesarum*, 'Divus Iulius', lxxxii. In *Julius Caesar* Shakespeare ignores this rumour, though in *2 Henry VI* he had made Suffolk refer to 'Brutus' bastard hand' as guilty of Caesar's death (4.1.136–7).

(only the Epilogue survives) may have originated the Latin form, doubtless also a variant of Suetonius. The first known occurrence of the tag itself is among the piratical additions to *3 Henry VI* in the 'bad quarto' of that play, *The True Tragedy of Richard Duke of York* (printed 1595); it reads 'Et tu Brute, wilt thou stab *Caesar* too?'[1] The identical line recurs in Samuel Nicholson's *Acolastus his Afterwit* (1600); and in Jonson's *Every Man Out Of His Humour* (1600) Carlo Buffone, threatened by Sir Puntarvolo, cries out '*Et tu, Brute*' (5.6.79). That Shakespeare climaxed the gravest moment of *Julius Caesar* with it suggests that in 1599 it was a familiar expression but not yet felt as melodramatic or comic cliché.

Appian's *Chronicle of the Romans' Wars* (as translated by W[illiam?] B[arker?], 1578) perhaps gave something. Around AD 160 Appian compiled Greek narratives of Roman history. His account of the plot against Caesar does not materially differ from Plutarch's though he is more ardently Caesarian, and where there are differences Shakespeare is almost always nearer to Plutarch. Yet in a few details he may reflect Appian,[2] and so in a fuller way may his treatment of Antony's oration. Appian presents the murder as a crime against a friend and benefactor, and against religion and the commonwealth, a crime visited by divine vengeance (all this is in Plutarch too, but expressed less vehemently). As for Antony's oration, Appian's account in general gives nothing not in Plutarch, yet it does elaborate the speech with a passion which might point the way for Shakespeare. Antony is portrayed as hymning Caesar as a god, 'holy and inviolate, father of the country, benefactor and governor, . . . direct[ing] his countenance and hands to Caesar's body, and with vehemency of words open[ing] the fact'.[3] Mixing 'pity and indignation' he commends the crowd for honouring Caesar's corpse, vows vengeance, girds his gown round him 'like a man beside himself', with raised hands rehearses Caesar's victories and booties (see 3.2.88–89), turns

[1] Some editions of Shakespeare – e.g. Peter Alexander's Tudor edition – do in fact include this in *3 Henry VI*, following 5.1.79.

[2] Appian and the Folio have the spelling 'Calphurnia', Plutarch 'Calpurnia'. Appian describes Antony as displaying Caesar's 'vesture' (Bullough, v. 158) – compare 'Our Caesar's vesture wounded' (3.2.193), where Plutarch has 'Caesar's gown' (*Brutus*, p. 129) and 'bloody garments' (*Antonius*, p. 189). In Appian the body is taken for burial in 'an holy place' (Bullough, v. 159) – compare 'We'll burn his body in the holy place' (3.2.247), where Plutarch refers to 'the most holy places' (*Brutus*, p. 129). But such resemblances are very slight.

[3] Bullough, v. 157.

from the theme of triumph to lament a dear friend 'unjustly used' while the people join in 'like a choir', and with 'most vehement affections' shows Caesar's body and gashed robe, speaking as if Caesar himself were accusing his killers of treachery and ingratitude. The crowd runs wild, tears Cinna to pieces leaving 'not one part to be put in grave' (see 3.3.28–35; Appian's Cinna, however, is a tribune, not a poet), fires the Senate House, and makes a funeral pyre. The oration in Appian has none of the brilliant ironies so conspicuous in the play, and its contents differ considerably from Shakespeare's version; but it certainly anticipates Antony's intoxicating tone, though there is none of the phrasal identity so notable when Shakespeare is following Plutarch. Whether Appian was an influence is uncertain but the consonance of spirit at this high point of the action is interesting.

Possibly, too, something came from the anonymous *Tragedy of Caesar and Pompey. Or, Caesar's Revenge.*[1] Acted at some unknown date at Trinity College, Oxford, and printed in 1607, it belongs in style to the early or middle 1590s. It covers far more ground than *Julius Caesar*, extending from Pompey's defeat at Pharsalia to the conspirators' fates at Philippi, whereupon, having periodically appeared as Chorus, Discord rejoices, and Caesar's ghost, having thrice haunted Brutus, celebrates his revenge. Though most of its resemblances to Shakespeare's play are traceable to Plutarch, certain common features are not entirely Plutarchan. After Calpurnia's bad dreams Caesar bombastically resolves to meet the Senate, until ill auguries dissuade him; in Plutarch he takes alarm from the start. As he goes to the Capitol, a well-wisher proffers a scroll of the conspirators' names:[2] in Plutarch this vaguely contains 'all that he meant to tell him'. On Caesar's death Antony enters with an impassioned monologue on his greatness, the horror of his killing, and the theme of vengeance; nothing in Plutarch corresponds. Discord recurrently invokes the infernal powers, as in Shakespeare Antony summons Ate 'hot from hell'; again Plutarch gives no lead.

[1] It is included in the Malone Society reprint series. Ernest Schanzer, in 'A Neglected Source of *Julius Caesar*', *N. & Q.*, 199 (1954), 196–7, thinks that very probably Shakespeare knew it, and judges it second only to Plutarch as a source. Bullough (v. 34–5) gives a useful brief comparison with *Julius Caesar*, analyses its contents (pp. 196–200), and prints excerpts (pp. 200–11).

[2] This occurs too in the 1587 addition to *The Mirror for Magistrates*; see *Parts Added to the Mirror for Magistrates*, ed. Lily B. Campbell (Cambridge, 1946), p. 301, ll. 361–2.

The ghost foretells to Brutus that 'Thine own right hand shall work my wished revenge', as in Shakespeare both Cassius and Brutus recognize the dead man's power presiding over their suicides; and in both plays Titinius kills himself with Cassius' sword. On these two points Plutarch is less clear, though he does observe that Caesar's 'fortune' pursued his killers to death and that Cassius killed himself with the sword that killed Caesar, and he could be misread as saying that Titinius slew himself with the same sword (*Brutus*, p. 161). None of this amounts to certain evidence. Shakespeare may have seen the earlier play in manuscript but there is nothing to prove it. To find the events of *Julius Caesar* treated by an aspiring but undistinguished contemporary is interesting, but there are no convincing signs of Shakespearian indebtedness.

No less doubtful are other proposed 'influences'. Writing *Henry V* shortly before *Julius Caesar*, Shakespeare may have found in R. Grenewey's translation of Tacitus' *Annals* (1598) the idea of the general's incognito night-watch among his men (as in *Henry V* 4.1); did he also follow Tacitus in presenting an Octavius thrusting to the front of Roman politics?[1] Perhaps, but the trait is much clearer in *Antony and Cleopatra*, and in any case is deducible from Plutarch. Did Shakespeare cast an eye on Kyd's *Cornelia* (1594), from the French of Jacques Garnier? If so, he could find, among many less relevant matters, that Caesar's ambitions would endanger Rome, that Cassius would shed his blood for Rome's sake and his own freedom (see Commentary on 1.3.90), that Brutus' ancestral traditions should stir him against the dictator, and that Caesar combines vaunting rhetoric with a desire for Rome's welfare, with heroism in peril, and with a preference for fame over long life (see Commentary on 2.2.32). Yet all these could readily come from Plutarch. It has been argued that Kyd's dialogue between Cassius, eager for Caesar's death, and the hesitant Brutus (*Cornelia* 4.1.1 ff.) closely anticipates their discussion in *Julius Caesar* (1.2.25 ff.) and that Shakespeare's Cassius, 'fiery yet shrewd, envious of Caesar yet full of a genuinely patriotic passion for liberty', owes much to Kyd's, whereas 'only the barest hints are suggested by

---

[1] For another possible origin of this see the Dion–Brutus Comparison, p. 23 above. Tacitus' supposed influence on *Henry V* may well have been overestimated; Anne Barton so argues in 'The King Disguised: Shakespeare's *Henry V* and the Comical History', in *The Triple Bond*, ed. Joseph G. Price (University Park, Pennsylvania, and London, 1975), p. 93, as also does Gary Taylor in his Oxford Shakespeare edition of *Henry V*.

Plutarch'.[1] But Plutarch makes clear Cassius' zeal for liberty and his powers of instigation, and sources need not be multiplied beyond what is necessary. Shakespeare may have known *Cornelia*, but that it gave him anything not already to hand in Plutarch is unproven.

As for the portents preluding Caesar's murder (in 1.3 and 2.2), most are in Plutarch – thunder and lightning, fire-charged tempest, slave with flaming hand, men parading in fire, ghosts, 'bird of night' hooting at noon in the market-place ('solitary birds': *Caesar*, p. 86), comets, sacrifice without a heart, and Calpurnia's dreams. Shakespeare interweaves others. Their precise source is uncertain since they are a general stock-in-trade, but three classical poets who treat of Caesar's death offer parallels. Ovid in particular, a favourite author with Shakespeare, has firebrands in the air, clouds dripping blood, a screech-owl (more specific than Plutarch's 'solitary birds'), armed warriors in the skies, howling dogs (in Shakespeare, neighing horses), and earthquakes (*Metamorphoses*, xv. 787–98). Lucan's *Pharsalia*, i. 522–82, along with several items shared with Plutarch and Ovid, has ominous birds and wild beasts (in Shakespeare, a lion prowling (1.3.20) and lioness whelping (2.2.17)). Virgil's *Georgics*, i. 466–92, along with features shared with the others, has thunderbolts. If Shakespeare wished to save himself trouble, Ovid was available in Golding's translation (1567) – which he certainly knew – and Lucan in Marlowe's (though this was in manuscript until 1600). From whatever source, such things were vivid in his mind, to be used again (open graves, wandering ghosts, meteors, and bloody rain) in his next tragedy, *Hamlet*.[2]

Shakespeare and Roman Values

'Shakespeare fully submits his imagination to the great idea of Rome', Harley Granville-Barker commented, writing on *Julius Caesar* in his *Prefaces to Shakespeare*. Does he really? Critics have differed. According to Nahum Tate, introducing his tragedy *The*

---

[1] *The Works of Thomas Kyd*, ed. F. S. Boas (Oxford, 1901), p. lxxxiii. Kenneth Muir, in *The Sources of Shakespeare's Plays* (1977), pp. 119–20, parallels *Cornelia* passages about indiscriminate slaughter (1.198–200, 2.142–3, 4.1.8–10 and 110) with Antony's vision of murderous chaos (*Julius Caesar* 3.1.274–5). But the resemblances are merely general. For a parallel with Marlowe's *Massacre at Paris* see the Commentary at 2.2.28.

[2] *Hamlet* 1.1.115–20.

Loyal General (1680), Shakespeare 'never touches on a Roman
story but the Persons, the Passages, the Manners, the Circumstances, the Ceremonies, are all Roman'. Dryden, as reported by
John Dennis in a letter to Richard Steele (26 March 1719), thought
Coriolanus 'truly Roman', and Pope considered Shakespeare 'very
knowing in the customs, rites and manners of Antiquity. In . . .
Julius Caesar, not only the Spirit, but Manners, of the *Romans* are
exactly drawn.'[1] Thomas Rymer, on the other hand, in his *Short
View of Tragedy* (1693; p. 148), derided *Julius Caesar* as absurdly
below Roman dignity and thought that it 'put [Brutus and Cassius]
in Fools Coats'. For Dennis, the mob in *Coriolanus* was an affront
to 'the Dignity of Tragedy . . . and the Majesty of the *Roman* People'
and that in *Julius Caesar* a regrettable 'Rabble'.[2] In the nineteenth
century Edward Dowden questioned whether Shakespeare was
ever as concerned about corporate life – for instance the conception
of Rome – as about the natures of individuals;[3] yet in the twentieth
Granville-Barker himself thought that, impressive though Shakespeare found 'the great idea of Rome', he left his Romans a little
bloodless, acting by set forms rather than as fully realized persons,
and the American critic Mark Van Doren similarly judged that
Shakespeare's Romans 'express their author's idea of antiquity
rather than his knowledge of life'.[4]

So what Tate, Dryden, and Pope admired, the 'Romanness' of
Shakespeare's Romans, has to other critics seemed not wholly
convincing, whether as to their Romanness or to their full humanity. Even Johnson, though defending Shakespeare from the charge
that he created stereotypes, found himself 'not much affected' with
the play except in the great quarrel scene. These Romans, one may
feel, spend so much of their time in discussion and speech-making.
Caesar enunciates positions as if a god; the rest of them debate, as
by second nature, perpetually announcing their attitudes to life.
Compared with Ben Jonson's 'tedious though well-laboured
Catiline' or 'irksome' *Sejanus*, *Julius Caesar* is alive; compared with
Shakespeare's English histories is it a little over-decorous, holding
the mirror up to a dignified selection from Nature rather than to

---

[1] D. Nichol Smith, *Eighteenth-Century Essays on Shakespeare* (Oxford, 1903; repr. 1963), p. 49.

[2] Ibid., p. 25.

[3] *Shakspere: A Critical Study of His Mind and Art* (1875), p. 277.

[4] *Shakespeare* (New York, 1939), pp. 180–1.

her full vitality? Yet what non-Shakespearian play on a Roman subject can approach it?

That a Roman subject meant something important to Shakespeare is incontestable. One readily surmises 'that Shakespeare knew what he was doing in writing Roman plays; that part of his intention was a serious effort at representing the Roman scene as genuinely as he could, . . . producing a *mimesis* of the veritable history of the most important people (humanly speaking) who ever lived'.[1] In the same spirit one can agree that *Julius Caesar* 'is full of *romanitas*, of an imaginative awareness of the unique greatness of Roman power, even in crisis, and of what it must have been like to be at the vortex of that power and to help to exercise it'.[2]

What was this unique greatness? Roman history offered some of the most impressive themes available to the Renaissance, an era when political lessons were ardently sought in antiquity – themes such as despotism and republicanism, strong rule good and bad, the stable and unstable realm, scrupulous and unscrupulous motives, the relations between rulers and subjects (particularly the populace), and so on. What, in general, Roman history presented was Roman arms triumphant abroad, and the Roman state stormily evolving at home. Faced in their own lands with intestine divisions, Renaissance scholars noted with awe the extent and continuity of Roman power, and with keen curiosity the contentions within Rome itself. They found in Livy, Caesar, Cicero, Suetonius, Tacitus, Lucan, Appian, and others the record of Rome's rise to greatness and her turbulent continuance in it. *Titus Andronicus*, as has been mentioned, with its violence and changes of fortune, accords more with Renaissance views of Roman metropolitan history than do the grandeurs of *Julius Caesar*, but once *Titus Andronicus* was left behind Shakespeare's sense of Roman history, under Plutarch's influence, breathed a different air, offering formidable conflicts – as in *Coriolanus* – but doing so on a grand scale and with an air of heroic dignity.

Shakespeare surely intended his Roman plays, like his English political ones, to be 'always a genuine piece of history'.[3] What did it mean for him to treat a Roman scene? To the Elizabethan, it has been said, a sense of greatness came naturally, and Rome was

---

[1] Spencer, p. 28.
[2] Ure, p. 13.
[3] Hunter (*Politics*), p. 110.

undeniably great. In *The Ruins of Rome*, which Spenser translated
from the French of Du Bellay, the city is

> Renown'd for fruits of famous progeny,
> Whose greatness by the greatness of none other
> But by herself her equal match could be.
>
> (Sonnet 6)

'*Rome* was th'whole world, and all the world was *Rome*' (Sonnet
26). Kyd's *Cornelia* abounds in heroic Roman patriotism; Caesar
celebrates his conquests and aspires to immortal fame (4.2.25,
93–7, 134–9), and his enemies invoke against him 'our honours
and our ancient laws' (5.1.126). Shakespeare's 'god-like Romans',
as Dryden was to call them in the prologue to *Aureng-Zebe* (though
in fact they are more human than that), reflect this sense of high
pitch, its *virtus*, its self-command, and its gift for noble utterance.
The concluding speeches of both *Julius Caesar* and *Coriolanus*, identifying heroism, virtue, and fame, relate to 'the composite heroic
image, language, and style' of classical epic.[1] Characters strike
impressive attitudes of body and mind, conforming, as Cleopatra
was to say, to 'what's brave, what's noble, . . . the high Roman
fashion', and making death proud to take them.

The Roman code presented bracing conceptions to which the
noble Roman would be true. Though it meant his living up to the
heroic image and, like Caesar and Brutus, fitting himself to a conscious role, it need not make him an automaton, though if carried
in literature to an extreme it could result in the stereotypes of
Senecan or neo-classical fashion. When less extreme it could
produce the demigod stances of a Caesar or Coriolanus. But more
sympathetically upheld it pointed towards an admirable distinction. Introducing his *History of Rome* Livy reflects on the Roman
ethos:

So great is the military glory of the Roman People that when they profess
that their Father and the Father of their founder was none other than
Mars, the nations of the earth may well submit to this . . . No state was ever
greater, none more righteous or richer in good examples, none ever was
where avarice and luxury came into the social order so late, or where
humble means and thrift were so highly esteemed and so long held in
honour.[2]

---

[1] Brower, pp. 29–30, 149.
[2] Livy, Book I, Preface (Loeb edition, i. 5–7).

Those, at least, were the early-republican virtues from which, Livy laments, later corruptions diverted the Roman state; his stress is on the older traditions. When in *The Merchant of Venice* Bassanio characterizes Antonio he does so in terms of 'the ancient Roman honour' (3.2.297); when in *2 Henry IV* Falstaff writes to Hal he aims to 'imitate the honourable Romans in brevity' (2.2.118) – it is 'honourable' that springs to his mind ; when in *Henry V* Fluellen defines military virtue his ideal is 'the pristine wars of the Romans' (3.2.76); when Horatio tries to follow the dying Hamlet he proclaims himself 'more an antique Roman than a Dane' (*Hamlet* 5.2.333); and so on. Throughout North's Plutarch the word 'noble' sounds recurrently, often for prowess in war (virtually restricted in *Coriolanus* to valour and patrician dominance yet still a word of glamour, even if haughty glamour), but often carrying also the sense of moral beauty – Brutus, for instance, in words Shakespeare follows closely, prays 'that he might be found a husband worthy of so noble a wife as Portia' (*Brutus*, p. 119). When in *Julius Caesar* Brutus proves 'the noblest Roman of them all' this is because of his 'general honest thought' for the public good, his 'gentle' (that is, generously ethical) life, and the equipoise of his temperament.

Such nobility means that one is above self-indulgence. As Rome's early-republican values wane, Caesar is supported by the sensual Antony and opposed by the spare Cassius, who hears no plays and loves no music – an imbalance in him towards the excess of restraint, as Antony's sensuality is an imbalance towards its defect. Whether austere or well-tempered, the true Roman seeks his country's well-being, to gain which Brutus will seek honour and death 'indifferently'. The Roman ideal, exalting liberty and fraternity, does not – unlike that of the French Revolution – include equality (though with high-minded vagueness Brutus offers the uncomprehending citizens 'a place in the commonwealth'; 3.2.42); patricians and plebeians are separate classes, yet meant to harmonize in the well-tuned Roman state. This is like the interdependence of 'high, and low, and lower, | . . . in one consent' which Exeter lauds in *Henry V* (1.2.180–1). At the patrician level the crux is whether Rome's ruler is first among equals or an autocrat; an authoritarian emperor and obsequious populace flout the traditions. In Jonson's *Catiline* (5.1.8–19) Petreius, campaigning against the tyrant Catiline, urges his soldiers to defend the Romans' ancient free honour:

> to retain what our great ancestors,
> With all their labours, counsels, arts, and actions,
> For us were purchasing so many years.
> ... for your own republic,
> For the raised temples of the immortal gods,
> For all your fortunes, altars, and your fires,
> For the dear souls of your loved wives and children,
> Your parents' tombs, your rites, laws, liberty,
> And, briefly, for the safety of the world.

The Roman achieves his highest selfhood through public service – in war or government or both. In either sphere, in victory or defeat, in life or death, he has one aim – honour: it is the subject of the Roman story, as of Cassius'. It is a concept Shakespeare had already evaluated. Hotspur had extravagantly idolized it, Falstaff as extravagantly derided it. Henry V, coveting it only as the heroic leader of his band of brothers, had truly embodied it.[1] In the English histories honour and glory are frequently objects of aspiration; in the Roman ones they are the presiding values, coupled with the idea of the noble, a word ranging from the self-assertion of a Coriolanus to the disinterested idealism of a Brutus. For Cassius, honour is the autonomy of the man 'born free as Caesar' and refusing to obey the fiat of another. 'Believe me for mine honour' is Brutus' appeal to his hearers. And even Antony's derision of the 'honourable men' has a curiously elevating effect. Though, as Antony insists, the deed which the conspirators think 'honourable' is in fact shocking, and though save for Brutus their motives are mixed, yet a kind of bracing high-mindedness presides over the conspiracy, as, in later plays, over the career of Coriolanus and over that side of Antony which struggles against Cleopatra. In one light the conspiracy is a shady affair activated by self-persuasion and personal antipathy, with a shrewd contriver, Cassius, manoeuvring a scrupulous patriot into a dreadful act. But *Julius Caesar* does not feel like that. The conspirators' lofty aims, if ambiguous in the mouths of Cassius and Decius, have in that even of the sardonic Casca a true ring (1.3.118–20), and to the revived Ligarius they promise 'Any exploit worthy the name of honour' (2.1.318). So often is the Roman ideal of virtue mentioned that it

[1] The play's values are in fact more complex than this, but this is the impression it generally makes on a popular audience.

becomes a colour-filter giving a high quality to acts in themselves dreadful. It is this quality, of high human distinction whatever failings the characters may have, that, as has been mentioned, puts the Roman plays into the Hegelian tragic category where good struggles not with evil but with incompatible good – republican virtue with imperial efficacy in *Julius Caesar*, heroic leadership with civic justice in *Coriolanus*, disciplined duty with erotic fulfilment in *Antony and Cleopatra*. The esteem earned by honour is not that of Hotspur's bravado, it is that deserved by courage, patriotic service, moral straightness, self-sacrifice when needed, constancy, and indomitableness.

The effects are striking. In these Romans there is much to admire, indeed to like. Yet, however they touch the heart by nobility of sentiment, and moving though their fates are, they remain at a certain small distance, not intimately known as Hamlet, Lear, and Macbeth are known (Othello may, in his different way, be analogous to them as the noble alien). And what they find out about themselves in the tragic action is not some new moral dimension, a discovered world within, but how their code enables them to face success or failure. 'In the process of achieving a maximum of loyalty and devotion from its citizens, Rome restricts their access to wisdom, especially to self-knowledge.'[1] That is the weakness of any code, yet its strength also, the acceptance of a form through which the individual disciplines himself, guided by what is expected and making his life a work of art as well as of nature. Brutus, his less friendly critics say, ends as he began, the man of virtue not doubting his motives or judgements or actions, gravely assured that more glory will accrue to him 'from this losing day' than his foes will win by their 'vile conquest', and consoled that no man has been untrue to him – the pure example of the *mens sibi conscia recti*. His code protects him from self-scrutiny. Yet the result is stirringly impressive, as indeed, granted greater qualifications, it is with the other characters. The Brutus of Plutarch, 'having framed his manners of life by the rules of virtue and study of philosophy, and having employed his wit, which was gentle and constant, in attempting of great things' (*Brutus*, p. 102), stands as a model for the others. The Brutus of Shakespeare, largely cleared of such blemishes as Plutarch still admits in him (ingratitude to

[1] Paul Cantor, *Shakespeare's Rome, Republic and Empire* (Ithaca, NY, 1976), p. 120.

Caesar, rivalry with Cassius, Caesar's doubts about him, and his killing of captured slaves), lives and dies by the best of Rome's ethics, so humanized that Johnson, asking the notable question 'What should books teach but the art of living?', might have had him in mind.

To the extent that Shakespeare's characters recognize what, as Romans, is expected of them, or what they expect of themselves, they look and sound like Romans. But they also look and sound like human beings. The sense of high pitch, honour, valour, and integrity is still that which we recognize in real life, and Shakespeare has again pulled off the feat of giving his personages a local habitation and a name – the great name of Rome – while yet, in the dramatic tensions this involves them in, making them convincingly human. Brutus knows what it is to be a virtuous republican, yet in deciding to act he goes through a phantasma or hideous dream. Cassius is the shrewd manipulating politician of old Roman faith, yet he yields to Brutus' moral prestige and proves poignantly vulnerable in his feelings. Even Caesar, behind the grand poses, has evident signs of the mortal man. Though Shakespeare makes us conscious of a formulaic ideal, his characters present the dilemmas of life.

Politics and Morality

What pointers does the play offer as it presents its Roman action? The first and fundamental point of attention is the antithesis between republican 'virtue' and imperial 'tyranny', both words in inverted commas since neither is a clear-cut case. Republican 'virtue' is blemished in a way which idealizations of 'liberty' ignore. Cassius on principle hates an overlord, yet much of his utterance suggests the 'envy of great Caesar' which motivates all save Brutus. Brutus kills in moral muddle, and he stands on his spotless principles while expecting to share in Cassius' extortions. His followers revere freedom, yet they misread Rome's prospects and are redeemed only by the dignity of their deaths. As for 'tyranny', that amounts merely to Caesar's imperiousness; Brutus himself admits his moderation, and only in Cassius' hostile bias are Plutarch's accusations of violent ambition reflected. Caesar is by turns grand, arrogant, pompous, fallible, genial, dignified, and (in his will) generous. His overthrow proves to be sacrilege. The second question the action poses is that of personal morality under political pressure, of private conscience under partisan strain.

The play bases itself on ambiguities, the central one being the ambiguity of Caesar, demigod and fallible man, monopolist of power yet the essential axle of Rome's wheel. The tenor of Shakespearian histories, English or Roman, suggests a Shakespeare sharing his countrymen's instincts for the settled order of society, constituted authority being revered as long as it serves its subjects' needs for justice. The conspirators cry out for 'Liberty, freedom, and enfranchisement', but this has really little graspable content. They equate the rights of all with their own senatorial dignities, and their 'pity for the general wrong of Rome', though nobly felt, directs itself to such 'wrong' as they feel about the infringement of their prerogatives. Caesar's authority and popularity are in fact Rome's safeguards, and the generosity his will reveals does more for the common good than does republican idealism. The symbolism of the storm, which Cassius takes for proof of Caesarian violence, is actually a supernatural warning of chaos to come; as Sir Thomas Elyot observes in *The Governor* (1531; I. ii), 'the best and most sure governance is by one king or prince, which ruleth only for the weal of his people'; contention for power 'bringeth all to confusion', as Caesar's murder is so fatally to do.

Nevertheless, the republican side is treated sympathetically, and the play can be taken as endorsing Brutus, a martyr for those liberties which are every man's birthright. Always in Shakespeare political attitudes stem from personality, and in *Julius Caesar* the conspiracy takes its tone mainly from Brutus, who aspires to turn politics into ethics. As for Cassius, he figures in Plutarch as choleric, cruel, and, though always a hater of 'tyrants', moved less by idealism than by jealousy of Caesar. But Shakespeare develops him from the shrewd intriguer to the emotionally sensitive and brave ally in a doomed cause, not incongruously mourned by Brutus as 'The last of all the Romans'. Whatever the political rights and wrongs of the situation, it is for most readers the republican cause which moves the heart.

If the play offers the figure of Caesar as its major ambiguity, it is only following centuries of tradition. 'The mightiest Julius' (*Hamlet* 1.1.114) presented a classic case of ambivalence. His extraordinary abilities, the enigma of his intentions, and the motives of his assailants were and are matters of inexhaustible interest. From his own time onwards there was no agreed view on these matters save that he was, as Brutus recognizes, 'the foremost man of all this world' (4.2.74), whose destruction at the climax of his power was the most stupendous reversal of fortune imaginable. Cicero and many others admired his abilities yet feared his ambitions. Dio Cassius' *Roman History* balanced his pride and clemency evenly, attributing his faults largely to his flatterers and his murder to a 'baleful frenzy' which seized his enemies through envy of his power.[1] Sallust, a beneficiary of his patronage, praised him for opposing senatorial corruption during the Catiline conspiracy and began the process of glorification which was to develop strongly: Gaius Velleius Paterculus, for instance, who had served in his wars, lauded him as being of divine descent and as one 'whose soul rose above the limits of man's nature'. On the other hand Lucan's *Pharsalia* supported his rivals Pompey and Cato and looked on him as a restless force of destruction. Plutarch is remarkable for the pros and cons he offers. In Caesar's favour are his eloquence, his courage and leadership in war, his mercy to opponents, and his popularity gained through courtesy. Against him stand his ambitious unscrupulousness and 'his covetous desire to be called king [which] made him mortally hated': yet, Plutarch admits, only 'an absolute Prince' could now govern Rome, and, this being so, his assassins were punished by the relentless gods. 'Shall Rome stand under one man's awe?' Cassius asks. Plutarch would answer that she could not do otherwise. Lucius Florus in his *Epitome of Livy* thinks back admiringly, like Livy, to republican days, yet he admits that Rome could only be ruled imperially; he praises Caesar, blames Brutus and Cassius. Appian highly honours Caesar, whom the Romans did 'fear as a lord, and honour ... as a merciful minister', who even promoted those who had fought against him. His dismissal of the tribunes, Appian admits, caused suspicions of tyranny since their office was holy; yet his killers destroyed 'such an officer, as never was the like, so profitable to all men and to his country and empire'.[2] As for Brutus and Cassius, Appian leaves open the interpretation of their motives – 'either for envy ... or, as they said, for the love of their country's liberty'.[3] Appian offers a dual theme, of Caesar's great nature and deeds, and of Brutus' and

[1] Schanzer, p. 15, citing Dio Cassius, *Roman History*, Book 44. 1.

[2] *Shakespeare's Appian*, ed. E. Schanzer (Liverpool, 1956), pp. 12–13, 67–8.

[3] Ibid., p. 15.

Cassius' lofty aims blemished by their ill-judged deed to one who had been magnanimous.

So, by the end of the classical epoch, 'the main features of the chief characters in the fall of the Republic were well established ... The ambivalence found in Cicero and developed by Plutarch affected the whole Caesar tradition.'[1] The great protagonists each displayed two contrasted aspects – Caesar the heroic leader and fine orator, kind and clement, yet ambitious and on occasion ruthless; Brutus the noble patriot, yet guilty of killing his benefactor and misinterpreting Rome's needs; Cassius the ardent republican, yet cunning and harsh; Antony the sensualist, emerging from indulgence to vindicate Caesar, yet relapsing through his infatuation with Cleopatra.

Medieval and Renaissance views were similarly varied. In popular tradition Caesar was the world conqueror, one of the Nine Worthies, and for his murder Dante consigned Brutus and Cassius to the lowest circle of Hell (*Inferno*, xxxiv. 61–6). In Orosius' *Historia adversus Paganos* (*c.* AD 500), his killing is stigmatized as a crime; Chaucer in *The Monk's Tale* (B3885–900) deplored his murder by 'This false Brutus and his othere foon' and Lydgate followed suit (*The Fall of Princes*, vi. 2862 ff.). Petrarch, though in his *Trionfi* exalting the republicans, in *De Viris Illustribus* condemned Brutus and Cassius as ungrateful and treacherous. Shakespeare's early views were favourable to Caesar, unfavourable to his opponents.[2] On the other hand many Renaissance sources idolized Brutus,[3] and for John Stow's *Chronicle* (1580) Caesar was 'the most ambitious and greatest traitor that ever was to the Roman state'. Often the same writers urged views for and against each side. As Plutarch had done, they stressed Caesar's value and dangerousness, Brutus' virtue and misjudgement. Montaigne highly praised Caesar yet offset his virtues with the superhuman ambitions which brought disaster to his country.[4] Elyot's *The Governor* likewise takes Caesar as an example of the great leader in war and peace (I. xvii, xxiii, II. v), yet in time becoming 'radicate in pride' (II. v), inordinately ambitious, and the subverter of 'the best and most notable public weal of the world' (III. xvi). As for Brutus and

[1] Bullough, v. 17–18.
[2] See pp. 5–6.
[3] Wilson, p. xxiii, quoting Burckhardt's *The Renaissance in Italy* (English trans., 1904), pp. 59–60.
[4] Ibid., quoting Florio's *Montaigne*, Book II, chap. 33.

Cassius, Elyot admits their 'excellent virtues' yet sees their deaths as 'convenient [i.e. appropriate] vengeance for the murder of so noble and valiant a prince' (III. vi). The Caesar of the 1587 *Mirror for Magistrates* not unnaturally laments the 'cruel bloody deed' against his 'noble heart' and takes his killers' deaths as proofs of Jove's justice, but then he recognizes that he was guilty of pride and tyranny and himself fell by Jove's will. And William Fulbecke's *The Continual Factions . . . of the Romans* (written 1586, printed 1601) admits that Caesar was an oppressor, yet condemns Brutus for political assassination.[1]

The variety of views sampled above – and others could be added – has been well documented.[2] It was reflected in the many plays which treated the Caesar story, starting with Marc Antoine Muret's Latin *Julius Caesar* of 1544 which provided a model. In it Caesar boasts his power and conquests, Brutus and Cassius kill him to restore liberty, and his ghost foresees doom for his killers and fame for himself; admiration and sympathy are accorded to both sides and fairly balanced in the choric commentaries.[3] Similar ambivalences recur, for instance in Jacques Grévin's *Julius César* (1561), Jacques Garnier's *Cornélie* (1574) which Kyd translated, the anonymous *Caesar's Revenge* (c.1594?), and Sir William Alexander's *Julius Caesar* (1604). The dual traditions on both sides, of great leader and ambitious braggart on Caesar's, and of virtuous republican and misguided killer on Brutus', are the seemingly incongruous elements which Shakespeare so strikingly made to coalesce. And he allows both sides to end with distinction. However faulty, Brutus and Cassius restore themselves after their quarrel; however fallible in life, Caesar in death is a majestic influence; however shocking the proscriptions, Antony and Octavius rise to magnanimity after their victory – Antony particularly, yet Octavius too unless his final speech is cynically misinterpreted.

Despite its apparent straightforwardness *Julius Caesar* reveals many subtle shadings and implications. The range of response runs all the way from Dowden's 'In the characters of *Julius Caesar* there is a severity of outline; they impose themselves with strict authority upon the imagination', to Wilson Knight's insistence in

[1] Spencer, p. 34.
[2] For example, by H. M. Ayres, 'Shakespeare's *Julius Caesar* in the Light of Some Other Versions', *PMLA*, 25 (1910), 183–227; MacCallum, pp. 1–72; Schanzer, pp. 10–23; Bullough, v. 4–35.
[3] MacCallum, p. 26.

The Imperial Theme on 'a brilliant erotic vision which sees a flaming spirit in history, in action, in man'.[1] The truth lies between these extremes. The Roman scene has something of 'strict authority', something too of 'erotic vision', but Dowden's view, unqualified, makes it too frigid, Knight's, unqualified, too emotional (though it does well to stress how often the participants express loving attachments to each other). Within the impressive decorum of Roman conduct there are passionate impulses, and the result is a presentation of Roman life as both disciplined and ardent.

To pass to the second aspect: if such is the play's balance of political consideration, what of its moral bearing, that 'imaginative statement about something of permanent importance, ... the connexion between observable events in the public world and their causes in the deeper places of personal life'?[2] Any such 'statement' can only be implicit, integral to the action. No one gives as much choric guidance as do Enobarbus in *Antony and Cleopatra* or various commentators in *Coriolanus*. There are brief pointers to judgement – Caesar assessing Cassius, Brutus admitting Caesar's impartiality, and Antony eulogizing the dead Brutus (his oration over Caesar, despite its memorable truths, is highly tendentious) – but moral evaluation is deducible only from the whole context. The main moral idea, the relationship between the public and private roles of those in power, is one already prominent in Shakespeare's English histories; it is the more evident in *Julius Caesar*, since *romanitas* firmly prescribes the public image controlling the private conduct. The implicit 'statement' (that political good cannot flow from moral evil) is still a clear by-product of Roman behaviour, though capable of wider relevance.

The question that so much role-playing provokes – and *romanitas* inevitably prescribes role-playing – is how far the roles limit the humanity which makes up true personality, how far distort the moral and understanding nature. How far does partisanship, even when high-minded, blind its practitioners to true values? Politics, like morals, should further humane relationships, and the moral tragedy framed within the political is that the two great leaders can form affectionate relationships yet allow im-

[1] E. Dowden, *Shakspere, his Mind and Art* (1875), p. 307; G. Wilson Knight, 'The Torch of Life', in *The Imperial Theme* (1931, revised 1951), p. 59.
[2] L. C. Knights, 'Personality and Politics in *Julius Caesar*', in *Further Explorations* (1965), pp. 33–4.

perious superhumanity on the one side and virtuous republicanism on the other to provide the formula for disaster. Caesar, the
demigod, elevates himself into those images of bird of prey,
colossus, lion, northern star, and Olympus which seem to justify
his assassination. Brutus, prompted by family tradition and his
own reputation, betrays the love which unites him and Caesar and
supplants what he knows with what he theorizes about his friend.
As for Cassius, encased in his affronted senatorial prerogatives, he
can see only the Caesar of his prejudices. His fellows adopt the
libertarian slogans of their upbringing as eternal truths. The op-
portunist Antony, on the other hand, unconditioned by conceptions of himself, and deeply moved by Caesar's death, adopts every
pose his strategy calls for. Octavius, too, reveals no discrepancy
between person and persona; he does not so much play a role as
identify himself with what the situation requires. When politics
takes over, humanity fades. But then Antony and Octavius are not
caught between ambiguous situations. Caesar, Brutus, and
Cassius are involved in a deep commitment to the welfare of Rome
and a histrionic sense of how to fulfil it, histrionic in the sense that
they act out their conceptions. This is apparent in almost every line
from Caesar. As for his opponents, they see themselves as 'heroes
of an archetypal drama':[1] Brutus urges his partners to bear themselves 'as our Roman actors do'; Cassius imagines future ages re-
enacting 'our lofty scene' (3.1.112).

Yet to be too admonitory over the restrictions of *romanitas* would
falsify our sense of the play. Whatever the strains imposed by the
high ideas they form of themselves these Romans are figures of
moving power, often noble in utterance, and accompanied in their
falls by our grieved admiration for aims so intended for the general
good. Throughout the English histories Shakespeare had shown
himself

profoundly impressed, in a way the modern artist is seldom impressed,
with the essential relation of the individual to that larger society which is
called a nation; and with the influences which a man's feelings towards
the community can have upon his whole life and character.[2]

This concern, explored poignantly in *Richard II*, triumphantly in

[1] John Anson, 'The Politics of the Hardened Heart', *Shakespeare Studies*, 2
(1966), 11–33; p. 11.
[2] E. de Selincourt, *English Poets and the National Ideal* (1915), p. 10.

Henry V (if with some shadings), is the groundwork of *Julius Caesar*. The 'nation' is less intimately felt than in the English plays, yet devotion to Rome promotes in her champions a courageous largeness of spirit; within this there is ample room for the warmth of attachments which time and again stir the heart. If implicitly *Julius Caesar* warns against the doctrinaire, or theories which supplant true knowledge, yet its human affections and dignities raise morality into wisdom and the Roman idea to moving distinction.

The Play's Style

The style is lucid and vigorous; the Roman world asks for temperate magniloquence, practical enough for real life in real locations (public walks, gardens, Pompey's Porch, Capitol, market-place), spirited for argument or the surge of action, uncomplicated and honourable, a style in which men firmly command their utterance, and words like 'virtue' and 'noble' have their full value. Styles which in Shakespeare's English histories had been strong and urgent, and in the comedies richly melodious, combine and temper these qualities to exactly what the Romans need, an unhurried cogency borne on fluent and assured rhythms with 'a limited perfection, . . . an impression of easy mastery and complete harmony, but not so strong an impression of inner power bursting into outer life'.[1] Yet if the strenuous pressures of the histories are generally (not always) forgone in favour of a dignified directness, yet the style is the perfect vehicle for the elevated character, orderly plot, and decorous tone so evident in the play. It is in a degree intellectual, with 'a philosophical air which . . . manifests itself not only in the judicious citation of "saws" and "common proofs" but also in the extraordinary orderliness of the whole'.[2] It looks predominantly clear and disciplined. Yet it is more than that: it can be passionate and picturesque, strong and direct certainly but also emotive, richly suggestive, and insistent in its drive. Along with 'philosophical' qualities there is a personal expressiveness, a perpetual presence of the human voice. Even the arguments are persuasions, coloured by temperamental appeal.

[1] A. C. Bradley, *Shakespearean Tragedy* (1904), p. 85. It has far more character than the 'extreme simplicity both of vocabulary and of phrasing. . . . sometimes . . . a stiffness, perhaps even a baldness, of diction', which Chambers noted in it (i. 399).

[2] Richard David, *The Janus of Poets* (1935), p. 47.

As presented through their historians and Plutarch, disciplined public speech and resonant cogency were the signs of the Romans' distinction, their badge of status. The predominant style of *Julius Caesar* is that of fine public address. Even when delivered privately it expounds, however sympathetically. The similes and anecdotes with which it enlivens its meanings are clear, illustrative analogies. What strikes the ear from the start is the exact balance between meaning and metre, the flow and adjustment of sense within line, and the unforced undulation of speeds and rhythms as though swing and poise were the most natural things in the world. Indeed, from these speakers who need seldom struggle for their meanings they *are* natural. This might be called 'rational lyricism', 'rational' in that firm ideas readily available are its content, and 'lyricism' in that the sense lithely recognizes the sway of the metre. From the moment when Marullus reproves the celebrating citizens, the lines sound with supple and living dignity. His words run almost to stanzaic phasing, the ideas not bursting out individually but offering themselves in coherent summations. As, reconciled, Brutus and Cassius contemplate the prospects of the battle (5.1.93–126), their manner, gravely courteous, bravely poignant, thoughtfully decisive and semi-oracular, is the central note of the play, the speech not of supermen but of a noble mortal race. The style has often the decorum of natural art, modulated by deep feeling; the thought and emotion, felicitously at one, give the verse spirit yet remain harmoniously contained within it.

The unforced patterns of phrasing show how well, with skill which is second nature, the speakers verbally command their strategies – 'command their strategies' because they are so often exercising modes of persuasion. The patterns are not those of show but of ideas evolved with intelligent order. Thus Cassius urges Brutus on, persuading him to emulate his forebears (1.2), Brutus instructs his allies (2.1), Portia pleads with him (2.1), Caesar enunciates his fiats (3.1, and elsewhere), Brutus and Cassius press their quarrelling arguments and later discuss battle strategy (4.2). Finally, brief though it is, Antony's eulogy over Brutus (5.5.69–76) has the same methodical lucidity as, line by line, it defines its subject's qualities. This controlled vigour of suasion reaches its climaxes in the orations of Brutus and Antony, that of Brutus so formed and formal, in wave-like successions of Euclidean sequence, that of Antony, its opposite in spirit and intention, yet equally controlled in balance and measure, trying position after position on its hearers' minds.

The passion of Antony's oration points to an essential quality in the play, the warmth of its feelings. But other aspects of clarity and assurance need mentioning first. One is the cogency which comes from characters who know their positions and formulate them indomitably. Caesar's mode consists of little else; with majestic resonance, grand or grandiose, it formulates, determines, pronounces, so that his mere 130 lines loom large through finality of meaning measured out with semidivine authority. In a different tone but with equal decisiveness, when Brutus expresses his Roman resolution (e.g. 1.2.82 ff., 162 ff.) there is a spare Wordsworthian strength (that, say, of the *Ode to Duty*), a selection of the language really used by men, purified from the commonplace and sounding with disciplined resonance. Brutus develops this manner in the great speech against oath-taking, public utterance inspired by enlightened resolution. In quieter, graver mood, but with like uncomplicated firmness, Portia invokes the spirit of Cato to vouch for her integrity.

This style can express arrogance but seldom does it sound mere bombast, the besetting fault of much 'classical' drama in English; the characters generally have too much integrity merely to make heroic noises. Caesar comes nearest to it, equating himself with the northern star, yet he does genuinely express the height of imperial objectivity, and his absoluteness sounds splendid. He may impose upon himself, yet it is with an ideal which, as Caesar, he ought to live up to. He is sometimes guilty of the thrasonical, but his general note is that of lofty majesty. To attack him is to attack the voice of Rome's imperial will and power.

Many devices of style convey the sense of status. Developing them,

Shakespeare was not 'following' anyone but 'growing' the kind of speech-manner that seemed right to the dramatic occasion, that would set these noble Romans apart from ordinary mortals to act their scene on the stage of history. The relatively bare and austere manner, more Latin than Latinate, is one of the ways in which Shakespeare, like Plutarch, turned the generals and politicians of history into noble heroes of an ideal antiquity.[1]

[1] Brower, p. 219.

Characters adopt the third person, for themselves or their addressees, as if they were autonomous human objects, the name standing for the individual. Status-ridden though this habit is with Caesar (damagingly so), the effect elsewhere is of characters living up finely to an ideal of themselves. To be 'Brutus' or 'Portia' or 'Cassius' is to stand for what the name represents. Indeed, names have a talismanic value; one should be what one's name implies since it is a proudly borne badge of worth, individual rather than individualistic, honoured for integrity. Then too there are the suasive devices of oratory, apostrophes, declarations, rhetorical questions, persuasions: speakers steer their utterance purposefully.

It is, up to a point, 'a direct and manly play; and one filled with straight talk'.[1] Yet it is more complex than a sequence of speakers unambiguously seeking to impress others. Not infrequently through the apparent confidence there show strains of the self-persuading, even the obsessive. Characters sway others by what they urge; equally, they sway themselves or, having already done so, show by tendentiousness the irrationality they are censoring from themselves. Cassius, cogent though his criticism of Caesar is, colours every expression with the tones of prejudice, and his obsessions, so compellingly enforced (to himself as well as to Brutus), betray through his insistence the jaundice of his judgement. Brutus argues himself into conviction that Caesar must die, yet beneath his self-persuasion he senses that the case is dubious ('Fashion it thus') and develops specious metaphors to validate the threat he hypothesizes from Caesar and his conviction that the murder will be a sacrifice. Caesar hypnotizes himself by self-idolizing diction, 'talking himself into consistency' amid his vacillations by verbal ruses which impose on himself.[2] These are the ironies of incomplete self-knowledge. Shakespeare's Romans, however concerned to be rational, are human enough to use rationality as a mask for assumption, and this shows by many a slant of diction, stress, or tone. 'Honesty to honesty engaged' is the ideal of their behaviour and of their address, but the inevitable ambiguities behind the openness make for interestingly conditioned expression.

[1] J. I. M. Stewart, *Character and Motive in Shakespeare* (New York and London, 1949), p. 50. The author, it should be made clear, is not limiting the play to these qualities; he recognizes the depths to which it suggests the opacities and ambivalences of motive.

[2] Traversi, p. 42.

This is not the diversion from the matter of style which it may seem. Varying 'the dilemmas . . . set out with Roman clarity, Roman simplicity'[1] there are pressures evident in such qualities of utterance as grandiloquence, excitability, high-mindedness, irritation, or (as with Antony's oration) tendentiousness. These shadings are effectively catered for by the way the written word demands the speaking voice. The varying tones of reproof, command, reserve, indignation, insistence, and the rest are all but audible from the page. The outstanding examples are the orations of Brutus and Antony, but speech after speech dictates its character of expression. To say this is to say the obvious: Shakespeare is the most expressive of dramatists, and dramatic writing is writing for the voice. Yet the play is often discussed as if it were formal and deliberate in its speech styles whereas hardly a line lacks temperamental nuance. Even Brutus' hesitation while he deliberates, subdued in tone though it is, has the speech poise of his adjudicating nature. To take the other extreme, while he and Cassius quarrel every word rings with acrimony or distress. The wide range of expressive styles should dispel any idea that Shakespeare sacrificed dramatic idiosyncrasy to *romanitas*. Everyone speaks a living idiom.

Nevertheless, *Julius Caesar* stands out among Shakespeare's plays as unelaborated in style, and this presumably suggests a 'Roman' air. Often, even when most impressive, it is very little figurative, depending rather on cogency of pronouncement, modulated rhythm, and speech tone. Some of Caesar's great utterances, such as that beginning 'Cowards die many times before their deaths' (2.2.32 ff.), make their effect by aphoristic directness as plain as a Doric portico. Once Brutus has finished exhorting his fellows (2.1.190) the rest of Act 2 has little imagic or metaphoric colour. The servant who enters as Antony's ambassador speaks finely but plainly (3.1.123 ff.), though this is not to say that his lines, hinting at significant action and strategy, and charged with thematic words ('noble, wise, valiant, and honest, . . . mighty, bold, royal and loving, . . . honour', and so on), lack dramatic life. What follows between Antony and the conspirators is a clear display of their positions, given spirit on both sides by expressive tone and rhythm. The riveting effect of Brutus' funeral oration results from the integrity of its manner and the pithy semantics of its phrasal

[1] See p. 7, n. 3.

balances. Such speeches, short or long, resound with spirit but do so by plain and direct means.

Yet there is much also of vivid picture and stimulating image. Little is abstract or generalized; Shakespeare abounds in sensory effects. Scores of details, untouched by Jonsonian deliberation, create the Roman scene, its trades and homely life as well as its public policies, its ceremonials and processions and flourishes of music as well as its swarming and excitable citizenry on stage or off, seen in their throngs, heard shouting for Caesar, or evoked by picture and allusion as once they hailed Pompey and now crowd after their new hero, or flee in panic, or rise in mutiny. Human moods, behaviour, and bodily or facial expressions are flashed on the mind's eye – the populace vanishing tongue-tied in guiltiness; Brutus neglecting the show of love once so evident to Cassius or, with himself at war, inwardly vexed; Caesar with the pallid lips of fever or the angry spot glowing on his brow; Cassius lean and seldom smiling; Portia intimately describing Brutus' abstraction, and he admitting 'All the charactery of [his] sad brows', and so on repeatedly. One may reverse Dryden's comment and say that when he describes anything 'you more than feel it, you see it too'. There is much vivid narration of off-stage events – the triumphs of Pompey, the Tiber swimming-match, Caesar spurning the crown 'with the back of his hand, thus', as the populace cast up their sweaty nightcaps, Casca and Calpurnia describing the portents of doom, Antony re-creating the murder of Caesar (which he never in fact witnessed); the list could be long. Actions are metaphorically rendered – Cassius holding before Brutus the mirror of self-recognition, or working Brutus' 'mettle', or whetting him against Caesar; Brutus sitting high in all the people's hearts, or urging a cause to steel melting spirits with valour, or refusing to stain the even virtue of their enterprise. Body and spirit are in vivid relationship; Romans are thewed like their ancestors yet degenerate in mind; the genius and mortal instruments within Brutus are in rebellious council; bodily and spiritual Caesar can equally be dominant; no earthly bounds 'can be retentive to the strength of spirit'. Such evident points should not need labouring, but they are often ignored in talk about stylistic austerity.

Within its prevalent clarity the play is strikingly picturesque. Time is made real, the historic past by vivid reminiscence, the present and future by frequent intimations – hours, days, dates, the Ides of March, clocks striking, appointments, rendezvous, what the morrow will bring, and how future ages will view the present action or shed glory on Brutus' 'losing day'. The tides in the affairs of men are dynamically felt. There are climatic and atmospheric colourings, night fearful with storm, apparitions and exhalations, dawn with grey lines that fret the clouds on the fatal day, the blood-red sun setting on Cassius' life and the conspirators' defeat. There are lively vignettes from the natural or mythical-natural worlds: Caesar as falcon, as wolf to the Roman sheep, as lion preying on hinds, yet in his vanity fooled with fables of deluded unicorns, bears, or elephants. In the subversion of order a lion 'glaze[s]' before the Capitol, owls hoot by day, a lioness whelps in the market-place, horses frenziedly neigh, and the heavens themselves blaze forth the death of princes. These details come mostly from Plutarch, Virgil, or Ovid, yet they are fresh on Shakespeare's page, re-created through the narrators' excitement, figuring not as melodrama but as supernatural symbolism of the calamities to follow. Blood likewise figures symbolically in many guises – the blood of noble race, the lifestream of heroic figures, the guarantee of Roman quality, the warmth of the heart, the enriching or shocking evidence of Caesar's death (whether as sacrifice or butchery), blood metaphorical or physical. There is in fact a great deal which presents the play's meanings in lively sensory form.

So to limit the play to an ordered dignity is to ignore its throbbing pulse, its variegated colour. It is animated with feelings which, however under command, play against 'philosophical' decorum. At one pole it shows the Roman ideal of self-mastery, at the other, the vitalities which that mastery cannot repress. As Pope would put it in *An Essay on Man* (i. 165–70),

> Better for us, perhaps, it might appear,
> Were there all harmony, all virtue, here; ...
> But All subsists by elemental strife,
> And Passions are the elements of Life.

Shakespeare's Romans are human, and of humanity passion is a deeper power than reason.

The Play in Performance

From 1599 onwards, with only temporary eclipses, *Julius Caesar* has been a stage draw.[1] Its productions have reflected prevalent outlooks, the Restoration's heroic flair, Augustan Whiggish patriotism idealizing the high 'Roman' mode, the early nineteenth-century grand style and beau ideal of classical elevation, the late nineteenth-century leaning towards populist 'realism' and crowd participation, and the twentieth-century directorial zest for 'relevance' and for dislodging the noble Romans from their pedestals. A play about politics responds to political prejudice: it can mirror heroic antiquity, acrid modernity, and various concepts in between. *Julius Caesar*'s ambivalences in all the leading parts invite differing interpretations. The eighteenth century, downgrading Caesar, exalted republican virtue. Around 1900 Beerbohm Tree was overbalancing the play with his own part, Antony, the heroic vindicator. The twentieth century has at times offered it as Fascism crushing the liberal intellectual. And there have been many other tendentious variants.

Few eyewitness accounts survive from the seventeenth century, though Leonard Digges's tribute to the quarrel scene (see p. 4) is notable. Beaumont and Fletcher may have recalled this scene as they set the noble Amintor and Melantius quarrelling in *The Maid's Tragedy*, 3.2 (1610), and Dryden praises it in the preface to his *Troilus and Cressida* (1679). The text hardly authorizes the virtual duel Digges describes, and the great Brutuses of the late seventeenth and early eighteenth century, Betterton and Barton Booth, seem to have stayed majestically restrained. But from other performers the sword-play thrill was long a theatrical draw. William Guthrie's *Essay Upon English Tragedy* (1747) comments that the actors of Brutus and Cassius 'have ever made a feint towards a duel [though] nothing could be more opposite to the poet's meaning',[2] and Smollett in *Peregrine Pickle* (1751; chap. 51) satirizes James Quin and (probably) Lacey Ryan for clashing their sword-hilts like 'a couple of merry-andrews endeavouring to raise the laugh of the vulgar'. As late as Thomas Davies's *Dramatic Miscellanies* (1783–4) the writer observes that 'their swords are half-drawn, and their hilts should meet and repel each other' (ii. 248). Even melodramatized the scene has great power.

---

[1] This section is much indebted to the admirably documented and amply descriptive study by John Ripley, *'Julius Caesar' on Stage in England and America, 1599–1973* (Cambridge, 1980), cited hereafter as 'Ripley'.

[2] Quoted in Sprague, p. 324.

2. Illustration to manuscript extracts from *Titus Andronicus*, attributed to Henry Peacham, *c.*1595.

How far Shakespeare's actors donned Roman dress is still uncertain. The earliest drawing of a Shakespeare play, that of *Titus Andronicus* about 1595, shows elements of classical costume. Titus, laurel-wreathed, wears armour to the waist, a robe draped from his shoulder and folded about his body, and what seem to be buskins on otherwise bare legs. Queen Tamora has a patterned voluminous gown of no specific period. Her sons and Aaron have close-fitting doublets (or body-armour?) above thigh-length skirts. Titus' commanders, holding long halberds, have a plumed helmet and a kind of turban above florid baldrics and baggy pantaloons. The effect is part-classical, part-Tudor. (There is an expert commentary on the drawing in Martin Holmes's *Shakespeare and his Players* (1972), pp. 150–4; see also the Oxford Shakespeare *Titus Andronicus*, pp. 2, 20–7.)

Within the next few years it seems that efforts were made towards more classical consistency. Henslowe's records for other plays mention a senator's gown and senators' capes, and make what look like other references to classical costumes.[1] A list of properties for plays done at Oxford in 1605 refers to 'Antique fashions', 'antique suits', and 'antique vizards', and in London it seems unlikely that *Sejanus* (1603) and *Catiline* (1611) 'were given

---

[1] *Henslowe's Diary*, ed. R. A. Foakes and R. T. Rickert (Cambridge, 1961), p. 317.

anything but a full-scale production in classical costumes'.[1] Elizabethan visual arts, in statues, tapestries, and the like, seem to show a well-established convention for classical costume during Shakespeare's lifetime – for warriors 'the Roman breastplate, shaped to the figure ..., the military skirt or kilt, the draped scarf, and plumed helmet',[2] for women ample robes often with shaped bodices. These modes, under Italian influence, were confirmed by masque designs in the early seventeenth century but they were not unfamiliar even before the death of Queen Elizabeth. *Julius Caesar* contains minor anachronisms (striking clocks, books with pages, unmasked actors, and so on), but its doublets, sleeved cloaks, and hats may be more classical and less Elizabethan than is often supposed. 'Doublet' might mean any close jacket (not merely Tudor),[3] and the Romans had various kinds of cloaks and hats. Other apparel mentioned in the play, such as aprons, scarfs, and kerchiefs, belongs to no particular period. Calpurnia and Portia would wear flowing gowns, the citizens any workaday dress. If the senators wore togas (like the 'wolvish toge' in *Coriolanus*, 2.3.112) and the leading warriors some Renaissance version of Roman armour, the effect would be plausibly classical.

There are few detailed accounts of *Julius Caesar*'s seventeenth-century productions before 1660 or so. Plays presented at Whitehall during the winter season of 1612–13 for the marriage festivities of Princess Elizabeth and the Elector Palatine included 'Caesars Tragedye', which may well be Shakespeare's, and other performances took place before the Court in January 1637 and November 1638.[4] After the Restoration the leads were taken by very notable actors; Charles Hart as Brutus and Michael Mohun as Cassius 'greatly signalized themselves, and especially Mohun ... for his excellent performance of Cassius'.[5] Antony, too, was well taken, by Edward Kynaston, and from the reputation of all

[1] The details are from Hal H. Smith, 'Some Principles of Elizabethan Stage Costume', *Journal of the Courtauld and Warburg Institutes*, 25 (1962), pp. 252–3.

[2] W. M. Merchant, 'Classical Costume in Shakespearian Productions', in *Shakespeare Survey 10* (Cambridge, 1957), 71–6; p. 71.

[3] Smith, 'Some Principles' (see n. 1), p. 254; this cites Maurice Charney, 'Shakespeare's Roman Plays' (unpublished Ph.D. dissertation, Princeton University, 1952), pp. 64–5, as pointing to the occurrence of 'doublet' in North's Plutarch. Charney's published study *Shakespeare's Roman Plays* (Cambridge, Mass., 1961) has a brief discussion of Elizabethan versions of Roman dress, pp. 207–9.

[4] Chambers, ii. 343, 353.

[5] Davies, ii. 201.

three for robust action it seems clear that the play was given less for psychological insights than for spirited personalities in a forceful plot. This one would expect in the age of Dryden.[1]

Thomas Betterton, the greatest actor of the late seventeenth century, played Brutus as a majestic philosophical stoic and long provided the approved model. His keynote was noble gravity, yet with much reserve of power. Colley Cibber vividly describes how he managed the quarrel scene: 'His spirit flew only to his eye; his steady look alone supplied that terror which he disdained an intemperance in his voice should rise to. Thus with a settled dignity of contempt, like an unheeding rock he repelled upon himself the foam of Cassius.'[2] Betterton made the play predominantly Brutus', and its tenor that of republican liberty against despotic encroachment. This remained its message through the first half of the eighteenth century, when it was very popular; between Betterton's last Brutus in 1708 and James Quin's last in 1751 only five seasons passed without a performance. Its Roman ideals struck a responsive chord ('All ancient authors, sir, all manly', was Johnson's reply when asked by Boswell about his early reading) and Roman precedents were powerful in Augustan culture – the term 'Augustan' itself, claiming for English taste a kinship with that of Rome, goes back at least to the early eighteenth century. The play became a simple contest between tyrannous ambition and autonomous freedom, freedom such as Britons prided themselves on having secured against absolutism. As a commentator observed, 'If powerfully inculcating one of the noblest principles that actuates the human mind, the love of national liberty, can stamp additional value upon works of genius, ... the tragedy before us, as to the subject of it, [is] highly deserving of attention from an English audience.'[3] The text was abridged for speed and to remove anachronisms and traits at odds with Roman dignity;[4] Brutus

---

[1] Ibid., iii. 161 – Davies surmises that it was the quarrel scene's power as Hart and Mohun presented it that prompted Dryden's 'generous confession of Shakespeare's superiority' in the Prologue to *Aureng-Zebe* (ll. 15–16), which admits how far short of the master he felt he came – 'when he hears his Godlike *Romans* rage | He, in a just despair, would quit the stage.'

[2] *An Apology for the Life of Mr Colley Cibber*, ed. R. W. Lowe, 2 vols. [1888], i. 103–4.

[3] Gentleman, ii. 1.

[4] For instance, the lines about the conspirators staining their hands and swords with Caesar's blood were seldom delivered, doubtless as too gruesome (Sprague, p. 321 on 3.1.105 ff., citing Bell's acting edition of 1774).

was spared some human failings, Caesar some bravado (though his part was reduced to that of the dangerous autocrat), Antony some unscrupulousness – the proscription scene (4.1) was generally cut. Characters were envisaged simply, spared Romantic or modern ambivalences, though not without earnest feeling, enhancing the drive of the plot.[1] Elocution made the most of oratorical occasions, and acting which modern taste would think histrionic provoked in its audiences not only willing suspensions of disbelief but melodramatic empathies of vicarious experience. Of William Milward, Antony to James Quin's Brutus in 1734–6, Thomas Davies records that his funeral oration cast his hearers into 'enthusiastic rapture' and was greeted with hardly conceivable applause.[2] Such audiences would have made nothing of Brechtian alienation; they wanted 'such violence of affected agitation as imposes upon the undiscerning spectator'.[3]

After Betterton retired in 1708 Barton Booth inherited his noble-Roman role as Brutus and, like his precursor, captivated audiences by i.npressive restraint, by moral distinction, and by the 'heart-piercing manner' in which he gave the news of Portia's death.[4] As with Betterton before him and James Quin after, his Brutus dominated the play; Caesar (considered an unrewarding part anyway) was merely the idol with feet of clay, and Antony merely the athletic young patrician. When Booth retired in 1728 Quin maintained a similar distinction, with the occasional extravagance pilloried in *Peregrine Pickle* yet with a command of grave feeling which made his announcement of Portia's death deeply impressive.[5] During the nearly seventy years from Betterton's debut to Quin's retirement in 1751 the interpretation as sketched above prevailed – Caesar the pompous bane of libertarian idealism; Brutus its soul; clear action free from psychological ambiguity or

[1] Voltaire, while thinking *Julius Caesar* an example of 'bizarre and barbarous' taste, admitted that its natural energy seized him – 'I began to be interested ... the piece held me' (*Théâtre de Corneille*, ii. 262, quoted in Furness, p. 421).

[2] Davies, ii. 245–6.

[3] T. Smollett, *Peregrine Pickle*, chap. 51. Not all acting was melodramatic. In *Tom Jones* (Book 16, chap. 5) the naïve Partridge complains that Garrick, playing Hamlet, did not rave on seeing the ghost but behaved as any actual man would. Garrick was the outstanding example of actors developing less flamboyant modes.

[4] W. Cooke, *Memoirs of Charles Macklin* (1804; second edn., 1806), p. 365.

[5] Davies relates that in the quarrel scene he spoke loudly and showed Cassius 'a look of anger approaching to rage' which compared ill with Booth's earlier, self-commanding, firmly quiet Brutus (ii. 248–9).

scenic elaboration or crowd prominence; and fine delivery in an age when oratorical skill counted highly. Then, surprisingly, until the end of the century *Julius Caesar* had very few revivals in England; in America, though as yet rarely staged, it was read in the enthusiastic spirit of republican patriotism (see p. 59).

The next major phase came when John Philip Kemble produced it at Covent Garden between 1812 and 1817, with himself as Brutus. The result proved a 'noble drama, with every attention to scenic splendour, and classical costume, which could represent the dignity of "the old heroic time" '.[1] Kemble, a friend of Sir Joshua Reynolds, was influenced by the ideals of noble art on which Reynolds discoursed to his Royal Academy students annually from 1769 to 1790. Translated into the theatre these resulted in handsome pictorial effects. Roman grandeur was to be realized not only, as hitherto, by fine elocution in strong acting roles, and by classical costumes posed against scene paintings populated by unobtrusive extras, but by the high art of scenic design before which the actors were grouped according to Reynolds's classical principles, while an impressive crowd of supporters reflected Rome's pomp and circumstance. That so large a theatre should be filled twice weekly was, a critic observed, 'highly creditable to the taste of the public', who were greatly impressed by 'Roman manners and greatness'.[2] Kemble sought advice from classical archaeologists though he allowed himself to prefer lavish imperial Rome to the austerer Republic,[3] and he engaged the best of scene painters. The results were notably fine:

Kemble's painted backgrounds owed much of their effect to his living scenery – processions and statuesque groupings of supernumeraries roughly comparable in function to drapery in beau idéal paintings. Costumes, based on antiquarian research, were relatively accurate, colours were simple and subdued, movement was kept to a minimum, and groupings were arranged according to the sculptural principles admired by Reynolds.[4]

The formality of movement and grouping struck the visiting German critic Ludwig Tieck, attending Covent Garden in 1817, as overritualizing the assassination which (perhaps too faithfully to

---

[1] *The Times*, 2 March 1812, quoted in Odell, ii. 105.
[2] *The Examiner*, 29 March 1812, quoted in Odell, ii. 106.
[3] J. R. Planché, *Recollections and Reflections*, 2 vols. (1872), i. 54.
[4] Ripley, p. 51.

Brutus' hopes) was a ceremonious rite rather than the butchery it should be. Caesar, enthroned at the rear centre, repulsed his petitioners in turn, while their fellows ranged themselves in a pyramid of which he was the apex. Casca struck, and Caesar turned to one side, receiving a second thrust. He turned the other way, receiving a third, and so alternately, staggering from side to side of the widening space, his enemies remaining motionless. Finally he reached Brutus downstage and died on the final thrust. 'The whole scene', Tieck remarks, was 'arranged like a clever ballet' but suffered from an air of 'pretentious majesty', and the effect was less majestic than artificial.[1]

Whether too formal or not in the interests of Roman decorum, the stage was set – literally and metaphorically – for the subsequent cult of pictorial magnificence. Action and speech resounded with stately grandeur. Groupings were manipulated for better balance than the text provided; Kemble cut some minor characters on Brutus' side, and added some on Antony's. His Brutus, the major interest, was (as hitherto) simplified to the lofty patriot, 'the idealized creation of David or Reynolds, not the intensely human, and often inconsistent, character created by Shakespeare'.[2] Antony, played by his brother Charles Kemble, was enhanced with a larger following and presented not as the astute politician (the proscription scene was still cut) but as 'the noble companion of Caesar who, from the purest motives, sets out to revenge his friend's death'.[3] Caesar, entering to processional music and choral shouts (his first appearance involved seventy-one participants), was allowed that grand dimension the eighteenth century had denied him; he was to be a ruler impressively worth supporting, or opposing, and would have been so had not the actor (Daniel Egerton) substituted pomp for the tragic majesty and human variations the part calls for; this was a further simplification of Shakespearian ambivalence. Charles Mayne Young as Cassius, intellectual, thrusting, and high-strung, with a fine range of delivery (later proving an even better Brutus than Kemble himself, and one of the best in all the part's history), played intense vitality against Kemble's deliberateness. Like his precursors, Kemble cut the text to sharpen the plot, reduced the supernatural

---

[1] *Kritische Schriften* (Leipzig, 1852), iv. 324, quoted in Furness, p. 440.
[2] Ripley, p. 53.
[3] Ripley, p. 55.

element, diminished the number of speaking parts (grouping them more symmetrically), and clarified characters. The grandeur, it should be added, was not insensitive; Brutus' forlorn end was felt the more poignantly for the glamour of earlier pageantry.[1]

What Kemble's splendid version missed was, in general, something the later nineteenth century, subtilizing its psychology, was slowly to develop, complex characterization alerting the audience to the intricacies of political motives. Kemble controlled the audience's response by heightening its sense of great natures but the shadings in the main characters were diminished by classical dignity and consistency. On the other hand, twentieth-century versions, bowing to naturalism and realism, often insist that all politicians are brothers under the skin and that *Julius Caesar* virtually prefigures Fascist/liberal dichotomy. This is further from the play's centre than too 'Roman' a version; Shakespeare was not writing any such parable. He was following Plutarch in locating universal human natures in the context of Roman prestige, the qualities of which reveal themselves in lofty actions and lucid utterance. Kemble's ideal classicism made it clear that the play was about Plutarch's 'noble Romans', however perennial their appeal. If the result was rather an idealization than the full problematical version, its merits were nonetheless outstanding; they allied the eighteenth century's robust classicism with the nineteenth's concern for scenic beauty, and they expressed a single mind's high directing intentions. For half a century, until Samuel Phelps played his last Brutus at Drury Lane in 1865, *Julius Caesar* with only brief intermissions held the popular stage with the distinction reflected from Kemble's achievement. After that, until Beerbohm Tree's spectacular revival in 1898, the United States was its principal home.

What developments offered themselves as the nineteenth century advanced? First, as Shakespeare's English histories were mounted with idealized medieval settings, his Roman ones were classically grand; this reflected the Romantic interest in the colourful past from which both medieval and classical interests benefited. Then again, reflecting Romantic sensibility, subtler analysis developed than Kemble's stateliness had allowed. *The Examiner* of 1 November 1829 articulated a growing sense that Shakespeare's

[1] Ripley, p. 66.

Romans were something other than classical archetypes. It remarked that to the modern mind ancient manners are a dead language, and their exponents, as sculpture records them, 'a stern, formal, severe, and unbending people', whereas to Shakespeare they were beings with the strengths and the weaknesses of men. Weaknesses, *The Examiner* observed, do not accord 'with the general notion of "classicality", . . . but Shakespeare thought that such familiarities were consonant with *nature*'.[1] (Concurrently, in the field of painting Constable was complaining of Academicians who 'stickle for the "elevated and noble" walks of art'.)

So W. C. Macready, reviving the play at Covent Garden in 1838–9 and Drury Lane in 1843 (and acting in it from 1813 to 1851), modified Kemble's stateliness. He retained the handsome and scholarly settings and the populous crowd scenes, but these latter he directed vigorously to set his protagonists in the context of a living society; Rome became a city not merely of patricians but of a populace involved in the actions of the great, a development which pointed towards the modern populist sense of history. *Julius Caesar*'s Rome was turning from a far-off classical scene to a mirror of social reality. The assassination, ballet-like under Kemble, became alive with universal alarm, stressing not the ritual Brutus intends but the violence he achieves. The onlookers registered not solemn awe but the historical shock of the deed. And the other development was the subtilizing of character. Macready at different times acted Cassius and Brutus. The former part, which he first played in 1819, gave him peculiar pleasure, he said, 'as one among Shakespeare's most perfect specimens of idiosyncrasy'.[2] Of his performance in 1822 he wrote: 'I entered *con amore* into the study of the character of Cassius, identifying myself with the eager ambition, the keen penetration, and the restless envy of the determined conspirator, which, from that time, I made one of my most real personations.' Though he monopolized the limelight he brought to his parts a devoted intentness, and in Cassius he ranged from fanatical intensity to poignant affection. At one stage, in 1836, he thought Brutus 'one of those characters that requires peculiar care . . . but . . . never . . . a part that can inspire a person with an eager desire to . . . see represented'. But his comments on

---

[1] Quoted in Ripley, p. 76.

[2] This and the following quotations are from W. C. Macready, *Reminiscences*, ed. F. Pollock, 2 vols. (1875), respectively i. 179, 235, ii. 53, 359, and 365.

his latest performances, in 1850 and 1851, were far warmer. On 18 November 1850, he 'Acted Brutus in my own opinion ... far beyond any performance I ever gave of the character', though the audience, while applauding his salient passages,

did not seem to watch the gentle, loving, self-subdued mind of Brutus which I tried to make manifest before them. The gentle touches were done with great care, and, I think, with skill – the remonstrances with Cassius in the third act about Caesar's funeral – and, in the fourth, the quarrel.

But his farewell performance, on 24 January 1851, he felt was wholly successful:

Acted Brutus as I never – no, never – acted it before, in regard to dignified familiarity of dialogue, or enthusiastic inspiration of lofty purpose. The tenderness, the reluctance to deeds of violence, the instinctive abhorrence of tyranny, the open simplicity of heart, and natural grandeur of soul, I never so perfectly, so consciously, portrayed before. I think the audience felt it.

In such a reading temperamental shadings far more subtle than those of the noble philosopher are emerging; character analysis is developing analogously with contemporary developments in the novel. And supporting Macready in psychological complexity were the Cassius of Samuel Phelps, turning the impetuosity of con- spiratorial temper to a wide spectrum from exasperation to tender- ness, and the Antony of James Anderson, spared the proscription's cynicism, since this was still not performed, but suggesting a mercurial variability from young sensualist to bereaved friend to virtuoso demagogue.

Phelps's productions at Sadler's Wells between 1846 and 1862 followed Macready's in time and in spirit but with sparer sets and fewer supers, the Wells being a humbler theatre. These losses he compensated by better integration and balancing of the parts. He played Brutus himself, avoiding Macready's stress on his own pre- eminence, with fine delivery, moving dignity, and an impressive command of pathos. With generally undistinguished and sometimes inexperienced supporting casts he managed well- adjusted and capable presentations, and with his farewell perfor- mance as Brutus at Drury Lane in 1865 his audience

witnessed the last great English Brutus of the nineteenth century and the end of a method of presentation which had lasted more than five decades. When next they saw the play more than thirty years later [produced by

Beerbohm Tree in 1898], the text would be vastly altered, settings would be on a scale beyond their wildest imaginings, and Brutus would no longer dominate the action as he had done for at least two centuries.[1]

The break conveniently allows a retrospect over the play's American fortunes. British libertarian patriotism of the early eighteenth century was still more headily sensed over the Atlantic, where the national mind ran to political doctrine and oratory. What the advertisement for the first performance, at Philadelphia on 1 June 1770, calls 'The noble struggles for Liberty by that renowned patriot Marcus Brutus' appealed very strongly as the colonies moved towards the fight for independence, and though only six more productions are recorded up to 1802 *Julius Caesar* was read for what an early critic called 'the growing spirit of liberty it breathes [and its] elegant and sublime language'.[2] The prestige of Roman subjects was high in a land where baptismal and local names often drew upon classical antiquity, and nineteenth-century presentations of the play, if less handsomely mounted than those in London, aimed at Roman dignity, virile feeling, and rotund delivery. The actors, Lewis Hallam, John Henry, Thomas Cooper, Edwin Booth, Junius Brutus Booth, William Augustus Conway, Edwin Forrest, Lawrence Barrett, and others, were generally men of commanding presence, and their performances invested with republican relevance the lofty idea of the public weal. As with Kemble, a stately high-mindedness prevailed through the first half of the century. For the two following decades the play then remained quiescent, to revive strongly in New York in 1870 with a Brutus by E. L. Davenport so humanely handled in its classical distinction as to establish a long tradition. Lawrence Barrett's Cassius (which he also acted to Edwin Booth's Brutus) was no less admirable, capturing the intensities beneath the conspirator's resolution so well as to become for decades the ideal rendering. Walter Montgomery's gallant and dynamic Antony completed a distinguished trio, and the revival, which a contemporary hailed as 'the most finished production of *Julius Caesar*, if not the most thoroughly satisfactory Shakespearian revival, yet seen upon the

---

[1] Ripley, p. 99.
[2] Both quotations are from Ripley, p. 100, to whose treatment of the whole subject this section is particularly indebted.

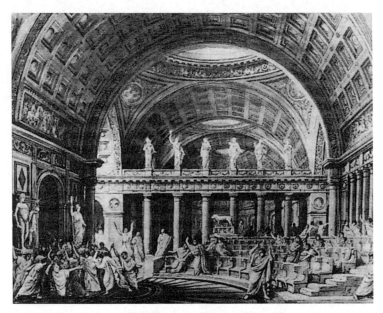

3. The Roman Senate in Edwin Booth's New York production, 1871.

4. Ludwig Barnay as Antony in the production by the Duke of Saxe-Meiningen's Company, brought to Drury Lane in 1881 (*The Illustrated London News*).

American stage',¹ restored the play to its traditional stirring and ardent heroism.

Two New York productions of the 1870s climaxed the play's first century in America, one by Edwin Booth in 1871, the other (indebted to it) by Henry Jarrett and Henry Palmer in 1875. Magnificently mounted and strongly acted, Booth's was an outstanding triumph of the intelligently popular stage. As Kemble had done, he set pictorially grouped and handsomely costumed figures in majestic settings; spiritually, he saw *Julius Caesar* as presenting 'a noble past which shamed a decadent present'.² His Brutus, no longer the mere heroic stereotype, expressed righteous perturbation, impassioned idealism, and tender chivalry, while yet recognizing the psychological complexities of human imperfection which the role offers, the 'poetic idealist . . . look[ing] towards a new century and its resolute, even wayward, attempts to plumb Brutus' unheroic and all-too-fallible humanity'.³

Later Booth switched to Cassius, and then to Antony, bringing to both an unusual sense of their varied qualities, his Cassius 'comet-like, rushing, and terrible – not lacking in human emotion but coloured with something sinister', his Antony 'politic, reckless, somewhat treacherous, . . . yet resolute, strong, and fierce', not without 'lighter and more winning qualities [of] patrician nobility and refinement'.⁴ In the 1875 revival, on the other hand, E. L. Davenport as Brutus turned from Booth's complex sensibility and for a while restored the unblemished dignity which two centuries had established as the main tradition of the part, and the play. For a century, then, American production paralleled British in defining two main intentions, those of idealized stateliness and of psychological complexity, within the architectural opulence of nineteenth-century popular stagecraft.

Back in Britain a word must go to a visiting company from Saxe-Meiningen in 1881, playing in German, and making the people of Rome integral to the political action. Brutus and Cassius lost their pre-eminence; Antony was commandingly played and he operated on the crowd with electrifying force. *The Daily Telegraph* (31 May)

---

¹ H. P. Goddard, in *Lippincott's Magazine*, April 1878, p. 463, quoted in Ripley, p. 112.
² Ripley, p. 117.
³ Ripley, p. 145.
⁴ W. Winter, *The Life and Art of Edwin Booth* (New York, 1893), pp. 216, 219.

5. The assassination of Caesar: Herbert Beerbohm Tree's staging at Her Majesty's Theatre, London, 1898 (Charles Fulton as Caesar, Lewis Waller as Brutus).

6. Antony's oration in Beerbohm Tree's production (Beerbohm Tree as Antony).

thought the result 'the most startling effect ever seen – those forests of hands and arms, those staccato shouts, that brilliancy of emphasis, the whirl and rout and maddened frenzy of an excited mob'.[1] For *The Times* of the same date, Antony's oration was

a masterpiece of scenic arrangement, such as has seldom been witnessed on the stage. The gradual change in the feeling of the crowd, the lessening approval at the mention of the name of Brutus and the other honourable men, the final outburst of popular fury – all this was indicated with a delicacy of gradation which fully warranted the enthusiasm elicited.

This sense of popular participation pointed towards the next century's awareness of mob politics and the hysteria of crowd response.

The nineteenth century, then, while generally maintaining Brutus at the play's focus, saw significant developments. Spectacle was greatly enhanced, with grandly authentic settings. The main characters' psychological ambiguities were recognized, and monumentality dwindled before natural humanity. Character interests were increasingly balanced for dramatic ambivalence; political realism magnified the role of the populace; and the play was felt rather as an organic whole than as an anthology of striking speeches and episodes.

And so to Beerbohm Tree's spectacular 1898 revival at Her Majesty's Theatre; this, with over a hundred performances on its first run and many more up to 1913, opened 'a new epoch in the history of Shakespeare on the London stage'.[2] As in the Saxe-Meiningen production, Brutus and Cassius sank, Antony (Tree's own role) rose, having 'the colour – the glamour of the play' (though, Tree admitted, 'I like Brutus best – he is so much deeper').[3] The text was adjusted to enhance his part which, as usual, was relieved of duplicity and particularly of the proscription scene. The funeral oration became the climax, and lest its impact be weakened the later scenes were much curtailed in respect of parts other than his own. To effect these changes, concentrate the action, and accommodate elaborate spectacle, about a quarter of

---

[1] See Odell, ii. 424, for this and the *Times* quotation which follows. See also Michael R. Booth, 'The Meininger Company and English Shakespeare', *Shakespeare Survey* 35 (Cambridge, 1982), 13–20.

[2] Odell, ii. 450–1.

[3] Tree writing to his wife in 1897, from Hesketh Pearson, *Beerbohm Tree* (1956), p. 104.

the text went. The rest fell into three Acts, displaying Antony in three dominating stances which might, John Ripley suggests, be designated 'Antony Introduced, Antony Contriving, and Antony Triumphant'.[1] Each of them culminated in a tableau centring upon him. The first ended with him prophesying vengeance over Caesar's body; the second was the scene of the funeral orations, insufficiency of text being padded out by plentiful 'business'; the third featured Antony's final supremacy. His importance was repeatedly stressed. In the second scene he was clearly Caesar's bosom friend. After the murder, the brutality of which debased the conspirators, he confronted them with tragic deliberation; their degradation was symbolized in the gesture by which Casca gruesomely smeared his forearm with blood (whereon Antony 'repressed a rising look of horror'[2]) and in the coarseness with which Cassius bestrode the corpse to accost Brutus (Lawrence Barrett had already done so in 1871). In the market-place the crowd gave Antony as hostile a reception as possible, to make his triumph the more remarkable. And the triumph was sensational; as *The Times* reported (24 January 1898),

the now unchained passions of the mob, clamouring for vengeance . . ., and brandishing their torches lighted at the pyre that has been prepared for the dictator's remains, combine to produce a scene which, for its moving effect upon the house, has probably never been equalled before on the stage.

The settings and costumes, designed by Sir Lawrence Alma-Tadema, Royal Academician and master of luxurious classical subjects, were superbly apt for what *The Times* called 'scenes of unexampled beauty and effect', and

the audience was so literally [*sic*] transported to ancient Rome that a considerable portion of the *Telegraph*'s scholarly review could be devoted to pointing out in some detail just what elements in the scenery, costume and colouring made it a replica not of the last days of the Republic but of the hey-day of the Empire. Tree's instinct was theatrically sound: . . . to make his Rome superbly, theatrically itself, he had to give back to his audience their idea of Rome made bigger and better and three-dimensional.[3]

[1] Ripley, p. 153.

[2] Account by Percy Simpson, quoted in Furness, p. 443.

[3] Muriel St Clare Byrne, 'Fifty Years of Shakespearian Production', *Shakespeare Survey 2* (Cambridge, 1949), 1–20; p. 3.

A fine Caesar (Charles Fulton) redeemed the part from its usual vacuity. And, unexpectedly, several imaginative touches naturalized the Romans so that the production was praised for its humanity. Kemble had launched the main nineteenth-century tradition; in Tree it culminated. The text was still adjusted to suit a partial vision, though primacy passed from Brutus to Antony. Other producers had sought a balance of roles and sensitive character analyses: Tree offered *Julius Caesar* as the magnificent frame for heroic personality, and for spectacle. As he commented in *The Academy* (26 February 1898), 'the business of the manager [is] to present Shakespeare in such a way as to commend him to the many, even at the risk of agitating the few'.

The twentieth century has seen versions too various to be neatly summarized, in many countries and in different media. In Britain some, like Frank Benson's between 1890 and 1933, sought a Kemble-like dignity, the text pruned for athletic action. Others, like those by W. Bridges-Adams at Stratford-upon-Avon from 1919 to 1934, and by Anthony Quayle and Michael Langham reviving it there in 1950, saw the play as a balanced whole and its characters not as ideograms but as lifelike participants in a realistic yet impartially-viewed political scene. *The Times* (3 May 1950) praised this first major post-war production as offering 'a reasonable measure of Roman grandeur [enlivened by] all the momentum that a flowing pace can give', with John Gielgud's Cassius 'beyond question the most important person of every scene in which he figures'. For the *Birmingham Post* of the same date his was 'a performance of pounding force and eagerness' driven by 'urgent pleading, fiery disagreement, and all the disturbing action of a man fretting after greatness but dragged back from it by his own infirmities'. Harry Andrews played Brutus with quiet dignity and deep, controlled feeling; Anthony Quayle as Antony was the reveller turned crowd-orator; and Andrew Cruickshank made Caesar the arrogant living legend, 'senile, unctuous, and sour-faced, . . . decidedly unsympathetic but not without a certain faded majesty'.[1] Sympathy lay predominantly, as is traditional, with Brutus and Cassius, but these interpretations did not distort the play in favour of some *parti pris*; the dignity of ancient Rome, and

---

[1] Ripley, p. 250. Gielgud's performance as Cassius is preserved in the notable film version of 1953, directed by Joseph L. Mankiewicz, of which there is an account in Jack Jorgens's *Shakespeare on Film* (Bloomington, 1977).

7. The armies and their leaders confront each other, Act 5, Scene 1;
Shakespeare Memorial Theatre, 1950.

the impressive eminence of ancient Romans, were still felt as
positive values, and the human worth of all the contestants was
justly recognized.

Yet as, increasingly, the age, and stage, leaned towards more
ruthless political realism, a problem emerged – how combine the
dignity proper to *Julius Caesar*'s full effect with the informality
modern taste looks for? Shakespearian characters are artistically
(if not morally) 'better' than the norm and they need such a degree
of distinction as does not overbalance into the affected. Great art
imposes greatness; humane art imposes humanity. Shakespeare's
art does both, and *Julius Caesar* should find humane greatness
congenial.

But as the skies darkened under Fascism the play was seen in a
different fashion, as ruthless power directing the mindless mass
against too credulous altruism. This theme was sensationally
sounded in New York in 1937 when Orson Welles's production,
subtitled *Death of a Dictator*, set the play within blood-red walls and

uncompromisingly updated it, for an unprecedented American run of 157 performances. For Welles Brutus was the perennial liberal, precipitating calamities even worse than those he seeks to avert. The text, heavily cut, was 'not divided into acts and scenes but follow[ed] the format of a radio or film script with episodes fading one into another, punctuated only by light, darkness, and sound effects'.[1] Despite the cuts, Cinna's murder (3.3) was for the first time on the American stage played in full;[2] it stood shockingly out as mob violence smashed the hapless innocent. The same harsh theme was heard in the mob's 'superbly orchestrated whispers, murmurs, shouts, chants, and screams' as, to the noise of pounding feet, Antony's oration let slip the dogs of war.[3] Drastic chiaroscuro, rhythmic percussion, and martial sounds kept the nerves throbbing. Costumes were street clothes and Fascist uniforms. Accentuated in shafts of light, Caesar projected totalitarian menace, with 'striding height, jutting chin, cross-belted military tunic, sleek modern breeches' (*Time*, 22 November 1937). Antony, the virtuoso rabble-rouser, gave his (hypocritical) eulogy of Brutus against vertical searchlights as if at the Nazi Nuremberg rally. Brutus, low-toned, scrupulous, intellectual, was the liberal whose fellow-conspirators shone with a heroism reflected from his own ethical light, a man whose tragedy is 'truly tragic because it is the destruction of virtuousness by the logic of its own virtue'.[4]

Welles's version, the most remarkable of many attempts to make Shakespeare urgently actual, was offered with revolutionary force. Less successful was London's counterpart, by Henry Cass in November 1939, modern-dress-Fascist, with Brutus the well-meaning democrat out of his element, Antony a Hitlerian henchman, Caesar 'a nervous hypochondriac wearing spectacles', and field commanders communicating by telephone.[5] It did not catch on; 'relevance' failed to compensate for lack of nobility. Other productions, in the post-war era of autocratic directors, have

[1] Ripley, p. 223. As well as Ripley's vivid account there is a good brief one by A. C. Sprague in *Shakespearian Players and Performances* (Cambridge, Mass., 1953; London, 1954), pp. 159–60.

[2] On both sides of the Atlantic it had been considered, to quote Gentleman, ii. 12, 'a most unessential scene, omitted in representation'.

[3] Ripley, p. 228.

[4] Archibald Macleish in *The Nation*, 4 December 1938.

[5] J. C. Trewin, *Shakespeare on the English Stage, 1900–1964* (1964), p. 185.

presented *Julius Caesar* with anti-heroic lack of glamour, symboliz-ing power's menace or tawdriness, holding up a tarnished mirror to an unillusioned world. The 1963 Royal Shakespeare Company's production, with sombre sets, drab colouring, and menacing leather costumes, was described by the *Birmingham Post*'s critic, J. C. Trewin, as comprising 'simply a dictator's murder, a grim little revolution and counter-revolution. Except, remarkably, for Caesar himself, the scale is much reduced; it is the new contemporary way with Shakespeare – that resolve to bring the whole thing down to earth.' A foreigner without English, Philip Hope-Wallace remarked in *The Guardian*, 'might have thought himself watching a scene from *Mother Courage* – the lighting, scrim walls, and cropped heads'; the conspirators, 'a poor stumbling band, fell upon Caesar in what seemed some deserted corner of a railway station'. Such a version is 'down to earth' indeed. The more relevance, the less resonance.

Modernization is legitimate if the play's greatness survives; charismatic dictatorship can hardly be ignored. So Caesar, previously an unrewarding part prematurely cut short, his name merely labelling a play belonging to Brutus or Antony, has moved into the centre. There were earlier examples as Fascism began to bite; in Stratford-upon-Avon's 1934 revival 'Caesar's tragedy [was] the key',[1] with the great leader, alive or dead, controlling the whole action. In Henry Cass's 1935 Old Vic version Cecil Trouncer gave Caesar the 'majesty a little over-matured which the part needs'.[2] In 1957 at Stratford-upon-Avon, Rome was symbolized by massive grey monoliths, at first ranged in order, later disarranged, and Caesar was neither the traditional figure-head nor the modern Fascist but the fount of authority he would have been to Elizabethans, 'treacherously assassinated by professed friends who then plunge their country into . . . civil wars'.[3]

And because, so conceived, Caesar is equivalent to Rome, symbolism conveyed the message. The sky darkened as disorder threatened, or reddened for fire or war; lightning crackled; and Antony's listeners were silhouetted at the stage front as though

[1] *Yorkshire Post*, 18 June 1934, quoted in Ripley, p. 206.
[2] Ivor Brown in *The Observer*, 27 October 1935, quoted in Ripley, p. 239.
[3] Roy Walker, 'Unto Caesar', *Shakespeare Survey* 11 (Cambridge, 1958), 128–35; p. 132. This article comments that 'No major play of Shakespeare's has suffered more from democratic distortion', and it gives an excellent account of the 1957 production and of its rehabilitation of Caesar.

8. The conspirators kneel before Caesar; Shakespeare Memorial Theatre, 1957 (Cyril Luckham as Caesar, Alec Clunes as Brutus, Geoffrey Keen as Cassius).

light were fading. Caesar's red-and-gold toga distinguished him in life and, covering his catafalque, also in death. As Antony cried, 'Here was a Caesar! When comes such another?' the northern star suddenly shone. It shone again when, over dead Cassius, Brutus exclaimed 'O Julius Caesar, thou art mighty yet!', and at the end,

The dead body of the tragically deluded liberator lay in the centre of the stage, not in Rome but in the wilderness he had helped to make of Rome, and high above him shone out the star of whose true-fixed and resting quality there is no fellow in the firmament.[1]

In John Barton's Fascist-flavoured 1968 production for the Royal Shakespeare Company, again Caesar (Brewster Mason) was in 'massive command' (*Birmingham Post*), his grandeur and hauteur recalling General de Gaulle.[2] In Trevor Nunn's 1972 Stratford revival, Caesar (Mark Dignam) dominated the scene, 'some time-

[1] Ibid., p. 134.
[2] Robert Speaight, in *Shakespeare Quarterly*, 19 (1968), 367–77; p. 373.

9. Caesar's statue dominates the stage in Trevor Nunn's Royal Shakespeare Theatre production, 1972 (Mark Dignam as Caesar).

less Mussolini', said the *Financial Times*. His overpowering image was symbolized by a colossal statue, its features spotlit in red as one by one his enemies perished. At the start an enormous red carpet spun right down the stage to a crash of martial sound, while Caesar, black-leather-clad, headed a surge of white, black, and red-robed subservient senators and populace given to heel-clicking and Fascist salutes.[1]

He bestrode the action of the early scenes like some omnipotent robot … At the same time he evinced a magnetism very nearly irresistible. One was forced to recognize his greatness, however malign; and one instantly understood Brutus' admiration for the man, and his reluctance to annihilate a veritable symbol of human potential. Although a bolder and less complex portrait than many of its predecessors, the impact of Dignam's Colossus was immediate, overwhelming, and all pervasive.[2]

[1] David, p. 150, gives interesting details.
[2] Ripley, p. 274.

Beneath this indomitable presence Brutus, a theorizing precursor of Hamlet, poignant in private affections and painfully strained before violence, led a confused and inexpert conspiracy to doom.

For three centuries *Julius Caesar* has inevitably reflected political assumptions. Still, Shakespeare himself takes no sides, or all sides. This survey, neglecting other revivals for lack of space, must close with one of the most recent, the BBC's television version (1978) which, without tendentious stressing, went less for Romans or politicians than for human beings, caught in an impetuous action. Settings not over-massive for the play's humanity yet grand enough for Rome's authority were modelled with cool clean lighting fitting the cool clean style. Countenances, costumes, manners, and gestures were those of the strong ethos of Rome. Above all, character shadings were scrupulously preserved. Caesar (Charles Gray), imperious, massively 'Roman', yet at times affable, suggested his infirmities by passing tremors and uncertain step; Antony discreetly supported him as he entered, and their intimacy was neatly established. Cassius (David Collings), courteous-rational rather than rasping-trenchant, lacked something of authority yet was acutely intelligent and emotionally sensitive; in the quarrel scene his sense of outrage and distress were equally striking. Brutus (Richard Pasco), self-reliant in evident virtue, rejected oath-swearing and Antony's death with an authority which half-persuaded one that murder could be clean-handed, yet by his unease revealed how deeply he felt the furtiveness of strategy, as the poignancy of his scene with Portia and his envy of Lucius' easy sleep hinted at the depth of his perturbation. The ambivalence of the conspiracy showed up well. On the surface there was 'honesty to honesty engaged' (2.1.127); beneath, the darkness of treachery. This, clear in Decius' flattery, became visually vivid in the murder, first when Caesar, gripped with courageous and stupefied anguish while being stabbed, reached to clasp Brutus in their final relationship as the climactic blow was given, and also when, in the blood-smearing, the semblance of ritual and the actuality of horror united in dreadful irony as 'the men that gave their country liberty' celebrated their revolting ceremony. As for Antony (Keith Michell), grand in bearing, deeply attached to Caesar, outraged by his murder, by turns strategic, unscrupulous, and honourable, rising finally to his eulogy over Brutus, yet edged out of primacy by Octavius, he compassed all the complexities the part can offer.

The result was a production which, if not outstanding for any particular feature, in justness of rendering, humanity of characterization, drive of action, and distinction of diction, kept in fine relationship the variant elements which Shakespeare provided, proving itself 'more concerned with interpreting the play than with playing an interpretation'.[1]

The play's problems are seldom all solved together, calling as they do for insight and sympathy over four great roles, each with integrally related virtues and failings, calling too for verse-speaking neither declamatory nor wholly naturalistic – what one may call unaffectedly stylized – and for characterization neither idealized nor simplified, taking distinction to be the right mode for those in high Roman station. Shakespeare has a political subject yet he draws on Plutarch's *Lives of the Noble Grecians and Romans* with its themes of great though human natures pursuing great though human actions. One remembers *Julius Caesar* not for diagrams of dictator, altruist, instigator, and demagogue, but for the depth of its insights into men and women in public and private life on whose behaviour great issues depend, and for its confirmation of the Aristotelian tenet that poetry is a higher and more philosophical thing than history.

*   *   *

The First Folio Text

Julius Caesar was first printed, and printed strikingly well, in the 1623 First Folio. The Folios of 1632, 1663, and 1685 have no independent authority; each derives from its precursor and differs textually only in minor corruptions and self-evident corrections. So too with the Quartos issued in the 1680s and 1690s in quick succession 'to supply the demand created by Betterton's fine presentation of Brutus'.[2] The first, dated 1684, seems to derive from the First Folio, with alterations reflecting stage practice. One

---

[1] This neat phrase is from Ripley, p. 260, where, however, it is used with the contrary application, to describe a production *less* concerned to interpret the play, etc.

[2] Henrietta Bartlett, 'Quarto Editions of *Julius Caesar*', *The Library*, third series, 4 (1913), 122–32; p. 130.

is dated 1691 (and is known as Q1691). Three others (Quartos 2–4) are undated, but their actors' lists show them to be not earlier than 1684; from their publishers' trade history they seem to fall between 1684 and 1688. Another, Q5, shows some resemblances to Rowe's Shakespeare of 1709 and may itself have appeared in or after 1709. They, and Q1691, appear to derive, immediately or mediately, from Q1684. The sole authority for the play, therefore, remains the First Folio.

What was the relationship between Shakespeare's manuscript and the Folio text? The text itself is unusually clean and (at first sight) problem-free, and that between Shakespeare's own papers (still evincing, presumably, the irregularities of composition) and the Folio a fair copy intervened seems evident. There is a striking orderliness and clarity of presentation, the efficiency of which (granted that such 'efficiency' perhaps conceals undetectable variations from what Shakespeare in fact wrote) points to a 'clean scribal transcript of Shakespeare's own working papers'.[1] That this fair copy was by a hand other than his seems evident, too – there are no 'Shakespearian' spellings such as elsewhere can be found when the compositor was following Shakespeare's own script, save for the name-forms discussed in the next paragraph. Even such compositorial slips as can be detected or suspected are infrequent and venial,[2] and this points to admirably legible copy. A few readings normally amended (as in this edition) may be what Shakespeare inadvertently wrote.[3]

Idiosyncratic spellings occur in some proper names. 'Murellus' or 'Murrellus', 'Caska', and 'Calphurnia' (for Plutarch's 'Marullus', 'Casca', and 'Calpurnia'), for instance, are insignificant changes carried through consistently and originating with either Shake-speare or the transcriber. More significant is 'Antony' ('Antonius' in Plutarch), since in other plays (*Romeo and Juliet*, *Much Ado About Nothing*, *Henry V*, *Macbeth*, and *Antony and Cleopatra*) the Folio

[1] Bowers, p. 23.

[2] 2.1.67 ('of a man' for 'of man'), 268 ('hit' for 'his'), and 281 ('tho' for 'the'); 3.1.113 ('State' for 'States') and 115 ('lye' for 'lyes'); 3.2.104 ('are' for 'art') and 214 ('writ' for 'wit'); 4.2.300 ('will it' for 'will'); and 5.4.17 ('thee' for 'the').

[3] 2.2.23 ('do'); 3.1.208 ('Hart'); 5.1.96 ('rests'); 5.3.104 ('Tharsus'). The Folio's 'first' at 2.1.40 (which editors amend to 'Ides'), '*Lucillius*' at 4.2.50 (most editors read 'Lucius'), and 'Let *Lucius*' at 4.2.52 (most editors read 'Lucilius') may be readings originally correct but rendered inappropriate (and inadvertently left standing) by subsequently added material; see the Introduction, p. 80, n. 1, the Commentary to 2.1.59, and Stirling, p. 193.

almost always spells the name with 'th', which suggests that probably Shakespeare did so too; *Julius Caesar*'s different version looks like a scribal preference. But an interesting example of presumably Shakespearian spelling transmitted through the transcript is the recurrence of Folio name-endings in 'io' where one would expect 'ius'. 'Antonio's' and 'Antonio' occur at 1.2.3, 4, 6, and 190, and at 1.3.37. 'Octauio's' occurs at 3.1.275.1 and 5.2.4, 'Claudio' at 4.2.292 (and thereafter through that scene, where conversely 'Varro' is given as 'Varrus'), and 'Flauio' at 5.3.108 (perhaps by attraction from the 'Labio' of Plutarch's 'Labio and Flavius'; *Brutus*, p. 169). In *Antony and Cleopatra* 'Anthonio's' occurs at 2.2.7 and 'Anthonyo's' at 2.5.26. Having in other plays offered characters with Italianate endings Shakespeare may have slipped into these 'io' spellings here, and as they would come spontaneously into his mind a case can be argued for retaining them. But they look eccentric in a classical context, and one assumes that had he given the matter thought he would have altered them, as most editors have done.[1]

The text's freedom from the irregularities common when copy has not been carefully prepared again points to a capable scribal transcript. Admittedly there are small abnormalities: '*Iulius Caesar*' (2.2.0.1) differs from the standard stage direction form '*Caesar*', and at 4.2.207.1 Lucius re-enters as '*Boy*', a variation probably resulting from later addition of lines 194 to 208 and 216 (see pp. 78–81). But these are very minor irregularities. There is a general absence of the loose or confused stage directions commonly found when no regulating hand has been at work; occasional examples (as at 4.2.0.1 or 5.4.1.1, 7.1) occur during complicated battle manoeuvres and appear questionable only on close inspection. The lineation is predominantly good, despite an occasional metrical jumble caused by faulty line division,[2] and a few single lines split into two even when the Folio's column width could easily accommodate them; in some cases, at least, this appears to be the result of faulty casting-off of copy.[3] Punctuation is generally clear and efficient; in almost all cases where a modern editor will change it

[1] 'Pluto's' for 'Plutus'' at 4.2.153 is, however, a different matter, this being a not uncommon Elizabethan alternative: see the Commentary at that point.

[2] See collation at 1.2.52–3, 79–80, 175–7; 1.3.39–40, 57–60, 139–41; 4.2.229–30, 274–5, 349–50; 5.1.71–2 (this last is trivial); and 5.3.36–7.

[3] See collation at 1.2.58, 178–9, and 300; 1.3.42 and 79; 2.4.39; and 3.2.253.

the Folio is not wrong but following a different convention. The main significant differences (and these merely venial slips) occur at 1.1.37, 1.2.166 and 252, and 1.3.125 and 129.

Speech prefixes are unusually uniform (within very narrow limits of variation) and speech attributions reliable. Many editors follow Capell and transfer 1.1.15 from the Folio's Flavius to Marullus; many, too, follow Pope and transfer 3.1.101–2 from Casca to Cassius; but neither change is necessary. At 4.2.34–6 the Folio names no speakers but different soldiers evidently repeat the command in sequence. At 5.4.7 the Folio has no speech prefix but slightly indents the line and, by what must be a scribe's or compositor's error, inserts the prefix '*Luc[ilius]*.' at line 9; Plutarch shows Lucilius to be the speaker also of lines 7 and 8.

But assuming a transcript efficiently regularizing the variations to be expected in Shakespeare's working papers, was it a preliminary to the prompt-book, was it transcribed from the prompt-book, was it annotated from the prompt-book, or did it serve as the prompt-book itself? It is hard to be sure. There would be little difficulty in using the Folio's copy as the prompt-book itself. Even though not all entrances, exits, deaths, and stage actions are noted (as is made clear below), the words of the text generally indicate what is to happen. Some directions, when they differ from the terse practicality expected in a prompt-book by added comments or descriptive detail, seem to reflect Shakespeare's mind sketching in or visualizing the action – directions such as those at 1.1.0 ('*Enter . . . certaine Commoners ouer the Stage.*'), 1.2.0 ('*Enter Caesar, Antony for the Course . . .: after them Murellus and Flauius.*'), 2.1.0 ('*Enter Brutus in his Orchard.*'), 2.2.0 ('*Enter Iulius Caesar in his Night-gowne.*'), or 4.2.286 ('*Enter Lucius with the Gowne.*').[1] These familiar touches may or may not be authorial, but they would not be ineffective in a prompt-book. And, as a more general point, one may wonder why such an efficient transcript should be made if it were not meant to be the prompt-book.

The balance of consideration, however, tilts slightly the other way. Though prompt-books could serve as printer's copy (it is generally agreed that *Macbeth*'s and – in all probability – *King Lear*'s did so), in general a prompt-book was too useful a property to be surrendered to the printing-house until the players had

---

[1] W. W. Greg, *The Editorial Problem in Shakespeare*, second edn. (Oxford, 1951), pp. 143–4.

entirely done with it, and since *Julius Caesar* seems to have continued popular and, apparently, to have been actively in the public mind in the 1620s when the Folio was being prepared (see p. 5), one would not expect its prompt-book to have been handed over. Moreover, though the Folio's stage directions (the main bases for determining prompt-book origins) are generally efficient, a prompt-book might be expected to provide rather more than the Folio does (though not as many as a modern edition).[1] There are no directions for the triumphal sounds which surely should accompany Caesar's procession at 1.2.0 (and are suppressed at 1.2.1), or for the music to which Casca and Caesar refer at 1.2.14 and 16, and which presumably must be heard at line 11. (Perhaps the absence of ceremonial music as Caesar returns at 1.2.177 reflects his soured temper, yet a 'Sennet' sounds as he leaves at line 214 and one might expect some signal of his re-entry too.) There are no directions for the entries of citizens at 1.2.0 (despite the 'press' and 'throng' at lines 15 and 21) or at 3.1.0 (though one would expect them to follow Caesar's progress),[2] for Popilius at 3.1.0, Caesar's carriers at 3.2.39, Lucilius, Lucius, and Titinius at 4.2.174, or Lucilius, Titinius, and Messala at 5.1.20.[3] At 4.2.0 the Folio has Titinius rather than Lucilius accompany Pindarus to meet Brutus, though (as lines 3 and 4 imply) it is Lucilius who has been with Pindarus at Cassius' camp.[4] The Folio gives no exits for Lucius at 2.1.60 and 76, Artemidorus and the Soothsayer at 3.1.12 (or thereabouts), Trebonius and Antony at 3.1.26, Cassius and his plebeians at 3.2.10, Lucilius, Titinius, or Lucius at 4.2.192, Lucius at 4.2.212 and 281, the Ghost at 4.2.336, Pindarus at 5.3.22 and

[1] Admittedly, as examination of prompt-books has shown, 'a good deal of untidiness [was] tolerated': W. W. Greg, *Dramatic Documents from the Elizabethan Playhouses*, 2 vols. (Oxford, 1931), i. 201.

[2] It is of course possible that since 3.1 requires fourteen entrants at its opening (thirteen specified in the entry direction, and the Popilius Lena omitted therefrom), and also Antony and his servant later on, the company lacked further actors to provide a crowd; on the size of the company see p. 1, n. 2.

[3] Not all these are clearly originally inadequate directions. At 3.1.0 a scribe or compositor might overlook Popilius because of the similarity of Publius. At 4.2.174 Lucilius (or, according to the Folio at 4.2.52, Lucius) and Titinius, guarding Brutus' tent, might be assumed self-evidently to enter with the intruder they are posted to keep out. And at 5.1.20 Lucilius, Titinius, and Messala might be covered by the Folio's '*Brutus, Cassius, & their Army.*'

[4] Such uncertainties may have arisen from Shakespearian confusion over military incidentals but one would expect them to be clarified as the stage action was being prepared.

50, Messala at 5.3.79, Brutus, Messala, and Flavius at 5.4.1, or Clitus, Dardanius, and Volumnius at 5.5.44. Exits, it is true, are often omitted in Elizabethan play texts, and most of these are patently self-evident, but, as Fredson Bowers observes, if a book-keeper were preparing the transcript as the prompt-copy 'the frequent omission would be more than ordinarily careless'.[1]

These deficiencies do not conclusively tell against the Folio's origin in the prompt-book, since one can tell from the Folio as it stands what practically all of the action must be. Yet collectively they do suggest that a prompt-book might be more fully annotated. Were there no prompt-book influences at all, the directions would probably be less efficient; were the prompt-book itself, or a transcript of it, actually the printers' copy, they should be more numerous than they are. The somewhat tentative assumption is that a clean scribal transcript of Shakespeare's working papers was either, as Fredson Bowers indicates, 'partly marked up by the book-keeper with a view to the later inscription from it of the official prompt-book, and then preserved in the theatre as a substitute file copy for the working papers',[2] or else partially annotated from the prompt-book in preparation for the printer.[3] These annotations would probably include the 'very full provision of stage noises and some apparent duplication'.[4] (The occasional omission of such noises has, however, been noted, on p. 76.) The marginal *'Thunder'* at 2.1.335 is unexpected after a scene atmospherically undisturbed, and may be the prompter's cue for the *'Thunder & Lightning'* with which, three words later, the next scene opens. The marginal *'Lowd Alarum'* at 5.2.2, following on the centred *'Alarum'* at 5.2.0.1, may be a prompt-book addition to stress the urgency of the situation; one would not expect Shakespeare himself to duplicate the instruction he had written two lines earlier. The *'Thunder still'* at 1.3.100, *'Low march within'* at 4.2.24 (anticipating *'Enter Cassius and his Powers'* six lines later), *'Low Alarums'* at 5.3.96 (following *'Alarum'* at line 90), *'Low Alarums'* at 5.5.23, and *'Alarum still'* at 5.5.29 look like prompt-book additions for extra effect. Such effects, not deducible from the course of the text

---

[1] Bowers, p. 27.

[2] Ibid., p. 24.

[3] A scribal copy partially annotated from the prompt-book supplemented quarto copy for the Folio printing of, for instance, *Love's Labour's Lost, A Midsummer Night's Dream,* and *Much Ado About Nothing.*

[4] W. W. Greg, *The Shakespeare First Folio* (Oxford, 1955), p. 290.

alone, may have resulted from experience during (or preparations for) rehearsals, and they somewhat favour the argument for annotation from (or anticipatory to) the prompt-book. How far, and at what stage, prompt-book influences may have operated is a question with little bearing on an editor's textual choices.

The Folio's Act divisions (after '*Actus Primus. Scœna Prima.*' there are no indications of scenes) would in all probability be editorial additions made as the copy was being prepared for the press.[1] Other alterations may well have been made either as Shakespeare was working the play over (as is indeed inevitable) or even after it was initially complete. Dover Wilson speculated that the discrepancies in Casca's character might result from later addition of the prose comedy of 1.2.215–91; if so, he thought, 'most of these inconsistencies would be explained'.[2] This idea, however, is merely supposition, and the 'inconsistencies' are only different aspects of an interesting individual. More cogently argued was the case presented by Brents Stirling, and strongly supported by Fredson Bowers, for thinking that on bibliographical and typographical evidence both Act 2, Scene 1 and Act 4, Scene 2 (lines 175–212, or thereabouts – the poet's incursion and the first account of Portia's death) can be proved to be revisions and indeed to demonstrate that Shakespeare, having 'completed' a play, could rework parts of it not merely for stage-practical reasons but for artistic and aesthetic ones.[3] Act 2, Scene 1, it was proposed, amalgamates an original two scenes, the one concerning a Cassius–Casca–Brutus meeting so clearly announced at 1.3.153–64, the other concerning a meeting of all the conspirators at Pompey's Porch (or Theatre) so clearly announced at 1.3.125–6, 136–9, and 147–52. In the former hypothesized scene, the three main plotters would take the basic decisions; in the latter, they would brief their fellows. But then, for speed and concentration, the two would be dovetailed together, to produce the powerful existing scene which, however, in discrepancies of time-scheme and in repeated motions for departure followed by repeated resumptions of business, shows signs of its disparate

[1] Eighteenth-century editors introduced the existing scene divisions. What this edition gives as a continuous 4.2 has traditionally been divided after line 52 into 4.2 and 4.3. The divisions between 5.1 and 5.2 and between 5.3 and 5.4 are odd, for in each case Brutus, having just left the stage, immediately rushes on again. But for this stage procedure the responsibility is Shakespeare's.

[2] Wilson, p. 97.

[3] See Stirling, pp. 187–205, and Bowers, pp. 23–36.

origins. As for the account of Portia's death, bibliographical and typographical 'proof' seemed for the first time to confirm the argument previously put, by a variety of critics, on grounds of character-appropriateness, that this earlier-occurring revelation was in fact a later-written insertion meant to show Brutus more deeply moved by his wife's death than did the phlegmatic coolness of the (assumedly) original one (lines 231–45), which it was meant either to replace or at least to explain as the outward mask behind which Brutus kept to himself his inward grief.

Space does not allow for the extended exposition which supported the case; in brief, it depended on the absence, in the Folio's printing of these two areas, of the '*Caffi.*' spellings otherwise all but invariable in the speech-prefixes for Cassius (these giving way to '*Caf.*' or '*Caff.*'). This change of practice, it was argued, pointed to a different scribal habit from that evident elsewhere and indicated that these passages were later additions to the script. Yet conclusive though the technical argument appeared, and skilful though its conduct, it has been met with an equally skilful and (it would seem) finally conclusive rebuttal, which indicates that the reason for the absence of these spellings hereabouts is merely the practical fact that supplies of the '*ffi*' ligatures (never very large) ran out, and such ligatures could not reappear until already-printed pages could have their type distributed into the cases for further use.[1]

Shakespeare may indeed have revised either or both of these scenes, but for the time being the argument about whether he did so must rest on normal critical grounds. It still seems tenable that revision lies behind Act 2, Scene 1, for though time discrepancies and loosenesses in the control of action can be found everywhere in Shakespeare (and generally are unimportant), certainly by the end of Act 1, Scene 3, Shakespeare has given every indication of intending the pair of scenes Stirling envisages, and in the conspiratorial parts of Act 2, Scene 1, there are, on close inspection, a good many apparent signs of dovetailing.[2] As for the two versions

[1] John Jowett, 'Ligature Shortage and Speech-Prefix Variation in *Julius Caesar*', forthcoming in *The Library*.

[2] The most striking pointer to a time discrepancy suggesting an alteration of Shakespeare's original plan is the Folio's 'first of March' at 2.1.40, which editors all (and inevitably) change to 'Ides of March'. Plutarch mentions 'the first day ... of March' (*Brutus*, p. 112) as the date on which Caesar was to be offered the crown

of Portia's death (4.2.194–208, to 'Speak no more of her.', and 231–45), that Shakespeare would not mean both to stand seems probable. On the stage, it is true, both are sometimes played, and in the onward course of the action the audience can well accept the impression that the first reflects Brutus' true feelings in private (under control though they are), while the second represents the noble self-command he shows in public, and his unwillingness to reopen the scene of his grief. The two episodes were very effectively played thus in – to take two notable instances – the 1972 Royal Shakespeare Company's production and the BBC television rendering.[1] Yet as one reads the text, and in the absence of any hint as to how to take the second occurrence (Shakespeare might be expected to offer guidance), Brutus' profession of ignorance (lines 232–4) about what he has so recently disclosed is a downright falsehood, and he can be relieved of this uncharacteristic untruthfulness only by assuming that when Shakespeare wrote this passage he had not in fact written the other, which was an afterthought intended to show Brutus' true feelings and redeem him from inhumanity. What seems likely is that he originally wrote the second passage but not the first, so that 'Lucius, a bowl of wine' (l. 192) or Cassius' 'I did not think you could have been so angry' (l. 193) led directly to 'In this I bury all unkindness, Cassius' (l. 209). Later, reflecting that Brutus must appear inhumanly unfeeling, he would add lines 194 to 208 (and also 216). He would mean lines 231–45 to be deleted, so that 'Cicero is dead, | And by that order of proscription' (ll. 229–30) would lead directly to 'Well, to our work alive' (l. 246). But by mischance the deletion was not made, or if made was overlooked, so that both versions survive, to put Brutus in a questionable light.

This seems a likely explanation of what on the face of it is a

(the 'tomorrow' of Casca's news at 1.3.85–8 and also of the midnight scene of 2.1). The fact that the same 'tomorrow' is now the Ides of March (15 March) suggests that Shakespeare originally intended an interval between the planning and the effecting of the assassination but on revision condensed the time-scheme while overlooking the time discrepancy. See also the Commentary on 2.1.61–2.

[1] For the successful playing of both 'Portia's death' scenes in these productions see, respectively, David, p. 154, and Thomas Clayton, 'Should Brutus Never Taste of Portia's Death But Once? Text and Performance in *Julius Caesar*', *Studies in English Literature*, 23 (1983), 237–55.

puzzle. If the surmised deletion could be proved without doubt to have been intended, ll. 231–45 should be cut, to conform with what would then be Shakespeare's demonstrable desire. But (as the above discussion about '*ſſi*' ligatures shows) what may seem to be proof may turn out otherwise; and in this case no more can be offered than seemingly strong likelihood. On less than certain evidence it would be wrong to prejudge the issue, so this text retains both versions of Portia's death and leaves this interesting problem for the reader's consideration.

Two further probable alterations need a word. The first concerns the conspirators who visit Caesar at 2.2.107 ff. Among them is the hitherto unheard-of Publius. Cassius, however, is missing, being either – critics have surmised – too honest to play the hypocrite, or too open a foe to appear as an alleged friend. But nowhere else does Cassius show such scruples, and Dover Wilson suggested that perhaps, as one would expect, Shakespeare originally wrote him in here, and not Publius.[1] But then, Wilson argued, the play's casting would encourage doubling 'lean' Cassius with 'lean' Ligarius (who, at 2.1.310, came on eighty lines after Cassius had left – time enough for change of robes and roles). So, the theory goes, when the play was cast, the simultaneous entry of both men had to be avoided, even though Shakespeare's script would surely have included both – Cassius obviously, and Ligarius because, having joined with Brutus at 2.1.332, he would automatically reappear with him here. The book-keeper could solve the problem by substituting Publius for Cassius (metrically the same) here and at 2.2.108–9. The effect, when one has time to think, is odd: the first visitor Caesar greets is a total newcomer. But the audience, without time to think, will not be struck by this, or by Cassius' absence. The idea that Publius was not initially involved gains some slight support (not apparently noted by previous commentators) from the Folio's entry direction at 3.1.0, which separates him from the others by inserting Artemidorus between him and them, as though he and they were different parties. Certainly if Publius were meant by Shakespeare as one of the plotters his stupefaction at 3.1.86 is odd.[2] So perhaps Cassius' absence at 2.2.107 results from a casting chance.

[1] Wilson, p. 96.
[2] Plutarch has no conspiratorial Publius at this stage but later mentions a

The final assumed alteration concerns Jonson's jibe about Caesar's never doing wrong 'but with just cause' (mentioned on pp. 4–5). Conceivably, from 3.1.46 onwards the original text ran something like:

> CAESAR
> I spurn thee like a cur out of my way.
> METELLUS
> Caesar, thou dost me wrong.
> CAESAR
> Caesar did never wrong but with just cause,
> Nor without cause will he be satisfied.

(This has the merit of eliminating the half-line with which the extant text ends Caesar's speech.) The apparent solecism is not actually – as Jonson held – 'ridiculous'; it may be taken to mean 'Caesar never acted hurtfully but for good reason'. But assuming that Jonson was not making it up, alteration (by Shakespeare or the book-keeper) might well seem desirable to avert derision, though if 'Caesar, thou dost me wrong' were (as Jonson alleged) in the original text its disappearance is odd, since there is nothing wrong with it. It might have been cut accidentally, or, though purporting to quote accurately, Jonson might sense that a plausible cue was needed and so invent one. Since he was retailing the joke in the 1620s the original version (if any) must have been current for some time in the theatre, but when, and by whom, revision (if any) was effected cannot be ascertained.[1]

As each sheet of the Folio was being printed certain errors were corrected, so some copies have the initial readings, others the alterations. Most variants consist of minor literals and the like, but three involve substantive corrections. At 5.3.97 'haue crown'd' became 'haue not crown'd'; at 5.3.101 'no teares' became 'mo teares'; and at 5.5.23.1 '*Loud Alarums*' became '*Low Alarums*'. The first two, being commonsense amendments, could have been

Publius Sicilius, whom the triumvirs execute for supporting Brutus (*Brutus*, pp. 136–7).

[1] See J. Dover Wilson, 'Ben Jonson and *Julius Caesar*', in *Shakespeare Survey 2* (Cambridge, 1949), 36–43; pp. 40–1. As late as 1657 a certain Thomas Plume could still note, in confused manuscript jottings, that 'One told Ben Johnson – Shakespear never studied for any thing he wrott. B. J. said – the more to blame He – said – Cesar never punishes any but for a just Cause' (Chambers, ii. 248).

effected without reference to copy but the third is not self-evident and it suggests that at least hereabouts some care was being taken over the readings.[1]

[1] Charlton Hinman, *The Printing and Proof-Reading of the First Folio of Shakespeare*, 2 vols. (Oxford, 1963), i. 298–300. Perhaps '*Lowd Alarum*' at 5.2.2 should also have been changed to '*Lowe Alarum*' (the page on which it occurs shows no signs of proof-correction); 'd' and 'e' are very similar in Shakespeare's hand. But '*Lowd*' here may well be correct; see the Commentary.

EDITORIAL PROCEDURES

THE present edition offers a text and stage directions as faithful to the Folio's as certain basic procedures allow. These consist of the revision or insertion of stage directions when needed for clear guidance, the correction of apparent errors, and the modernization of punctuation and spelling.[1] Such flexibilities in the Folio's punctuation are preserved as convey dramatic fluency and expressiveness without conflicting with modern practice (see, for instance, the Commentary at 2.1.330–2 and 3.1.240–2). Obsolete, variant, or ambiguous spellings are adjusted to appropriate modern ones.[2] 'And', for 'if', becomes 'an'. In the Introduction and Commentary, quotations from sixteenth and seventeenth-century texts are given in modern spelling.

Past forms need a word of comment. In *Julius Caesar* the Folio is generally methodical in indicating the syllabic value of these for metrical purposes. In verse it nearly always shows non-syllabic endings by shortened forms (for example, 'deckt', 'laught', and 'roar'd') or by adjusted spelling (for example, 'cride', 'cry'de'). At times metre is served instead by medial elision (for example, 'unnumbred', 'engendred'). All such forms are here rendered by normal past participles or tenses. As a result, the Folio's various versions of past forms in such a line as 'refresht, new-added, and encourag'd' (4.2.259) are here uniform. When the Folio gives the unelided form in verse it normally means the ending to be syllabic ('touched', 1.2.8; 'Vexed', 1.2.39, and the like): the syllabic value is indicated in this edition by '-èd'. But the Folio wavers over past forms of which the root ends in a vowel sound, often spelling them in full yet not implying a sounded syllable.[3] Whatever the form,

---

[1] For a full discussion of editorial procedures in the Oxford Shakespeare see Gary Taylor's edition of *Henry V*, pp. 75 ff. For a discussion of the problems of modernization, see Wells (*Modernizing*), pp. 3–36.

[2] For example, the Folio's 'soules' (1.1.14, soles); 'where' (1.1.61, whe'er (whether)); 'loose' (1.2.124, lose); 'swoonded', 'swound' (1.2.246, swooned; 1.2.249, swoon); 'disgest' (1.2.298, digest); 'moe' or 'mo' (2.1.72, 5.3.101, more); 'Y'haue' (2.1.238, You've); 'too blame' (2.2.119, to blame); 'earnes' (2.2.129, yearns); 'Coarse' (3.1.199), 'course' (3.1.291), or 'Corpes' (3.2.57, 158), all modernized to 'corpse'; 'Hart' (3.1.208, heart); and so on.

[3] For example, 'buried' (1.2.49), 'cried' (1.2.127)' 'signified' (2.2.90 and elsewhere), 'followed' (3.2.175, but see 'allow'd' (3.2.59) and 'swallow'd'

this edition keeps to modern practice and metrical requirements, spelling – for instance – the Folio's 'rendred' (3.2.7, 10) 'renderèd'. Through accidents of calligraphy or press certain Folio spellings would by Elizabethan conventions produce an unmetrical syllable; these are here regularized according to modern practice, and no extra syllable is called for despite the Folio's 'quartered' (3.1.268), 'moued' (3.2.264), 'loued'st' (4.2.157, 158 – this is monosyllabic), or 'ordered' (5.5.80). In prose the Folio treats past forms indiscriminately; this edition observes normal modern practice.

Alterations to the Folio's stage directions and speech prefixes are noted in the collation. If not indisputable they appear in the text between broken brackets (⌈ ⌉); otherwise they are not singled out. Scene numberings after Act 1, Scene 1 ('*Actus Primus. Scœna Prima.*' in the Folio) are editorial. They are not recorded in the collation. All directions for a speech to be spoken aside or to a particular character are editorial, and are usually not recorded. Rowe, in 1709, was the first editor to list the characters, though with some omissions which Theobald, in 1733, remedied to provide the basic pattern for later editions.

The collation records substantive departures from the Folio's readings, including variations in names, speech prefixes, and stage directions. If a subsequent edition's reading is adopted, the collation, in most cases, ignores minor differences irrelevant to the point at issue (e.g. insignificant differences in spelling, typography, punctuation, and the like). Necessary added stage directions for action are noted as '*not in* F' but not, in general, attributed to an originating editor. Likewise unattributed are such self-evident adjustments as the rendering of the Folio's '*Manet*' or '*Manent*'. The collation also records amended lineation, punctuation changes significantly affecting sense or syntax, and a few rejected but interesting variants from editions later than the First Folio. It does not record unimportant editorial variants or conjectures, straightforward modernization of obsolete forms, or punctuation changes which do not affect the sense or syntax.

Abbreviations and References

Line-numbers and quotations from other Shakespeare plays are taken from Peter Alexander's Tudor edition of the *Complete Works*

(4.2.206)), 'misconstrued' (5.3.84). 'Mortified' (2.1.325) has, however, four syllables – 'mortifièd'.

(London and Glasgow, 1951). Titles and illustrative quotations are normally given in modern spelling. In the collation, dates are added when an edition is later than the first. The place of publication is London unless otherwise stated. F1 is specified when the First Folio needs to be distinguished from the others.

EDITIONS OF SHAKESPEARE

F, F1	The First Folio, 1623 (*uncorr.* and *corr.* refer to readings before and after press-correction)
F2	The Second Folio, 1632
F3	The Third Folio, 1663
F4	The Fourth Folio, 1685
Q1684	The Quarto of 1684
Q2, Q3, Q4	Undated Quartos between 1684 and *c*.1688
Q1691	The Quarto of 1691
Q5	Undated Quarto between 1684 and early 18th century
Cambridge	W. G. Clark and W. A. Wright, *Works*, The Cambridge Shakespeare, 9 vols. (Cambridge, 1863–6)
Capell	Edward Capell, *Comedies, Histories and Tragedies*, 10 vols. (1767–8)
Collier 1858	John Payne Collier, *Works*, second edition, 6 vols. (1858)
Collier 1877	John Payne Collier, *Works*, third edition, 8 vols. (1875–8)
Delius	Nicolaus Delius, *Shakespeares Werke*, 2 vols. (Eberfeld, 1854)
Dorsch	T. S. Dorsch, *Julius Caesar*, new Arden Shakespeare (1955)
Dyce	Alexander Dyce, *Works*, 6 vols. (1857)
Dyce 1866	Alexander Dyce, *Works*, second edition, 9 vols. (1864–7)
Furness	H. H. Furness, Jr., *Julius Caesar*, New Variorum Edition (Philadelphia, 1913)
Globe	W. G. Clark and W. A. Wright, The Globe Edition (1864)
Hanmer	Thomas Hanmer, *Works*, 6 vols. (Oxford, 1743–4)
Hudson	H. N. Hudson, *Works*, 11 vols. (Boston, 1851–6)
Hudson 1879	H. N. Hudson, *Julius Caesar* (Boston, 1879)
Hunter	Mark Hunter, *Julius Caesar*, College Classics Series (Madras, 1900)
Johnson	Samuel Johnson, *Plays*, 8 vols. (1765)
Johnson, S. F.	S. F. Johnson, *Julius Caesar*, in *The Complete Works*, gen. ed. Alfred Harbage, revised Pelican Shakespeare (Baltimore and London, 1969)

Keightley	Thomas Keightley, *Plays*, 6 vols. (1864)
Kittredge	G. L. Kittredge, *Complete Works* (Boston, 1936)
Knight	Charles Knight, *Works*, Pictorial Edition, 8 vols. (1838–43)
Macmillan	M. Macmillan, *Julius Caesar*, The Arden Shakespeare (1902)
Malone	Edmond Malone, *Plays and Poems*, 10 vols. (1790)
Marshall	F. A. Marshall, *Julius Caesar*, The Henry Irving Edition (1869)
Pope	Alexander Pope, *Works*, 6 vols. (1723–5)
Pope 1728	Alexander Pope, *Works*, 10 vols. (1728)
Rann	Joseph Rann, *Dramatic Works*, 6 vols. (Oxford, 1786–94)
Rowe	Nicholas Rowe, *Works*, 6 vols. (1709)
Rowe 1709b	Nicholas Rowe, *Works*, 6 vols. (second issue 1709)
Rowe 1714	Nicholas Rowe, *Works*, 8 vols. (1714)
Sanders	Norman Sanders, *Julius Caesar*, New Penguin Shakespeare (Harmondsworth, 1967)
Singer 1856	S. W. Singer, *Dramatic Works* (second edition), 10 vols. (1856)
Sisson	C. J. Sisson, *Complete Works* (1954)
Steevens	Samuel Johnson and George Steevens, *Plays*, 10 vols. (1773)
Taylor	Gary Taylor, *Henry V*, The Oxford Shakespeare (Oxford, 1982)
Theobald	Lewis Theobald, *Works*, 7 vols. (1733)
Warburton	William Warburton, *Works*, 8 vols. (1747)
White	R. G. White, *Works*, 12 vols. (Boston, 1857–66)
Wilson	John Dover Wilson, *Julius Caesar*, The New Shakespeare (Cambridge, 1949)
Wright	W. A. Wright, *Julius Caesar*, The Clarendon Shakespeare (Oxford, 1878)

OTHER WORKS

Abbott	E. A. Abbott, *A Shakespearian Grammar*, second edition (1870)
Antonius	See 'Plutarch'

Bowers	Fredson Bowers, 'The Copy for Shakespeare's *Julius Caesar*', *South Atlantic Bulletin*, 43 (1978), 23–36
Brook	G. L. Brook, *The Language of Shakespeare* (1976)
Brower	Reuben Brower, *Hero and Saint: Shakespeare and the Graeco-Roman Heroic Tradition* (Oxford, 1971)
Brutus	See 'Plutarch'
Bullough	Geoffrey Bullough, *Narrative and Dramatic Sources of Shakespeare*, 8 vols. (1957–75)
Caesar	See 'Plutarch'
Capell (*Notes*)	Edward Capell, *Notes and Various Readings to Shakespeare*, 3 vols. (1779–83)
Cercignani	Fausto Cercignani, *Shakespeare's Works and Elizabethan Pronunciation* (Oxford, 1981)
Chambers	E. K. Chambers, *William Shakespeare: A Study of Facts and Problems*, 2 vols. (Oxford, 1930)
Coleridge	S. T. Coleridge, 'Notes on the Tragedies of Shakespeare . . . *Julius Caesar*', in T. M. Raysor, ed., *Samuel Taylor Coleridge: Shakespearean Criticism*, 2 vols. (1960)
Craik	G. L. Craik, *The Language of Shakespeare illustrated in a philological commentary on his 'Julius Caesar'* (1857)
David	Richard David, *Shakespeare in the Theatre* (Cambridge, 1978)
Davies	Thomas Davies, *Dramatic Miscellanies*, 3 vols. (1783–4)
Essays and Studies	*Essays and Studies . . . Collected for the English Association*
Farmer	Richard Farmer, *An Essay on the Learning of Shakespeare* (Cambridge, 1767)
Gentleman	Francis Gentleman, *The Dramatic Censor*, 2 vols. (1770)
Granville-Barker	H. Granville-Barker, *Prefaces to Shakespeare*, first series (1927; reprinted 1958)
Herr	J. G. Herr, *Scattered Notes on the Text of Shakespeare* (Philadelphia, 1879)
Hulme	Hilda M. Hulme, *Explorations in Shakespeare's Language* (1962)
Hunter (*Politics*)	Mark Hunter, 'Politics and Character in *Julius Caesar*', *Essays by Divers Hands, Transactions of the Royal Society of Literature*, NS, 10 (1931), 109–40

Jonson	Ben Jonson, *Complete Plays*, ed. G. A. Wilkes, 4 vols. (Oxford, 1981–2), based on vols. iii–vi of the edition by C. H. Herford and P. and E. Simpson (Oxford, 1925–52)
Jowett	John Jowett, 'Ligature Shortage and Speech-prefix Variations in *Julius Caesar*', in *The Library*, forthcoming
MacCallum	M. W. MacCallum, *Shakespeare's Roman Plays and their Background* (1910), reprinted with a new introduction by T. J. B. Spencer (1967)
North	Sir Thomas North, *The Lives of the Noble Grecians and Romans* (1579)
N. & Q.	*Notes and Queries*
McKerrow	*The Works of Thomas Nashe*, ed. R. B. McKerrow, 5 vols. (1910); revised edition ed. F. P. Wilson (Oxford, 1958)
Odell	G. C. D. Odell, *Shakespeare – from Betterton to Irving*, 2 vols. (New York, 1920), reprinted with a new introduction by R. H. Ball (New York, 1966)
OED	*The Oxford English Dictionary*, 13 vols. (Oxford 1933), and Supplements 1–2 (1972, 1976)
Onions	C. T. Onions, *A Shakespeare Glossary* (Oxford, 1911; rev. edn 1919)
Palmer	John Palmer, *Political Characters of Shakespeare* (1945)
Plutarch	*Shakespeare's Plutarch*, ed. T. J. B. Spencer (Harmondsworth, 1964)
PMLA	*Publications of the Modern Language Association of America*
Ringler	W. A. Ringler, 'The Number of Actors in Shakespeare's Early Plays', in *The Seventeenth-Century Stage*, ed. G. E. Bentley (Chicago and London, 1968)
Ripley	John Ripley, *'Julius Caesar' on Stage in England and America, 1599–1973* (Cambridge, 1980)
Saunders	J. W. Saunders, 'Staging at the Globe, 1599–1623', in *The Seventeenth-Century Stage*, ed. G. E. Bentley (Chicago and London, 1968)
Schanzer	Ernest Schanzer, *The Problem Plays of Shakespeare* (1963)
Sisson (*New Readings*)	C. J. Sisson, *New Readings in Shakespeare*, 2 vols. (Cambridge, 1956)
Spencer	T. J. B. Spencer, 'Shakespeare and the Elizabethan Romans', in *Shakespeare Survey 10* (Cambridge, 1957), 27–38

Sprague	A. C. Sprague, *Shakespeare and the Actors* (Cambridge, Mass., 1944)
Spurgeon	Caroline Spurgeon, *Shakespeare's Imagery* (1935)
Stirling	Brents Stirling, '*Julius Caesar* in Revision', *Shakespeare Quarterly*, 13 (1962), 188–205
Styan	J. L. Styan, *Shakespeare's Stagecraft* (Cambridge, 1967)
Thomson	J. A. K. Thomson, *Shakespeare and the Classics* (1952)
Tilley	M. P. Tilley, *A Dictionary of the Proverbs in England in the Sixteenth and Seventeenth Centuries* (Ann Arbor, 1950)
Traversi	D. A. Traversi, *Shakespeare: the Roman Plays* (1963)
Upton	J. Upton, *Critical Observations on Shakespeare* (1746)
Ure	P. Ure, ed., *Shakespeare: 'Julius Caesar'; A Casebook* (1969)
Walker (*Crit.*)	W. S. Walker, *A Critical Examination of the Text of Shakespeare*, 3 vols. (1860)
Walker (*Vers.*)	W. S. Walker, *Shakespeare's Versification and its apparent irregularities explained* (1854)
Wells (*Modernizing*)	Stanley Wells, 'Modernizing Shakespeare's Spelling', in Wells and Taylor, *Modernizing Shakespeare's Spelling, with Three Studies in the Text of 'Henry V'* (Oxford, 1979)
Whiter	W. Whiter, *A Specimen of a Commentary on Shakespeare* (1794), ed. A. Over and M. Bell (1967)

Julius Caesar

THE PERSONS OF THE PLAY

JULIUS CAESAR

MARK ANTONY (Marcus Antonius)
OCTAVIUS CAESAR } triumvirs after the death of Julius Caesar
LEPIDUS (Marcus Aemilius Lepidus)

MARCUS BRUTUS
CAIUS CASSIUS
CASCA
DECIUS BRUTUS
CINNA } conspirators against Julius Caesar
METELLUS CIMBER
TREBONIUS
CAIUS LIGARIUS

PORTIA, wife of Brutus

CALPURNIA, wife of Caesar

FLAVIUS
MARULLUS } tribunes of the people

CICERO
PUBLIUS } senators
POPILIUS LENA

A SOOTHSAYER

ARTEMIDORUS, a teacher of rhetoric

CINNA (Caius Helvius Cinna), a poet

ANOTHER POET

LUCIUS, attendant on Brutus

LUCILIUS
TITINIUS
MESSALA } friends and supporters in the armies of Brutus and Cassius
YOUNG CATO
VOLUMNIUS
STRATO

VARRO ⎫
CLAUDIUS ⎬ soldiers in the armies of Brutus and Cassius
CLITUS ⎭

CAESAR'S SERVANT

ANTONY'S SERVANT

OCTAVIUS' SERVANT

PINDARUS, a freed bondman of Cassius

DARDANIUS, a servant of Brutus in the army

A CARPENTER ⎫
⎬ plebeians
A COBBLER ⎭

FIRST, SECOND, THIRD, FOURTH and FIFTH PLEBEIANS

FIRST, SECOND, and THIRD SOLDIERS in the army of Brutus

FIRST and SECOND SOLDIERS in the army of Antony

A MESSENGER

LABEO ⎫
⎬ officers in the army of Brutus
FLAVIUS ⎭

Other Senators, Plebeians, Soldiers, and Attendants

Julius Caesar

1.1 *Enter Flavius, Marullus, and certain commoners, one a
Carpenter, another a Cobbler, over the stage*

FLAVIUS

Hence! Home, you idle creatures, get you home!
Is this a holiday? What, know you not,
Being mechanical, you ought not walk
Upon a labouring day without the sign
Of your profession? Speak, what trade art thou?   5
CARPENTER Why, sir, a carpenter.

MARULLUS

Where is thy leather apron and thy rule?
What dost thou with thy best apparel on? –

1.1] F (*Actus Primus. Scœna Prima.*)   0.1 *Marullus*] THEOBALD;   *Murellus* F   0.1–2 *one . . .
Cobbler,*] not in F   7 MARULLUS] THEOBALD;   *Mur.* F (*so throughout the scene*)

1.1 The play covers the period from Julius
Caesar's triumph over the sons of Gneius
Pompeius, October 45 BC, through the
assassination of Caesar on 15 March 44
BC, to the death of Brutus after the battle
of Philippi in the autumn of 42 BC. The
first three Acts and the first scene of Act
4 take place in Rome.

0.1 *Flavius, Marullus* As tribunes of the
people (*tribuni plebis*) Flavius and
Marullus (*Murellus* in F, doubtless by a
slip; a/u and u/e were easily misread)
should guide the populace in obedience,
i.e. to the republican tradition. But the
plebeians 'are thoroughly monarchical in
sentiment. They have not the slightest
desire to be "free" in the conspirators'
sense' (Hunter).

0.2 *over the stage* A theatre term for a cross-
ing of the stage before any dialogue, effected, Allardyce Nicoll suggests, from the
floor of the pit up to the stage and down
again (*Shakespeare Survey 12*, Cambridge,
1959, pp. 47–55); alternatively, from
one stage door and across to the other.
The play opens with an exuberant
popular incursion which, on encounter-
ing the tribunes, provokes a dramatic
rebuke, or with the tribunes driving the

mob before them (as in l. 70).

2–5 **Is this . . . profession** 'In Elizabethan England holidays and the attire associated
with them were regulated by statute. The
same is assumed to be true of Roman
workmen. . . . The costumes imply one
thing – a holiday, and so a rejoicing over
Caesar's defeat of Pompey. The alternative costumes would imply opposite
attitudes – a resolute support for
Republican Rome' (G. K. Hunter, 'Flat-
caps and Bluecoats', in *Essays and Studies*,
33 (1980), pp. 35–6). 'Holiday' was not
distinguished in usage from 'holy day'.

3 **mechanical** (a) artisans, working-men
(as in Plutarch – 'Thinkest thou that they
be cobblers, tapsters, or suchlike base
mechanical people, that write these bills
. . . ?': *Brutus*, pp. 112–13); (b) vulgar,
contemptibly base.

4–5 **sign . . . profession** mark of your occupation

6 **carpenter** More restricted in its
Elizabethan than its modern sense: one
who does heavy work in wood
(framework of houses, ships, etc.), as opp-
osed to the more skilled and respected
'joiner' (cabinet-maker).

You, sir, what trade are you?

COBBLER Truly, sir, in respect of a fine workman, I am but,   10
as you would say, a cobbler.

MARULLUS
But what trade art thou? Answer me directly.

COBBLER A trade, sir, that I hope I may use with a safe
conscience; which is indeed, sir, a mender of bad soles.

FLAVIUS
What trade, thou knave? Thou naughty knave, what
trade?

COBBLER Nay, I beseech you, sir, be not out with me. Yet if
you be out, sir, I can mend you.

MARULLUS
What mean'st thou by that? Mend me, thou saucy
fellow?

COBBLER Why, sir, cobble you.

FLAVIUS Thou art a cobbler, art thou?   20

COBBLER Truly, sir, all that I live by is with the awl. I meddle
with no tradesman's matters, nor women's matters, but

---

14 soles] F (soules)   18 mean'st thou by] F;   mean'st by STEEVENS *conj.*

---

10 **in respect . . . workman** in comparison
with a skilled worker
11 **cobbler** (a) botcher, clumsy fellow (b)
mender of shoes
12 **directly** plainly, without quibbling
14 **soles** 'soules' in F, and the occasion of
many puns in Elizabethan drama, as in
Merchant 4.1.123–4 – 'Not on thy sole
but on thy soul, harsh Jew, | Thou mak'st
thy knife keen.' Knight was the first to
modernize as 'soles'; earlier editors
followed F4's 'soals'.
15 **FLAVIUS** Most editors, following Capell,
give this to Marullus, since he takes the
Cobbler's reply to be addressed to him
(l. 18), but there is no good reason for
change; 'theatrically it is good to keep
both tribunes busy' (Sisson, *New Readings*, ii. 181).
naughty good-for-nothing (a stronger
sense than the present one)
16–17 **out . . . out** out of temper . . . out at
heel
17 **mend you** (a) mend your shoes (b) set you
right
18 **What . . . fellow** The tribunes' status is

signified by metrical speech. This line is
presumably either roughish metre as it
stands or, if Shakespeare wrote
'meanest', a hexameter; or the first *thou*
may be a printer's or scribe's error – the
line reads metrically without it.
21 **all . . . awl** A not infrequent pun. Tilley
A406 gives as proverbial 'Without *awl*
(*all*) the cobbler is nobody'.
21–2 **I meddle with no tradesman's matters**
(perhaps) 'as an ordinary workman I take
no part in trade organizations (e.g. craft
guilds).'
meddle This could mean 'have sexual
intercourse with'; *OED, v.* 5, cites
Lodowick Lloyd's *Pilgrimage of Princes*
(1583) – 'women . . . for all men at all
times to meddle with'. So also *Coriolanus*
4.5.46–8 – 'Do you meddle with my master? . . . Ay, 'tis an honester service than
to meddle with thy mistress.'
22 **women's matters** women's affairs, but
also, by innuendo, women's sexuality;
compare 'country matters', as Hamlet
teases Ophelia indecently (*Hamlet*
3.2.112–13).

with all – I am indeed, sir, a surgeon to old shoes; when
they are in great danger I recover them. As proper men
as ever trod upon neat's leather have gone upon my
handiwork.

FLAVIUS

But wherefore art not in thy shop today?
Why dost thou lead these men about the streets?

COBBLER Truly, sir, to wear out their shoes, to get myself
into more work. But indeed, sir, we make holiday to see   30
Caesar, and to rejoice in his triumph.

MARULLUS

Wherefore rejoice? What conquest brings he home?
What tributaries follow him to Rome,
To grace in captive bonds his chariot-wheels?
You blocks, you stones, you worse than senseless things!
O you hard hearts, you cruel men of Rome,
Knew you not Pompey? Many a time and oft

---

23 with all – I] F4 (withal, I); withal I F1 ; with all. I CAPELL; with awl. I FARMER *conj.*
32 Wherefore . . . home] ROWE; *as two lines, breaking after* 'reioyce' F   37 Pompey? . . . oft]
Q5 (*reading* 'many time and oft'), ROWE 1714; *Pompey . . . oft?* F

---

23 **with all – I** The dash is meant to let the
preceding and following words be linked
or separated, suiting the various quibbles
implied by F's 'withal I'; i.e. (a) with them
all. I (b) for all that, I (c) with my awl I.
24 **recover** (a) re-cover (*OED v.²*), repair (b)
restore to health
    proper good, fine
25 **as ever . . . leather** as ever walked on
cowhide – a proverbial phrase common
in various forms. Tilley M66 cites many
examples.
    neat cattle
    gone walked
27 **shop** workshop
31 **triumph** (a) victory (b) triumphal
procession (celebrating Caesar's defeat of
Pompey's sons at Munda in Spain, 45 BC).
Shakespeare transfers the triumph,
October 45 BC, to the Feast of Lupercal, 15
February 44 BC (see l. 67), so concentrat-
ing his time-scheme. It offended many in
Rome since it celebrated victory not over
barbarians but over noble sons of the
republic – 'men did not think it meet for
him to triumph so for the calamities of his
country' (*Caesar*, pp. 76–7).
32–55 **Wherefore . . . ingratitude** This is the

first development of the lucid lyrical
rhetoric of public address typical of the
play's 'Roman' dignity.
32 **conquest** booty (*OED*, Conquest, 4)
32–3 **home . . . Rome** To Shakespeare not
necessarily a rhyme, *Rome* being often
pronounced 'room' (see Commentary,
I.2.156).
33 **tributaries** captives, payers of tribute
34 **chariot-wheels** Captives were chained to
their conquerors' chariots.
35 **senseless** insensible, inanimate (though
the modern sense was available)
37 **Pompey** Gneius Pompeius, 'the Great',
106–48 BC, an outstanding commander
in Spain and the East, colleague and son-
in-law of Caesar himself but ultimately
his rival. Caesar defeated him first in
Spain and finally in Thessaly at Pharsalus: he fled to Egypt and was murdered.
37–47 **Many a time . . . shores** This, not
derived from Plutarch, suggests an actual
London scene, like similarly vivid evoca-
tions (*Richard II* 5.2.7–21, Bolingbroke's
entry into London; *I Henry IV*
3.2.46–59, Bolingbroke's progress;
Henry V 5.0.22–34, Essex's imagined
triumphal return from Ireland in 1599).

Have you climbed up to walls and battlements,
To towers and windows, yea, to chimney-tops,
Your infants in your arms, and there have sat   40
The livelong day, with patient expectation,
To see great Pompey pass the streets of Rome.
And when you saw his chariot but appear,
Have you not made an universal shout,
That Tiber trembled underneath her banks
To hear the replication of your sounds
Made in her concave shores?
And do you now put on your best attire?
And do you now cull out a holiday?
And do you now strew flowers in his way   50
That comes in triumph over Pompey's blood?
Be gone!
Run to your houses, fall upon your knees,
Pray to the gods to intermit the plague
That needs must light on this ingratitude.

FLAVIUS

Go, go, good countrymen, and for this fault
Assemble all the poor men of your sort.
Draw them to Tiber banks, and weep your tears

The tumultuous excitement over Essex's departure that spring may, Wilson suggests, have fired Shakespeare's mind. A contemporary description of Essex's departure is cited in the Introduction to the Oxford Henry V, p. 5.

39 **chimney-tops** (*OED*'s first occurrence)
45, 47 **her banks . . . her concave shores** 'Father' Tiber was traditionally masculine. Shakespeare usually treats rivers as neuter ('it') or masculine, as in *K. John* 3.1.23 ('river peering o'er his bounds'), *Richard II* 5.3.62–3 ('this stream . . . | Hath held his current and defiled himself'), and *1 Henry IV* 3.1.108, 112, 114 ('he bears his course', 'a little charge will trench him here', 'he runs straight'). The feminine form may arise here because, in accordance with Pompey's heroic masculinity, there is a heady emotion-

alism in the welcome the hero receives, and the river shrinks timorously before the force of his reception.

46 **replication** reverberation, echo (*OED*'s first example of this sense, which seems to be Shakespeare's extension of the normal meaning 'repetition')
47 **concave** Either, or both, (a) scooped out (b) curved.
49 **cull out** pick out, select (for show, like the 'flowers' of l. 50)
50 **strew flowers** 'some . . . cast flowers . . . as they commonly use to do unto any man when he hath obtained victory' (*Caesar*, p. 52).
51 **Pompey's blood** Pompey's sons; with the secondary, literal, implication of Pompey's own life-blood.
54 **intermit** suspend
57 **sort** rank

Into the channel, till the lowest stream
Do kiss the most exalted shores of all.   60
                    Exeunt all the commoners
See whe'er their basest mettle be not moved.
They vanish tongue-tied in their guiltiness.
Go you down that way towards the Capitol;
This way will I. Disrobe the images,
If you do find them decked with ceremonies.
MARULLUS May we do so?
You know it is the feast of Lupercal.
FLAVIUS
It is no matter. Let no images
Be hung with Caesar's trophies. I'll about,
And drive away the vulgar from the streets.   70
So do you too, where you perceive them thick.
These growing feathers plucked from Caesar's wing
Will make him fly an ordinary pitch,
Who else would soar above the view of men,
And keep us all in servile fearfulness.   *Exeunt*

61 whe'er] F (where)

59–60 **till . . . all** till even at its lowest the
water is level with the highest banks
61 **whe'er** whether (a frequent form, as at
5.3.97, 5.4.30)
mettle (a) disposition (b) substance (as at
1.2.293, 306). This and 'metal' are 'dif-
ferentiated spellings of the same word'
(Onions).
63 **the Capitol** The south-west summit of
the Capitoline Hill, overlooking the
Forum. It was the site of a great temple
of Jupiter where sacrifices were offered
and triumphs celebrated.
64 **Disrobe the images** 'Caesar's flatterers
. . . did put diadems upon . . . his images
. . . to allure the common people to call
him King' (*Brutus*, p. 110). *Disrobe*, however, rather suggests festoons, the
'trophies' of l. 69, the 'scarfs' of 1.2.282.
In *Antonius* (p. 187) one of the tribunes
plucks off Caesar's image the 'laurel
crown' Antony has offered Caesar (as at
1.2.220).
65 **ceremonies** ornamental trappings as
symbols of rule, as in *Henry V* 4.1.105

– 'His ceremonies laid by' – and *Measure*
2.2.59 – 'No ceremony that to great
ones longs, | Not the king's crown nor
the deputed sword, | The marshal's trun-
cheon nor the judge's robe . . .'.
67 **Lupercal** A fertility festival on 15 February, honouring Faunus or Pan. It
centred on the Lupercal, the cave on the
Palatine Hill believed to be where a wolf
suckled Romulus and Remus, founders
of Rome. Plutarch (*Caesar*, p. 82)
describes how naked youths ran striking
any woman who wished to escape barrenness (see 1.2.6–9).
70 **vulgar** common people
72–3 **These growing feathers . . . pitch**
Caesar is imaged as a bird of prey, the
plucking of whose feathers will hinder it
from flying high. *Pitch* is the highest
point of a hawk's flight.
74 **above the view of men** The soaring
hawk perhaps becomes an analogy for
the godhead Caesar is accused of assuming at 1.2.60, 116.

1.2   ⌜*Flourish.*⌝ *Enter Caesar, Antony for the course,*
         Calpurnia, Portia, Decius, Cicero, Brutus, Cassius,
         Casca, a Soothsayer; after them, Marullus
         and Flavius⌜; citizens following⌝

CAESAR
  Calpurnia!
CASCA   Peace, ho! Caesar speaks.
CAESAR   Calpurnia.
CALPURNIA Here, my lord.
CAESAR
  Stand you directly in Antonius' way
  When he doth run his course. Antonius!
ANTONY Caesar, my lord?
CAESAR
  Forget not in your speed, Antonius,
  To touch Calpurnia; for our elders say,
  The barren, touchèd in this holy chase,
  Shake off their sterile curse.
ANTONY   I shall remember.
  When Caesar says 'Do this', it is performed.   10

1.2.0.1 Flourish] ROWE (*subs.*);   *not in* F   0.2 *Calpurnia*] F (*Calphurnia*);   *so throughout the play*
0.3 *Casca*] F (*Caska*);   *so throughout the play*   *Marullus*] THEOBALD;   *Murellus* F   0.4 *citizens*
following] *not in* F   3 Antonius'] POPE;   *Antonio's* F   4, 6 Antonius] POPE;   *Antonio* F
9 remember.] ROWE;   remember, F

1.2.0.1 Shakespeare   skilfully   revises
Plutarch, in whose pages Caesar, without
Calpurnia, watches the Lupercalia from a
golden chair, and the soothsayer's warning has been uttered some days earlier
(*Caesar*, pp. 82, 87). Shakespeare wants
the processional pomp, wants Calpurnia,
wants to show Caesar desiring an heir,
and wants to juxtapose the celebrations
with the cryptic warning (Thomson, pp.
233 ff.).
  Flourish A ceremonial trumpet call.
  for the course 'Antonius, who was Consul at that time, was one of them that ran
this holy course' (*Caesar*, pp. 82–3): see
1.1.67, Commentary.
0.2 *Calpurnia* So spelt in Plutarch (the normal classical form), though 'Calphurnia'
throughout F.

0.2 *Cassius* He should be perceptibly older
than Brutus; see 4.2.83 and Commentary.
  3 **Antonius'** F *Antonio's*; see the Introduction, p. 74 (similarly at ll. 4, 6).
7–9 **our elders ... curse** 'Many noblewomen
and gentlewomen ... stand in their way,
... persuading themselves ... being barren, that it will make them to conceive
with child' (*Caesar*, p. 82). Plutarch does
not mention Calpurnia's barrenness but
in the play Caesar presumably hopes to
found a dynasty. His concurrence with
popular tradition ('For he is superstitious
grown of late', 2.1.196) allies him with
the Roman populace against the rationalism of Brutus and the sceptical
Epicureanism of Cassius.
  9 **sterile curse** curse of sterility

CAESAR

Set on, and leave no ceremony out.

⌜*Sennet*⌝

SOOTHSAYER Caesar!

CAESAR Ha! Who calls?

CASCA

Bid every noise be still. Peace yet again!

CAESAR

Who is it in the press that calls on me?

I hear a tongue, shriller than all the music,

Cry 'Caesar!' Speak. Caesar is turned to hear.

SOOTHSAYER

Beware the Ides of March.

CAESAR   What man is that?

BRUTUS

A soothsayer bids you beware the Ides of March.

CAESAR

Set him before me. Let me see his face.   20

CASSIUS

Fellow, come from the throng. Look upon Caesar.

CAESAR

What sayst thou to me now? Speak once again.

SOOTHSAYER Beware the Ides of March.

11.1 *Sennet*] This edition; *Musick; and the procession moves.* CAPELL; *not in* F

11.1 *Sennet* A processional trumpet flourish.

17 **Caesar is turned to hear** An impersonal, mechanical impassivity sounds in *is turned*. This is the sixth enunciation of *Caesar* in seventeen lines: the name becomes a status-loaded formula. Adopting the third person, Caesar 'collaborates ... in his own deification' (Palmer, p. 37). The procedure is most noticeable in him, though not unknown with other characters (Brutus frequently, Cassius sometimes, Portia once) – a sign of Roman role-playing. In Plutarch Caesar generally speaks of himself as 'I', though for strategic reasons he can invoke the power of his name – 'thou hast Caesar and his fortune with thee' (*Caesar*, p. 60) – and one of his flatterers adjures him, 'do you not remember that you are Caesar

...?' (*Caesar*, p. 82). The idea that Caesar habitually referred to himself as 'Caesar' may have originated in his doing so in his *Commentaries*, works highly regarded in the sixteenth century (T. J. B. Spencer, *Shakespeare: the Roman Plays*, 1963, p. 24). The status significance of proper names in the play (including that of Rome itself) is admirably discussed in Madeleine Doran's *Shakespeare's Dramatic Language* (Madison, 1976), pp. 120–53.

18 **Beware ... March** 'A certain soothsayer ... had given Caesar warning long time afore, to take heed of ... the Ides of March (which is the fifteenth of the month), for on that day he should be in great danger' (*Caesar*, p. 87–8).

19 **A soothsayer ... March** This, Brutus' first remark, is unwittingly ironical.

CAESAR

He is a dreamer. Let us leave him. Pass.

Sennet. Exeunt all but Brutus and Cassius

CASSIUS

Will you go see the order of the course?

BRUTUS Not I.

CASSIUS I pray you do.

BRUTUS

I am not gamesome. I do lack some part
Of that quick spirit that is in Antony.
Let me not hinder, Cassius, your desires.   30
I'll leave you.

CASSIUS

Brutus, I do observe you now of late;
I have not from your eyes that gentleness
And show of love as I was wont to have.
You bear too stubborn and too strange a hand
Over your friend that loves you.

BRUTUS   Cassius,

Be not deceived. If I have veiled my look,
I turn the trouble of my countenance

24.1 *all but*] F (*Manet*)

24 **He is ... Pass.** A line of magisterial finality ('pure gold', Granville-Barker, p. 374), and yet a grave error of judgement.
Pass proceed

25 **the order of the course** how the chase is managed

28–9 **I am ... Antony** The contrast between Brutus' self-control and Antony's self-display is marked at once. *Gamesome* (both 'sport-loving' and 'jaunty') and *quick spirit* (at once 'brisk', 'athletic', and 'responsive') do not necessarily imply contempt, but they certainly recognize a different temperament. Brutus later wholly misjudges Antony, thinking him 'but a limb of Caesar', given 'To sports, to wildness, and much company' (2.1.166, 190).

32–4 **Brutus ... wont to have** In Plutarch the two were estranged by rivalry for the praetorship (chief magistracy), for which Caesar preferred Brutus. Shakespeare clears their relationship from any competitiveness.

33–4 **that gentleness ... as** A frequent usage for 'that ... which'; see Abbott 280 and Brook, p. 80.

34 **show** manifestation (not 'mere outward appearance')

35–6 **bear ... Over** behave too stiffly and aloofly towards (as a rider curbs his horse too hard); *strange* = unfriendly, cold in demeanour (*OED, a.* 11).

36 **friend that loves you** The play has recurrent themes of deeply-grounded affections, counterbalancing the sterner virtues of public duty, stoic control, and so on. They are well displayed in G. Wilson Knight's 'The Eroticism of *Julius Caesar*', in *The Imperial Theme* (1931, revised 1951) – 'The word "lover" is strangely emphatic, sometimes meaning little more than "friend" but always helping to build a general atmosphere of comradeship and affection' (p. 63).

37–9 **If ... myself** if I have been reserved to you it is to keep my anxieties to myself

38–41 **I turn ... to myself** Brutus' inner

Merely upon myself. Vexèd I am
Of late with passions of some difference,   40
Conceptions only proper to myself,
Which give some soil, perhaps, to my behaviours.
But let not therefore my good friends be grieved –
Among which number, Cassius, be you one –
Nor construe any further my neglect
Than that poor Brutus, with himself at war,
Forgets the shows of love to other men.

CASSIUS

Then, Brutus, I have much mistook your passion,
By means whereof this breast of mine hath buried
Thoughts of great value, worthy cogitations.   50
Tell me, good Brutus, can you see your face?

BRUTUS

No, Cassius; for the eye sees not itself
But by reflection, by some other things.

CASSIUS 'Tis just;

And it is very much lamented, Brutus,
That you have no such mirrors as will turn
Your hidden worthiness into your eye,
That you might see your shadow. I have heard

52–3 No . . . things] ROWE; *as three lines, ending 'Cassius', 'reflection', 'things'* F   58 That . . .
heard] ROWE; *as two lines, breaking after* 'shadow' F

world of self-scrutiny and spiritual
separateness foreshadows Hamlet's. In
public Brutus behaved so 'that no man
could discern he had anything to trouble
his mind. But when night came that he
was in his own house, then he was clean
changed' (*Brutus*, p. 116). In Plutarch,
however, his perturbation arises from the
perils he involves his friends in, not from
moral and ethical self-examination.

39 **Merely** entirely (a different sense from the
modern one)

40 **passions of some difference** Either, or
both, (a) conflicting emotions (b) strong
feelings which come between me and my
friends.

42 **soil** blemish

45 **construe any further** interpret any otherwise. *Construe* is accented on the first syllable.

48 **passion** feelings

49 **By means whereof** for which reason

50 **worthy cogitations** reflections of great
value (*worthy* had a stronger sense than
now – 'Having worth; . . . good; excellent', *OED a.* A.I.1)

52–8 **the eye . . . shadow** Elizabethan
literature offers many parallels for the
idea of seeing oneself only by reflection
from others; Tilley E231a lists examples.
These lines seem to echo Sir John Davies's
Nosce Teipsum (1599) – 'Is it because the
mind is like the eye, | . . . | Not seeing itself
when other things it sees?' (stanza 27),
and 'Mine eyes, which view all objects,
nigh and far, | Look not into this little
world of mine, | Nor see my face wherein
they fixèd are' (stanza 47). Shakespeare
treats the idea again in *Troilus*
3.3.95–111.

57 **worthiness** excellence

58 **shadow** reflected image

58–62 **I have heard . . . his eyes** In Plutarch,

Where many of the best respect in Rome –
Except immortal Caesar – speaking of Brutus,   60
And groaning underneath this age's yoke,
Have wished that noble Brutus had his eyes.
BRUTUS
Into what dangers would you lead me, Cassius,
That you would have me seek into myself
For that which is not in me?
CASSIUS
Therefore, good Brutus, be prepared to hear.
And since you know you cannot see yourself
So well as by reflection, I, your glass,
Will modestly discover to yourself
That of yourself which you yet know not of.   70
And be not jealous on me, gentle Brutus.
Were I a common laughter, or did use
To stale with ordinary oaths my love
To every new protester; if you know
That I do fawn on men, and hug them hard,

---

63 Into . . . Cassius] ROWE; *as two lines, breaking after* 'you' F   72 laughter] F;   laugher Q5,
ROWE; lover HERR *conj.*

Cassius, taking Brutus' hand, says, 'What, knowest thou not that thou art Brutus? . . . the noblest men and best citizens . . . specially require . . . the taking away of the tyranny, being fully bent to suffer any extremity for thy sake, so that thou wilt show thyself to be the man thou art taken for, and that they hope thou art' (*Brutus*, pp. 112–13).

59 **of the best respect** most highly regarded
60 **immortal** Sarcastic; i.e. 'Caesar has become a god'.
62 **had his eyes** Either (a) would see how things stand, or (b) saw things as any anti-Caesarian does.
66 **Therefore** Cassius may be ignoring Brutus' query and impetuously continuing his own train of thought, but more probably he is noting the question (though not directly answering) and urging Brutus to act.
69 **modestly discover** temperately reveal
71 **jealous on** distrustful of

71 **gentle** The Elizabethan sense can include the modern one (see 3.1.255) but is normally much stronger – here, virtually 'noble', as at 3.2.140 and 5.5.74.
72 **laughter** This, F's word, is often emended to 'laugher' (= jester), sometimes to 'lover'. But in Elizabethan English 'abstract nouns are often used for concrete' (Brook, p. 115, citing 'baseness' for 'base fellow' in *Merry Wives* 2.2.17, 'blasphemy' for 'blasphemer' in *Tempest* 5.1.218, and 'my diligence' in *Tempest* 5.1.241 – although his examples are all of vocatives, which permit such a usage more easily than the indicative). F's reading is defensible, meaning, probably, 'one not to be taken seriously' (Dorsch), 'the sort of person that is generally . . . ridiculed' (Sisson, *New Readings*, ii. 182).
73 **ordinary** commonplace; perhaps also suggesting bibulous familiarity, an *ordinary* being a tavern.
74 **protester** one who effusively professes friendship (*OED*'s first occurrence)

And after scandal them; or if you know
That I profess myself in banqueting
To all the rout, then hold me dangerous.
   Flourish, and shout
BRUTUS
What means this shouting? I do fear the people
Choose Caesar for their king.
CASSIUS   Ay, do you fear it?   80
Then must I think you would not have it so.
BRUTUS
I would not, Cassius, yet I love him well.
But wherefore do you hold me here so long?
What is it that you would impart to me?
If it be aught toward the general good,
Set honour in one eye, and death i'th' other,
And I will look on both indifferently;
For let the gods so speed me as I love
The name of honour more than I fear death.
CASSIUS
I know that virtue to be in you, Brutus,   90
As well as I do know your outward favour.
Well, honour is the subject of my story.
I cannot tell what you and other men
Think of this life; but for my single self,
I had as lief not be as live to be

79–80 What . . . king] ROWE; *as two lines and a part line, breaking after* 'Showting', 'Caesar' F

76 **scandal** slander
77 **profess myself** proclaim friendship
78 **rout** rabble. Though convinced that they act for all Romans, Brutus and Cassius show themselves essentially patricians, and their isolation from the plebeians is a basic weakness.
82 **I love him well** Again the theme of deep affection (see Commentary, l. 36), and here the root of Brutus' dilemma.
86–9 **Set honour . . . fear death** In Plutarch, Brutus tells Cassius, 'I mean not to hold my peace . . . and rather die than lose my liberty' (*Brutus*, p. 112). In Shakespeare, he seems, rather oddly, to say, first that he views death and honour equally (*indifferently* = impartially), and then that he values honour more than death.

The image he has in mind, however, amends any inconsistency: he imagines himself facing a destiny which offers honour and death simultaneously, and he will gaze unmoved because, accepting both equally, he will, even by his death, gain the honour which is his highest good. The sentiment is that of Hotspur on danger and honour (*1 Henry IV* 1.3.195–208), but the steady tone differs from Hotspur's extravagance.
88 **speed** prosper
91 **your outward favour** the features you present to the world
92 **honour** For Brutus *honour* is integrity for the general good. For Cassius it is personal prowess and repute.
95 **as lief** just as soon

In awe of such a thing as I myself.
I was born free as Caesar, so were you;
We both have fed as well, and we can both
Endure the winter's cold as well as he.
For once, upon a raw and gusty day,   100
The troubled Tiber chafing with her shores,
Caesar said to me 'Dar'st thou, Cassius, now
Leap in with me into this angry flood
And swim to yonder point?' Upon the word,
Accoutred as I was, I plungèd in
And bade him follow; so indeed he did.
The torrent roared, and we did buffet it
With lusty sinews, throwing it aside,
And stemming it with hearts of controversy.
But ere we could arrive the point proposed,   110
Caesar cried 'Help me, Cassius, or I sink!'
I, as Aeneas, our great ancestor,
Did from the flames of Troy upon his shoulder
The old Anchises bear, so from the waves of Tiber
Did I the tirèd Caesar. And this man
Is now become a god, and Cassius is
A wretched creature, and must bend his body
If Caesar carelessly but nod on him.

97–9 **I was born . . . as he** Though professing high public spirit Cassius is moved by personal hostility: 'Cassius being a choleric man and hating Caesar privately, more than he did the tyranny openly, he incensed Brutus against him' (*Brutus*, p. 109).

100–115 **For once . . . Caesar** This match is Shakespeare's invention to convey Cassius' sense of superiority. In fact Caesar was a strong swimmer: Plutarch tells how at Alexandria, having to elude Egyptian enemies, 'with great hazard [he] saved himself by swimming' even while holding a load of books above water with one hand (*Caesar*, p. 70). The same story is told in Elyot's *The Governor* (1. xvii). Even without such evidence of Caesar's prowess, it is clear that Cassius' scornful account produces nothing to his detriment.

101 **chafing with** raging against

104 **point** used especially of a promontory or cape (*OED* 2b)

105 **Accoutred** fully armed

109 **stemming** breasting, making headway against (usually of a ship)
of controversy keen to contend (with the waves, and each other)

110 **arrive the point** Abbott 198 illustrates this and other omissions of prepositions after verbs of motion.

112 **Aeneas, our great ancestor** Virgil relates how the Trojan hero Aeneas, rescuing his father Anchises from burning Troy, went on to found the Roman nation (*Aeneid*, ii. 721 ff.); similarly in *2 Henry VI* 5.2.62 – 'As did Aeneas old Anchises bear'. The story had become a familiar example of filial devotion.

117 **creature** 'one who is actuated by the will of another, or is ready to do his bidding; an instrument or puppet' (*OED* 5)

He had a fever when he was in Spain,
And when the fit was on him I did mark   120
How he did shake. 'Tis true, this god did shake!
His coward lips did from their colour fly,
And that same eye whose bend doth awe the world
Did lose his lustre. I did hear him groan –
Ay, and that tongue of his, that bade the Romans
Mark him, and write his speeches in their books,
Alas, it cried 'Give me some drink, Titinius,'
As a sick girl. Ye gods, it doth amaze me
A man of such a feeble temper should
So get the start of the majestic world   130
And bear the palm alone.
    Flourish. Shout

131.1 *Flourish. Shout*] *Shout. Flourish.* F

119–28 **He had a fever . . . sick girl** This,
prompted by Cassius' hostility, goes clean
contrary to Plutarch's account of how,
though 'lean, white, and soft skinned,
and often subject to headache, and . . . the
falling sickness' (epilepsy, afflicting him
first in Spain), Caesar 'yielded not to the
disease of his body . . . but, contrarily,
took the pains of war as a medicine to
cure his sick body, fighting always with
his disease, travelling continually, living
soberly, and commonly lying abroad in
the field' (*Caesar*, p. 37). Up to the
assassination, things are presented mainly from the opposition's point of view;
after it, mainly from Caesar's. The actor
of Cassius has to decide how much emphasis to give to Cassius' genuine feeling
of his case, how much to the recklessness
suggested by his impetuous special pleading.

122 **His coward . . . fly** One expects the
colour to fly from the lips as in proverbial
reference (Tilley C773), yet the reversed
idea is striking. By a half-submerged pun
colour suggests the battlefield ensign,
symbol of heroism (modern 'colours'),
from which the coward soldier flees.

123 **bend** Often glossed 'look', 'glance', but
suggesting something more formidable,
from under folded brows; 'gaze', 'fixed
look', perhaps. *OED* has '*sb.⁴* I.3 Inclination of the eye in any direction', citing
only this line.

124 **his** This was the prevailing neuter form
as well as the masculine, 'its' being a
newcomer (not found, for example, in the
1611 Bible: see 2.1.252 and Abbott
228).

126 **books** Presumably, books of
memorabilia, or historical records.

127 **Alas** Editors often place this within inverted commas (F has none) as part of
Caesar's appeal, but it sounds an unlikely
start to his cry and is surely part of
Cassius' mock-regrets over him.
Titinius 'one of Cassius' chiefest friends'
(*Brutus*, p. 159), and an ally later in the
play. Mention of him so early is odd. In
Plutarch he is unheard of until the scene
of Cassius' death, and in the play he does
not appear until 4.2.0 or speak until
4.2.288. The reference here must result
from fortuitous recollection of his name.

129 **feeble temper** Dwelling on Caesar's
physical frailties, Cassius basically means
'bodily weakness'. But *temper* covers
'temperament' too, Caesar's failures in
greatness of spirit.

130 **get the start of** outstrip (so gaining the
palm of victory)
majestic (*OED*'s first occurrence)

131.1 *Flourish. Shout* F's direction at l.
78.1 and Casca's description (ll. 220–22)
indicate that the order of F's direction
here needs to be reversed: the flourish
heralds the offering of the crown and the
shout hails Caesar's refusal.

BRUTUS Another general shout?
    I do believe that these applauses are
    For some new honours that are heaped on Caesar.
CASSIUS
    Why, man, he doth bestride the narrow world
    Like a colossus, and we petty men
    Walk under his huge legs and peep about
    To find ourselves dishonourable graves.
    Men at some time are masters of their fates.
    The fault, dear Brutus, is not in our stars,   140
    But in ourselves, that we are underlings.
    'Brutus' and 'Caesar': what should be in that 'Caesar'?
    Why should that name be sounded more than yours?
    Write them together, yours is as fair a name.
    Sound them, it doth become the mouth as well.
    Weigh them, it is as heavy. Conjure with 'em,
    'Brutus' will start a spirit as soon as 'Caesar'.
    Now in the names of all the gods at once,
    Upon what meat doth this our Caesar feed
    That he is grown so great? Age, thou art shamed!   150
    Rome, thou hast lost the breed of noble bloods!
    When went there by an age, since the great Flood,

139 some time] F3; sometime F1

135 **bestride** bestraddle (first recorded use in this sense)
136 **a colossus** A gigantic statue, particularly that in bronze of Apollo as sun-god at Rhodes, traditionally reputed to be over thirty metres high and to straddle the harbour entrance, one of the seven wonders of the world.
137-8 **peep about . . . graves** are so humiliated that we only look furtively forward to the ignominious deaths of bondmen
139 **Men . . . fates** Here, and at 4.2.268-74, Cassius and Brutus, self-directed republicans, believe that circumstances must be turned to advantage. By the play's end they recognize defeat by a prevailing destiny.
    at some time F reads 'at sometime', which *OED* defines as '. . . in former times, formerly', its last example being of 1579. If Shakespeare wrote 'Men at sometime were . . .' Cassius, very fittingly, would be lamenting Rome's fall from sturdy independence (see ll. 150-61). But the

evidence is not certain enough to warrant emending F's 'are' to 'were' (as John Jowett suggests).
142 **'Brutus' and 'Caesar'** 'The name Caesar, in fact, until Julius had made it famous, was an insignificant name in history, but *Brutus* – why, it was the greatest name in Roman annals' (Kittredge); see l. 159, note.
143 **be sounded** (a) resound (b) be celebrated
146 **Conjure with 'em** pronounce them as spells to raise the dead. Wilson (p. 112) notes appropriately that only the names of gods could raise the dead.
147 **spirit** (monosyllabic, as often)
149 **meat** food (of any kind; still so used in Scotland)
152 **the great Flood** Both the Bible (Genesis 6-8) and Greek mythology tell of a universal flood. In the classical version Zeus drowns all mankind for wickedness, save Deucalion (son of Prometheus, who warned him to prepare a boat) and his wife Pyrrha, spared for their virtues; see Ovid, *Metamorphoses*, i. 187 ff.

Julius Caesar

But it was famed with more than with one man?
When could they say, till now, that talked of Rome,
That her wide walks encompassed but one man?
Now is it Rome indeed, and room enough,
When there is in it but one only man.
O, you and I have heard our fathers say
There was a Brutus once that would have brooked
Th'eternal devil to keep his state in Rome   160
As easily as a king.

BRUTUS

That you do love me, I am nothing jealous.
What you would work me to, I have some aim.
How I have thought of this, and of these times,
I shall recount hereafter. For this present,
I would not, so with love I might entreat you,
Be any further moved. What you have said
I will consider; what you have to say
I will with patience hear, and find a time
Both meet to hear and answer such high things.   170
Till then, my noble friend, chew upon this:

155 walks] F (Walkes); walls ROWE 1714   166 not, so with ... you,] THEOBALD (subs.);   not so (with ... you) F

153 **famed with** renowned for
155 **walks** Since *encompassed* (= encircled) suggests a boundary, Rowe's emendation 'walls' is generally adopted. But at 3.2.239 Caesar bequeaths to the citizens 'all his walks' (and gardens), and the idea of extensive strolling places surrounding the city is natural. In *Paradise Lost*, iv. 586, Milton describes Satan as lurking 'within the circuit of these walks' (i.e. the Garden of Eden). Shakespeare does not elsewhere use *wide* of walls but in *Titus* 2.1.114 he does apply it to *walks* ('The forest walks are wide ...').
156 **Rome ... room** Similarly 3.1.288-9, and *K. John* 3.1.180 – 'That I have room with Rome to curse awhile'. In *Lucrece* (ll. 715, 1644) *Rome* rhymes with 'doom' and 'groom', and this pronunciation lasted until the mid nineteenth century. But Elizabethan English also allowed the alternative, as at *1 Henry VI* 3.1.51 – 'Rome shall remedy this. – Roam thither, then.'
159 **a Brutus once** 'Marcus Brutus came of that Junius Brutus for whom the ancient Romans made his statue of brass to be set

up in the Capitol with the images of the kings, holding a naked sword in his hand, because he had valiantly put down the Tarquins from their kingdom of Rome' (*Brutus*, p. 102). About 509 BC he had ousted the tyrant Tarquinius Superbus and become one of the first two Roman consuls: 'the great opinion | That Rome holds of his name' (ll. 315-16) refers to Brutus' own repute but also to the reverence in which the very name 'Brutus' was held.
160 **devil** (often monosyllabic)
162-70 **That you ... things** The clipped controlled phrasing anticipates that of Brutus' funeral oration; see Commentary, 3.2.13-33, for Plutarch's account of this style.
162 **nothing jealous** not at all doubtfully mistrustful
163 **work** persuade
   aim idea (and intention)
167 **moved** pressed, urged
170 **meet** fitting
171 **chew** ruminate (not necessarily jocose in Elizabethan English)

III

Brutus had rather be a villager
Than to repute himself a son of Rome
Under these hard conditions as this time
Is like to lay upon us.

CASSIUS   I am glad
That my weak words have struck but thus much show
Of fire from Brutus.

    Enter Caesar and his train

BRUTUS

The games are done, and Caesar is returning.

CASSIUS

As they pass by, pluck Casca by the sleeve,
And he will, after his sour fashion, tell you   180
What hath proceeded worthy note today.

BRUTUS

I will do so. But look you, Cassius,
The angry spot doth glow on Caesar's brow,
And all the rest look like a chidden train.
Calpurnia's cheek is pale, and Cicero
Looks with such ferret and such fiery eyes
As we have seen him in the Capitol,
Being crossed in conference by some senators.

CASSIUS

Casca will tell us what the matter is.

CAESAR Antonius!   190

ANTONY Caesar?

CAESAR

Let me have men about me that are fat,
Sleek-headed men, and such as sleep a-nights.

175–7 I . . . Brutus] DYCE 1866 (*conj.* Walker, *Crit.*); *as two lines, breaking after* 'words' F
178–9 The . . . sleeve] ROWE; *as four lines, breaking after* 'done', 'returning', 'by' F   190
Antonius] POPE; *Antonio* F

175–7 **I am glad . . . Brutus** Whether this brief reply shows an 'eager response' (F. C. Kolbe, *Shakespeare's Way*, 1930, p. 167) or disappointment at Brutus' deliberateness is unclear. It sounds dubious, as if Brutus were flint from which only a spark or two can be struck.

177.1 *Enter Caesar* There are no trumpet flourishes; the mood is angry.

184 **chidden** *OED*'s first occurrence in *Troilus* is antedated by this example.

186 **fiery eyes** 'The eyes [of the ferret] small, but fiery, like red-hot iron' (Edward Topsell, *History of Four-footed Beasts*, 1607, p. 218).

188 **conference** debate

190 **Antonius** F *Antonio*; see the Introduction, p. 74.

192–5 **Let me . . . dangerous** The ambivalences of Caesar's nature are teasing: if delivered pompously this famous generalization suggests a Caesar of closed

Yon Cassius has a lean and hungry look;
He thinks too much. Such men are dangerous.

ANTONY

Fear him not, Caesar, he's not dangerous;
He is a noble Roman, and well given.

CAESAR

Would he were fatter! But I fear him not.
Yet if my name were liable to fear,
I do not know the man I should avoid   200
So soon as that spare Cassius. He reads much,
He is a great observer, and he looks
Quite through the deeds of men. He loves no plays,
As thou dost, Antony; he hears no music.
Seldom he smiles, and smiles in such a sort
As if he mocked himself, and scorned his spirit
That could be moved to smile at anything.
Such men as he be never at heart's ease
Whiles they behold a greater than themselves,
And therefore are they very dangerous.   210
I rather tell thee what is to be feared
Than what I fear; for always I am Caesar.
Come on my right hand, for this ear is deaf,

mind and defective sense, yet if touched
with sardonic humour it agrees with the
shrewdness of his next speech. '[Caesar]
said on a time to his friends: "What will
Cassius do, think ye? I like not his pale
looks." Another time, when Caesar's
friends complained unto him of Antonius
and Dolabella, . . . he answered them
again: "As for those fat men and smooth-
combed heads," quoth he, "I never
reckon of them. But these pale-visaged
and carrion-lean people, I fear them
most" – meaning Brutus and Cassius'
(*Caesar*, p. 85; similarly *Brutus*, p. 109).
Shakespeare strikingly applies this to
Cassius alone.

194 **Yon** A modernization of F's 'yond'; see
      the Oxford *Henry V* Commentary, 4.2.16.
197 **well given** well disposed
199 **if my name . . . fear** if, named Caesar, I
      could fear (Caesar's name has for him
      become a talisman of superhuman
      status. Despite his arrogance, however,
      his insight into Cassius is masterly.)

202–3 **looks . . . men** sees the motives hidden
        within men's actions
203–4 **He loves . . . Antony** Antony 'passed
        away the time in hearing of foolish plays'
        (*Antonius*, p. 183).
204 **no music** By Platonic doctrine derived
      from Pythagoras, for whom the universe
      was governed by numerical proportions
      of a musical kind, music was held to sym-
      bolize the metaphysical harmony of
      natural order and the equable balance of
      human temperament, as in *Merchant*
      5.1.81–8 – 'naught so stockish, hard,
      and full of rage | But music for the time
      doth change his nature. | The man that
      hath no music in himself, | Nor is not
      moved with concord of sweet sounds, | Is
      fit for treasons, stratagems, and spoils. |
      . . . | Let no such man be trusted.' Brutus,
      the man of harmonious temper
      (5.5.74–6), loves music (4.2.306–22).
212–13 **always . . . deaf** Again the irony of
        the overweening role embodied in the
        fallible person. Caesar's deafness is
        Shakespeare's invention.

And tell me truly what thou think'st of him.

       Sennet. Exeunt Caesar and his train, except Casca

CASCA You pulled me by the cloak. Would you speak with me?

BRUTUS

  Ay, Casca; tell us what hath chanced today

  That Caesar looks so sad.

CASCA Why, you were with him, were you not?

BRUTUS

  I should not then ask Casca what had chanced.

CASCA Why, there was a crown offered him; and being   220
  offered him, he put it by with the back of his hand, thus;
  and then the people fell a-shouting.

BRUTUS What was the second noise for?

CASCA Why, for that too.

CASSIUS

  They shouted thrice. What was the last cry for?

CASCA Why, for that too.

BRUTUS Was the crown offered him thrice?

CASCA Ay, marry, was't, and he put it by thrice, every time
  gentler than other; and at every putting-by, mine honest
  neighbours shouted.   230

CASSIUS Who offered him the crown?

CASCA Why, Antony.

BRUTUS

  Tell us the manner of it, gentle Casca.

214.1 *except Casca*] *not in* F

217 **sad** serious, grave, sorrowful
220 **a crown offered him** Antony 'carried a laurel crown in his hand, having a royal band or diadem wreathed about it, which in old time was the ancient mark and token of a king. When he was come to Caesar, . . . he did put this laurel crown upon his head, signifying thereby that he deserved to be king' (*Antonius*, pp. 186–7).
225 **thrice** See 3.2.96–7. Plutarch says that Caesar departed after two refusals, the people twice shouting approval (*Caesar*, p. 83), but also that there were several offers, refusals, and outbursts of applause (*Antonius*, p. 187). Drawing on both accounts, Shakespeare falls into a slight discrepancy. F's directions record shouting only after ll. 78 and 131; a third occasion might be after l. 147.
228 **marry** indeed (originally 'by the Virgin Mary')
229 **gentler** i.e. more reluctantly
    other For such uses of *other* in the singular, without 'the', see Abbott 12.
    honest 'a vague epithet of appreciation or praise, especially as used in a patronizing way to an inferior' (*OED a.* 1c).
230 **neighbours** Literally, those standing near him; but also widely used as a familiar form of address, or to mean 'fellow countrymen', or even (in the wider Christian sense) 'fellow creatures'.
233 **gentle** noble (as frequently)

CASCA I can as well be hanged as tell the manner of it. It was
mere foolery; I did not mark it. I saw Mark Antony offer
him a crown – yet 'twas not a crown neither, 'twas one
of these coronets – and, as I told you, he put it by once;
but for all that, to my thinking, he would fain have had
it. Then he offered it to him again; then he put it by again;
but, to my thinking, he was very loath to lay his fingers   240
off it. And then he offered it the third time; he put it the
third time by; and still as he refused it the rabblement
hooted, and clapped their chopped hands, and threw up
their sweaty nightcaps, and uttered such a deal of stink-
ing breath because Caesar refused the crown that it had
almost choked Caesar, for he swooned and fell down at it.
And for mine own part, I durst not laugh, for fear of
opening my lips and receiving the bad air.

CASSIUS

But soft, I pray you; what, did Caesar swoon?

CASCA He fell down in the market-place, and foamed at   250
mouth, and was speechless.

BRUTUS

'Tis very like; he hath the falling sickness.

252 like; he] ROWE (like, he); like he F

242 **still as** whenever. This instance antedates *OED*'s only recorded use.
242–3 **the rabblement … hands** This adapts
two phrases in Plutarch (a) 'all the whole
people shouted' (*Caesar*, p. 83) (b) 'all the
people together clapped their hands'
(*Antonius*, p. 187); *hooted* expresses
Casca's scorn of the mob, not the mob's
rejection of Caesar.
242 **rabblement** (a common Elizabethan
synonym for 'rabble')
243 **chopped** chapped, roughened
244 **nightcaps** Casca seems to be contemptuously caricaturing what they actually
wear. Nightcaps were normally for wearing to bed. To help the wool industry, in
1571 an Act of Parliament enjoined the
wearing of a woollen cap on Sundays and
holy days by every male above the age of
six years except certain officials (see
Shakespeare's England, ii. 111). Shakespeare may have been transferring the
Elizabethan custom to the Roman holi-

day. These caps are elsewhere referred to
as a mark of social disparagement.
'Nightcaps' were also, it seems,
associated with cuckoldry (Cyrus Hoy,
*Introductions, Notes, and Commentaries to
… 'The Dramatic Works of Thomas Dekker'*
(Cambridge, 1980), ii. 173, quoting from
R. Davenport's *The City Night-Cap*, Act 4,
and J. Shirley's *The Royal Master*, 1.1).
Casca assimilates the citizens' daytime
headgear with their (or their wives')
nightly pranks.
249 **did Caesar swoon** Cassius ironically
stresses *Caesar*.
250–1 **foamed at mouth** This detail is Shake
speare's invention. For 'the' omitted in
such cases see Abbott 90.
252 **like; he hath** F's 'like he hath' sound
as though Brutus were guessing. B
Plutarch positively refers to Caesar's fa
ing sickness – epilepsy (*Caesar*, pp. 3
81) – and Brutus would know the cau
and not speculate.

115

CASSIUS

No, Caesar hath it not; but you, and I,

And honest Casca, we have the falling sickness.

CASCA I know not what you mean by that, but I am sure
Caesar fell down. If the tag-rag people did not clap him
and hiss him, according as he pleased and displeased
them, as they use to do the players in the theatre, I am no
true man.

BRUTUS

What said he when he came unto himself?   260

CASCA Marry, before he fell down, when he perceived the
common herd was glad he refused the crown, he plucked
me ope his doublet and offered them his throat to cut. An
I had been a man of any occupation, if I would not have
taken him at a word, I would I might go to hell among the
rogues. And so he fell. When he came to himself again, he
said, if he had done or said anything amiss, he desired
their worships to think it was his infirmity. Three or four
wenches where I stood cried 'Alas, good soul!' and for-
gave him with all their hearts. But there's no heed to be   270
taken of them; if Caesar had stabbed their mothers they
would have done no less.

BRUTUS

And after that he came thus sad away?

CASCA Ay.

CASSIUS Did Cicero say anything?

---

254 **we have . . . sickness** i.e. we suffer
(political) collapse

256 **tag-rag** riff-raff. Tilley T10 offers many
parallels. *OED* glosses '*a*. Of or belonging
to the rabble'. Now 'ragtag and bobtail'.

258 **use** are accustomed

262–3 **plucked . . . cut** As in ll. 225, 242–3,
Shakespeare combines two accounts in
Plutarch. One (*Caesar*, p. 81) is nearer the
play's phrasing but occurs in quite a different context when, having offended the
Senate by discourtesy, Caesar 'departed
home . . . and, tearing open his doublet
collar, making his neck bare, he cried out
aloud to his friends that his throat was
ready to offer to any man that would
come and cut it' (an extravagance he
then blames on lightheadedness caused

by 'the falling evil'). The second (*Antonius*,
p. 187) is, as in the play, immediately
consequent on the crown-refusal, but is
less close in phrasing and does not refer
to the falling sickness.

262–3 **plucked me ope** On such usages
Abbott 220 comments that 'the *me* seems
to appropriate the action to the speaker,
and to be equivalent to "mark *me*" '.

263 **doublet** close-fitting jacket

264 **man . . . occupation** 'mechanic, one of
the plebeians to whom he offered his
throat' (Johnson), but implying also, sar-
donically, 'man who knew his business
(and how to act)'.

271 **stabbed** A bawdy equivocation for the
man's sexual penetration of the woman.

273 **sad** serious, grave, sorrowful

CASCA Ay, he spoke Greek.

CASSIUS To what effect?

CASCA Nay, an I tell you that, I'll ne'er look you i'th' face
again. But those that understood him smiled at one
another and shook their heads; but for mine own part, it   280
was Greek to me. I could tell you more news too: Marullus
and Flavius, for pulling scarfs off Caesar's images, are put
to silence. Fare you well. There was more foolery yet, if I
could remember it.

CASSIUS Will you sup with me tonight, Casca?

CASCA No, I am promised forth.

CASSIUS Will you dine with me tomorrow?

CASCA Ay, if I be alive, and your mind hold, and your dinner
worth the eating.

CASSIUS Good, I will expect you.   290

CASCA Do so. Farewell both.   *Exit*

BRUTUS

What a blunt fellow is this grown to be!

He was quick mettle when he went to school.

CASSIUS

So is he now in execution

Of any bold or noble enterprise,

However he puts on this tardy form.

This rudeness is a sauce to his good wit,

Which gives men stomach to digest his words

With better appetite.

281 Marullus] THEOBALD; *Murrellus* F

276 **he spoke Greek** i.e. being cautious he
spoke to be understood only by the elect.
According to Plutarch Cicero was an able
orator in Greek (*Life of Cicero*, Loeb
edition, p. 93).

281 **Greek to me** Already a common expression in Shakespeare's time (Tilley
G439).

282 **scarfs** *OED* gives one example, from
1655, of *scarf* as 'scroll . . . bearing an
inscription', which might suggest such
wax-fixed placards as Cassius refers to at
1.3.145–6; but Flavius' 'Disrobe the
images' (1.1.64) points to some kind of
draperies – sashes (*OED*, Scarf, *sb.* 1),

streamers, festoons, and the like.
Plutarch's image – 'diadems' – is quite
different (*Caesar*, p. 83).

282–3 **put to silence** This looks like a
euphemism for 'put to death', but
reference to Plutarch makes it less odious
– 'deprived . . . of their Tribune-ships'
(*Caesar*, p. 84; similarly *Antonius*, p. 187).

292 **blunt** blunt-witted, downright

293 **quick mettle** quick-spirited

296 **tardy form** slow-witted manner

297 **rudeness** rough manner (not the
modern 'impoliteness')
wit intelligence

298 **stomach** capacity, inclination

BRUTUS

And so it is. For this time I will leave you.   300
Tomorrow, if you please to speak with me,
I will come home to you; or, if you will,
Come home to me, and I will wait for you.

CASSIUS

I will do so. Till then, think of the world.   *Exit Brutus*
Well, Brutus, thou art noble, yet I see
Thy honourable mettle may be wrought
From that it is disposed. Therefore it is meet
That noble minds keep ever with their likes;
For who so firm that cannot be seduced?
Caesar doth bear me hard, but he loves Brutus.   310
If I were Brutus now, and he were Cassius,
He should not humour me. I will this night,
In several hands, in at his windows throw,
As if they came from several citizens,
Writings, all tending to the great opinion
That Rome holds of his name, wherein obscurely
Caesar's ambition shall be glancèd at.
And after this let Caesar seat him sure,
For we will shake him, or worse days endure.   *Exit*

300 And . . . you] ROWE; *as two lines, breaking after* 'is' F

301–3 **Tomorrow . . . wait for you** Brutus'
    hesitancy (ll. 162–70) has turned into
    urgent resolve under the seeming
    evidence of Caesar's ambitions. Shakes-
    peare telescopes Plutarch's time-scale, for
    swift, developing action.
304 **the world** the way things are going
305 **Brutus, thou** To Brutus Cassius uses the
    respectful 'you', away from him the
    familiar 'thou'; see Abbott 233.
305–7 **thou art noble . . . disposed** This plays
    on the alchemistical idea that *noble* metal
    (gold, silver) cannot be transmuted into
    anything inferior: Brutus is to be the ex-
    ception. *Mettle*, as often, unites the senses
    of 'substance (metal)' and 'tempera-
    ment'.
307 **that it is disposed** For the omitted
    relative ('that to which') see Abbott 244,
    396.
    meet fitting
309 **For who . . . seduced** This works two
    ways: Brutus is vulnerable (a) to Cassius'
    instigations (b) to Caesar's seductions.

310 **doth bear me hard** bears me ill-will.
    'Cassius . . . did egg him [Brutus] on the
    more, for a private quarrel . . . against
    Caesar; . . . Caesar also had Cassius in
    great jealousy and suspected him much'
    (*Caesar*, p. 85).
312 **He should not humour me** *He* may be
    Brutus: if so, the sense is, 'If Brutus and
    I changed places, he should not sway me
    as I sway him.' But ll. 310–12 seem to
    mean, 'Caesar is my enemy but Brutus'
    friend; if I were in Brutus' place, Caesar
    should not cajole me.' Plutarch records
    that Brutus 'might have been one of
    Caesar's chiefest friends and of greatest
    authority and credit about him' but was
    warned by Cassius' friends 'to beware of
    Caesar's sweet enticements . . . [which
    were meant] not to honour his virtue but
    to weaken his constant mind' (*Brutus*,
    p. 108).
313 **several hands** different handwritings
316 **obscurely** cryptically
317 **glancèd** hinted

1.3 *Thunder and lightning. Enter Casca, with sword drawn,*
and Cicero, meeting

CICERO

Good even, Casca. Brought you Caesar home?
Why are you breathless, and why stare you so?

CASCA

Are not you moved, when all the sway of earth
Shakes like a thing unfirm? O Cicero,
I have seen tempests when the scolding winds   5
Have rived the knotty oaks, and I have seen
Th'ambitious ocean swell, and rage, and foam,
To be exalted with the threat'ning clouds;
But never till tonight, never till now,

1.3.0.1 *with sword drawn*] *not in* F   0.2 *meeting*] *not in* F

1.3.0.1 **Thunder and lightning** These were
produced by the reverberation of heavy
metal or by drum-rolls (see Jonson, *Every
Man In His Humour*, Prologue 18–20 –
'rolled bullet heard, | To say, it thunders',
or 'tempestuous drum | Rumbles, to tell
you that the storm doth come') and the
flash of explosive devices (ll. 17–18 –
'nimble squib is seen to make afeard | The
gentlewomen'). *A Warning for Fair
Women*, Induction 51–3, notes sarcastic-
ally how 'a little rosin flasheth forth, | Like
. . . | . . . a boy's squib.'

 1 **Brought . . . home** Presumably from the
Lupercalia, after the supper to which
Casca was bound at 1.2.286. Shakespeare annuls the month interval between this (15 February) and the eve (14
March) of the Ides of March. The action
is tightly continuous.

 3 **all the sway of earth** the whole order of
things. *Sway* is 'governance' (though the
sense 'swing, rock' has an obvious
relevance). 'Certainly destiny may easier
be foreseen than avoided, considering the
strange and wonderful signs that were
said to be seen before Caesar's death'
(*Caesar*, p. 86). Though not mentioning a
storm Plutarch lists a long series of
unnatural phenomena.

 4 **unfirm** (a) unstable (*OED a.* 4) (b) infirm,
physically weak (*OED a.* 3). In both these
senses this passage antedates *OED*'s first
example.

 6 **rived** split

 7 **swell, and rage, and foam** As well as their
literal relevance to the storm, these verbs
carry on the personification implicit in
'ambitious': *swell* meaning 'to show
proud or angry feeling in one's action or
speech' (*OED v.* 9); *rage* obviously for
angry violence; and *foam* 'often . . . a
hyperbolical description of vehement
rage or wrath' (*OED v.* 1).

 8 **exalted** with raised as high as

9–28 **But never . . . shrieking** Plutarch
mentions 'fires in the element and spirits
running up and down in the night, and
also the solitary birds to be seen at noon-
days sitting in the great market-place',
'divers men . . . going up and down in
fire', 'a slave . . . that did cast a marvellous
burning flame out of his hand, . . . but . . .
he had no hurt' (*Caesar*, pp. 86–7).
Shakespeare had already in *1 Henry VI*
1.1.55–6 borrowed from Ovid's account
of how on his death Caesar became a star
(*Metamorphoses*, xv. 840–2; 944–7 in
Golding's translation, 1567), and several
others of Ovid's prodigies preceding his
murder reappear here or among Calpurnia's observations at 2.2.14–24:
Ovid mentions clashing arms heard
among storm-clouds, firebrands flashing
in the heavens, clouds dripping blood,
ghosts, wailing voices, owls hooting, and
earth tremors (*Metamorphoses*, xv.
783–98; 879–96 in Golding).

Did I go through a tempest dropping fire.   10
Either there is a civil strife in heaven,
Or else the world, too saucy with the gods,
Incenses them to send destruction.

CICERO

Why, saw you anything more wonderful?

CASCA

A common slave – you know him well by sight –
Held up his left hand, which did flame and burn
Like twenty torches joined, and yet his hand,
Not sensible of fire, remained unscorched.
Besides – I ha' not since put up my sword –
Against the Capitol I met a lion,   20
Who glazed upon me; and went surly by,
Without annoying me. And there were drawn
Upon a heap a hundred ghastly women,
Transformèd with their fear, who swore they saw
Men, all in fire, walk up and down the streets.
And yesterday the bird of night did sit,
Even at noonday, upon the market-place,
Hooting and shrieking. When these prodigies
Do so conjointly meet, let not men say

---

10 tempest dropping fire] F (Tempest-dropping-fire)   21 glazed] F (*subs.*);   glar'd ROWE 1709b;
gaz'd MALONE (*conj.* Johnson)

10 **tempest dropping fire** F's 'Tempest-dropping-fire' may reflect some scribal inclination for hyphens. 'High-sighted-Tyranny' occurs at 2.1.118, 'hony-heauy-Dew' at 2.1.231, and 'Low-crooked-curtsies' at 3.1.43.

12 **saucy** *OED a.*¹2, defines it as 'insolent . . . presumptuous', quoting *Every Man Out Of His Humour* 5.5.45 – 'that saucy, stubborn generation, the Jews'. Since Shakespeare's time the sense has weakened.

14 **anything more** anything else (rather than 'anything even more')

18 **sensible of** sensitive to
   unscorched (*OED*'s first example as participial adjective)

19 **put up** sheathed

20 **Against** over against

21 **Who** Abbott 265 illustrates *who* with 'irrational antecedents' such as animals, natural forces, and so on.
   glazed stared glassily (often emended to 'glared' or 'gazed'). *OED* comments '*Obs. exc. dial.*' and quotes only this example

and two from the nineteenth century, one being Cornish dialect. Kittredge, however, adds four from Middle English and Tudor texts, for eyes or stars gazing or shining.

22 **annoying** doing harm to

22–3 **drawn | Upon a heap** huddled together

23 **ghastly** ghostly white

25 **men all in fire** See Commentary, ll. 9–28.

26–8 **bird of night . . . shrieking** See Commentary, ll. 9–28, and Pliny, *Natural History* (trans. Philemon Holland, 1601), x. 12 – 'The screech owl betokeneth . . . heavy news, and is most execrable and accursed . . . He is the very monster of the night.' Alternatively, the raven; Tilley R33 gives many allusions to its ominous croak, as in *Much Ado* 2.3.76–7 – 'I had as lief have heard the night raven, come what plague could have come after it'.

28 **prodigies** omens, portents

29 **conjointly** *OED*'s first occurrence here is antedated by *K. John* 2.1.379.

29–30 **let . . . natural** Superior though

'These are their reasons, they are natural';   30
For I believe they are portentous things
Unto the climate that they point upon.

CICERO

Indeed it is a strange-disposèd time.
But men may construe things after their fashion,
Clean from the purpose of the things themselves.
Comes Caesar to the Capitol tomorrow?

CASCA

He doth, for he did bid Antonius
Send word to you he would be there tomorrow.

CICERO

Good night then, Casca. This disturbèd sky
Is not to walk in.

CASCA   Farewell, Cicero.   *Exit Cicero*   40

    Enter Cassius

CASSIUS

Who's there?

CASCA   A Roman.

CASSIUS   Casca, by your voice.

CASCA

Your ear is good. Cassius, what night is this!

CASSIUS

A very pleasing night to honest men.

CASCA

Who ever knew the heavens menace so?

CASSIUS

Those that have known the earth so full of faults.
For my part, I have walked about the streets,

37 Antonius] POPE; *Antonio* F   39–40 Good . . . in] ROWE;   *as two lines, breaking after 'Caska'*
F   42 Your . . . this] ROWE;   *as two lines, breaking after* 'good' F

Brutus and Cassius (and Cicero) are to 'prodigies', the play persistently implies that (as in *Lear*, *Macbeth*, and elsewhere) political subversion really does derange the whole natural order. Cassius' initial Epicurean scepticism (see 5.1.77–8) ultimately yields before proofs of supernatural outrage.

32 **climate** region, a 'clime' (*OED, sb.* 1b.)
   point direct their (malign) influence (an astrological idea)

34 **construe** Accented on *con-*.

35 **purpose** true bearing

37 **Antonius** F *Antonio*; see the Introduction, p. 74.

46–52 **For my part . . . of it** Later Cassius partly credits 'things that do presage' (5.1.78–89). Here, though rationally a sceptic, he is emotionally excited by the sense that the heavens are significantly intervening. He is in effect as superstitious in his flouting of celestial wrath as are those cowed by it; he actively invites the lightning stroke. Defiance of supernatural power has its own extravagance.

Submitting me unto the perilous night,
And thus unbracèd, Casca, as you see,
Have bared my bosom to the thunder-stone;
And when the cross blue lightning seemed to open   50
The breast of heaven, I did present myself
Even in the aim and very flash of it.

CASCA

But wherefore did you so much tempt the heavens?
It is the part of men to fear and tremble
When the most mighty gods by tokens send
Such dreadful heralds to astonish us.

CASSIUS

You are dull, Casca, and those sparks of life
That should be in a Roman you do want,
Or else you use not. You look pale, and gaze,
And put on fear, and cast yourself in wonder,   60
To see the strange impatience of the heavens.
But if you would consider the true cause
Why all these fires, why all these gliding ghosts,
Why birds and beasts, from quality and kind,

57–60 You ... wonder] ROWE; *as five lines, ending 'Caska'*, 'Roman', 'not', 'feare', 'wonder' F

47 **Submitting me** 'Me', 'him', and so on for 'myself', 'himself' and so on are Middle English usages current in Elizabethan English: Abbott 223.

48 **unbracèd** with doublet unbuttoned

49 **thunder-stone** thunderbolt, supposedly a fiery missile projected from the sky. The belief goes back at least to Pliny (*Natural History*, Loeb edition, xxxvii. 55, under 'Brontea, or thunderstone, ... supposed to fall from thunderclaps'). Stephen Batman, *Uppon Bartholome* (1582), Book II, chap. 15, fol. 164, equates it with Latin *fulgur* and observes that it 'cometh down with great violence . . . and cleaveth, and renteth'. Baring his bosom to it, Cassius is almost hysterical with daring.

50 **cross** forked, jagged; with, seemingly, an implication of 'hostile', as in *OED a*. 4, 'Adverse, ... unfavourable, untoward'.

52 **Even in the aim** at the very point it was aimed at (at the climax of Cassius' hyperbolical defiance)

54 **part** function

55 **tokens** signs

56 **astonish** stun, astound (a very strong sense). Along with the still extant 'amaze,

surprise greatly' *OED* includes as obsolete senses '2. To stun mentally; to shock one out of one's wits' and '3. ... to dismay, terrify.'

58 **want** lack

60 **put on ... cast yourself** Cassius half-consciously dramatizes the situation: as a spirited Roman, Casca should be undismayed – instead he enacts terror. Shakespeare often images emotion as an outward dressing, perhaps from the actor's gift for presenting externally what inwardly he is supposedly feeling, as in *Much Ado* 4.1.144 ('I am so attired in wonder'), *Lucrece* 1601 ('attired in discontent'), and *Macbeth* 1.7.35–6 ('the hope ... | Wherein you dressed yourself'); see 2.1.226.

63 **gliding ghosts** See Commentary, ll. 9–28.

64–5 **Why birds ... calculate** The syntax is impetuous. Johnson thought l. 65 might precede l. 64; others have suspected some omission between the two. But Cassius is so urgent that some disorder is natural; his meaning comes through the more forcibly for the dislocation.

64 **from quality and kind** against their characters and natures. *Kind* as 'natural

Why old men, fools, and children calculate,
Why all these things change from their ordinance,
Their natures and preformèd faculties,
To monstrous quality, why, you shall find
That heaven hath infused them with these spirits
To make them instruments of fear and warning   70
Unto some monstrous state.
Now could I, Casca, name to thee a man
Most like this dreadful night,
That thunders, lightens, opens graves, and roars
As doth the lion in the Capitol –
A man no mightier than thyself or me
In personal action, yet prodigious grown
And fearful, as these strange eruptions are.

CASCA

'Tis Caesar that you mean. Is it not, Cassius?

CASSIUS

Let it be who it is; for Romans now   80
Have thews and limbs like to their ancestors;

79 'Tis . . . Cassius] ROWE;   *as two lines, breaking after* 'meane' F

disposition or character' was common
until about 1600 (Onions).

65 **old men . . . calculate** Some editions read
'old men fool'; i.e. old men (normally
thoughtful) prove silly; children (normally thoughtless) prove prophets. 'The
meaning of F is plain: so obvious and so
numerous are the portents that any
dotard, fool, or infant can interpret them'
(Wilson). Tilley C328 illustrates the belief
that children and fools (a) reveal the
truth, and (b) foresee the future.
calculate foretell (from astrological
reckoning)
66 **ordinance** due function (as Providence
has ordained)
67 **preformèd** foreordained, congenital (*OED*'s
first occurrence of the verb 'preform')
68 **monstrous quality** unnatural, deformed
condition
71 **Unto . . . state** pointing to some fearful
condition (implying also, perhaps, the
Roman state under tyranny). Casca takes
the disturbances as incomprehensible
warnings, Cicero as natural phenomena,
Cassius as symbols of Caesar's 'tyranny';
they do indeed 'construe things after their

fashion' (l. 34), a striking instance of the
play's recurrent theme of opinion-
forming. Characters are always seeking
interpretations and deducing conclusions.
72–8 **Now could I . . . eruptions are** Cassius'
prejudices equate Caesar with the
destructiveness of abnormal Nature,
whereas no evidence has appeared of
anything remotely like it.
75 **the lion in the Capitol** Perhaps the surly
creature of l. 20. Shakespeare's audience
might well think of the lions of the royal
menagerie in the Tower; 'to have seen
the lions' was proverbial for seeing the
sights of London.
76 **no mightier** Repeatedly Cassius insists
that Caesar is no greater than the rest, if
as great; see 1.2.92–131, 142–7.
77 **prodigious** monstrous, ominous
78 **eruptions** upheavals (from abnormal tensions), as in *1 Henry IV* 3.1.27–8 –
'Diseasèd Nature oftentimes breaks forth
| In strange eruptions.'
80 **Let . . . is** Cassius is unexpectedly
secretive: he has not yet had the meeting
with Casca mooted at 1.2.287–90; in
any case he likes mystery.

But – woe the while! – our fathers' minds are dead,
And we are governed with our mothers' spirits.
Our yoke and sufferance show us womanish.

CASCA

Indeed, they say the senators tomorrow
Mean to establish Caesar as a king,
And he shall wear his crown by sea and land
In every place save here in Italy.

CASSIUS

I know where I will wear this dagger then;
Cassius from bondage will deliver Cassius.   90
Therein, ye gods, you make the weak most strong;
Therein, ye gods, you tyrants do defeat.
Nor stony tower, nor walls of beaten brass,
Nor airless dungeon, nor strong links of iron,
Can be retentive to the strength of spirit;
But life, being weary of these worldly bars,
Never lacks power to dismiss itself.
If I know this, know all the world besides,
That part of tyranny that I do bear
I can shake off at pleasure.
        Thunder still

CASCA   So can I.   100
So every bondman in his own hand bears
The power to cancel his captivity.

---

82 **woe the while** alas for the times
84 **yoke and sufferance** servitude and sub-
   mission
85–8 **Indeed . . . Italy** In Plutarch, Decius
   tells Caesar that the senators 'were ready
   . . . to proclaim him king of all the
   provinces . . . out of Italy, and that he
   should wear his diadem in all other
   places, both by sea and land' (*Caesar* p. 90).
   The historical reason was that according
   to prophecy only under a king's generalship could Rome vanquish the Parthians,
   against whom Caesar was about to lead
   a campaign to avenge the defeat and
   death of his colleague Marcus Crassus
   (*Caesar*, p. 81). In *Antony and Cleopatra*
   3.1.1–3 Ventidius, the Roman general,
   announces the victory which has
   achieved this.
89–115 **I know . . . indifferent** The thought
   of heroic autonomy rouses Cassius to

heady exultance.
90 **Cassius . . . Cassius** This is close to Kyd's
   Cornelia 4.1.147–50 (see the Introduction, p. 27) – 'But know, while Cassius
   hath one drop of blood | To feed this
   worthless body that you see, | What reck
   I death to do so many good, | In spite of
   Caesar, Cassius shall be free.'
91, 92 **Therein** i.e. by the option of suicide
94 **airless** (*OED*'s first occurrence)
95 **be retentive to** keep captive
102 **cancel** Prompted by 'bond[man]', this is
   the legal term for annulling a contract.
   Shakespeare repeatedly presents life as a
   bond which death terminates, as in
   Richard III 4.4.77 ('Cancel his bond of
   life'), *Macbeth* 3.2.49 ('Cancel . . . that
   great bond'), and *Cymbeline* 5.4.27–8
   ('Take this life, | And cancel these cold
   bonds.').

124

CASSIUS

And why should Caesar be a tyrant then?
Poor man, I know he would not be a wolf
But that he sees the Romans are but sheep.
He were no lion were not Romans hinds.
Those that with haste will make a mighty fire
Begin it with weak straws. What trash is Rome,
What rubbish, and what offal, when it serves
For the base matter to illuminate   110
So vile a thing as Caesar! But, O grief,
Where hast thou led me? I perhaps speak this
Before a willing bondman; then I know
My answer must be made. But I am armed,
And dangers are to me indifferent.

CASCA

You speak to Casca, and to such a man
That is no fleering telltale. Hold, my hand.
Be factious for redress of all these griefs,
And I will set this foot of mine as far
As who goes farthest.

CASSIUS   There's a bargain made.   120
Now know you, Casca, I have moved already
Some certain of the noblest-minded Romans
To undergo with me an enterprise
Of honourable-dangerous consequence;
And I do know, by this they stay for me

124 honourable-dangerous] F (*not hyphenated*)   125 know, by this] ROWE;   know by this, F

103 **tyrant** 'Cassius even from his cradle
    could not abide . . . tyrants' (*Caesar*,
    pp. 109–10).
104–5 **wolf . . . sheep** A version of the
    proverb, 'He that makes himself a sheep
    shall be eaten by the wolf' (Tilley S300).
106 **hinds** (a) deer (b) menials (c) peasants
108 **What trash is Rome** 'As men start a
    huge fire with worthless straws or shav-
    ings, so Caesar is using the degenerate
    Romans of the time to set the whole world
    ablaze with his own glory' (Hudson).
108–9 **trash . . . rubbish . . . offal** Virtual
    synonyms, reflecting Cassius' insistent
    exasperation. *Trash* = prunings, hedge-
    cuttings (which blaze readily), *rubbish* =

'debris, litter, refuse' (*OED*, *sb*. 1) from
broken buildings, *offal* = woodworkers'
chippings (off-fall).
110 **base** (a) nethermost (b) despicable
    matter substance (specifically, fuel)
114 **My answer . . . made** I must pay the
    penalty
115 **indifferent** immaterial
117 **fleering** gibing, sneering. The impli-
    cation here is probably that of the in-
    former laughing in his sleeve at his
    treachery.
    Hold, my hand enough said: I offer my
    hand
118 **Be factious . . . griefs** form a faction,
    party, to redress these grievances

In Pompey's Porch; for now, this fearful night,
There is no stir or walking in the streets,
And the complexion of the element
In favour's like the work we have in hand,
Most bloody-fiery, and most terrible.　　　　　　　　　130
　　　Enter Cinna

CASCA
Stand close awhile, for here comes one in haste.
CASSIUS
'Tis Cinna, I do know him by his gait;
He is a friend. Cinna, where haste you so?
CINNA
To find out you. Who's that? Metellus Cimber?
CASSIUS
No, it is Casca, one incorporate
To our attempts. Am I not stayed for, Cinna?
CINNA
I am glad on't. What a fearful night is this!
There's two or three of us have seen strange sights.
CASSIUS
Am I not stayed for? Tell me.
CINNA　　　　　　　　　　Yes, you are.
O Cassius, if you could　　　　　　　　　　140

129 In favour's] Q1691; Is Fauors, F; Is fev'rous Q5; Is feav'rous ROWE; Is favour'd
CAPELL; It favours, STEEVENS　bloody-fiery] F (*not hyphenated*)　137 I . . . this] ROWE;　*as two
lines, breaking after* 'on't' F　139–41 Yes . . . party –] SINGER 1856 (*conj.* Walker, *Vers.*);　*as
three lines, ending* '*Cassius*', '*Brutus*', 'party –' F

126 **Pompey's Porch** 'one of the porches
about the Theatre, in which . . . was
set up the image of Pompey which the
city had . . . consecrated in honour of
him', a place of good omen for the plotters
since Pompey had been an enemy of
Caesar (*Brutus*, p. 119). In Plutarch it is
the Senate's meeting-place and the scene
of Caesar's assassination: Shakespeare
takes this to be the Capitol, though he
retains on the scene the statue of Pompey, to be stained with the blood of the
murder (as in *Caesar*, p. 95).
128 **complexion of the element** disposition of
the heavens
129 **In favour's like** in appearance is like. F's
'Is Fauors, like' has been variously
emended. Its comma lends plausibility to
Q5's reading, 'Is fev'rous, like' (Rowe, 'Is

feav'rous, like'), which some editors
adopt. But Cassius' idea seems to be that
the heavens have the same aspect
('favour') as their own stormy work,
which he would hardly call 'fev'rous',
even though 'most bloody-fiery and most
terrible'.
130 **Most bloody-fiery** The hyphen (for F's
comma) saves *fiery* from limping along
without a *most*, and moreover makes
graphic sense – 'covered over with fiery
meteors of a blood-red colour' (Walker,
Crit.).
131 **Stand close** stay still
134 **Metellus** So in *Caesar* (p. 92); Tullius in
Brutus (p. 123).
135–6 **incorporate** | To integrally part of
137 **glad on't** i.e. that Cinna is one of us

But win the noble Brutus to our party –
CASSIUS

    Be you content. Good Cinna, take this paper,
    And look you lay it in the praetor's chair,
    Where Brutus may but find it; and throw this
    In at his window. Set this up with wax
    Upon old Brutus' statue. All this done,
    Repair to Pompey's Porch, where you shall find us.
    Is Decius Brutus and Trebonius there?
CINNA

    All but Metellus Cimber, and he's gone
    To seek you at your house. Well, I will hie,   150
    And so bestow these papers as you bade me.
CASSIUS

    That done, repair to Pompey's Theatre.   *Exit Cinna*
    Come, Casca, you and I will yet ere day
    See Brutus at his house. Three parts of him
    Is ours already, and the man entire
    Upon the next encounter yields him ours.
CASCA

    O, he sits high in all the people's hearts;
    And that which would appear offence in us

142–6 **Good Cinna . . . statue** In Plutarch this is done spontaneously by various plotters: Shakespeare concentrates it in Cassius' control. Plutarch's plotters 'durst not come to [Brutus] themselves . . . but in the night did cast sundry papers into the Praetor's seat where he gave audience' (*Caesar*, p. 84). For their contents see Commentary, 2.1.46.

144 **may but** must surely

145 **Set . . . wax** Proclamations, epitaphs, and the like were often affixed with wax to walls, monuments, and so on.

148 **Decius** So in *Caesar* (p. 89); actually Decimus. Like Brutus he had been strongly favoured by Caesar, who 'put such confidence [in him] that . . . he had appointed him to be his next heir, and yet was of the conspiracy with Cassius and Brutus' (*Caesar*, p. 90). His participation is gross treachery, and carried through most unscrupulously.

150 **hie** go speedily

154 **at his house** This suggests (like

ll. 162–4) a direct route to Brutus' house, whereas the others will gather at Pompey's Theatre (l. 152), yet at 2.1.70–2 they arrive together. Small discrepancies are natural hazards in the press of composition and pass unnoticed on the stage. For possible revision of the text, see Introduction, p. 78.

157–60 **O . . . worthiness** Obsequious in 1.2.1 ff., derisive in 1.2.220 ff., and scared in 1.3.3. ff., Casca has steadied into the resolute admirer of Brutus' virtue. Finding virtually no guidance in Plutarch for him (very brief notes in *Caesar*, p. 93, and *Brutus*, pp. 120–1, 124), Shakespeare drew him at will. Is the result 'a bundle of contradictions [with the] impassioned eulogy of Brutus . . . a finishing touch of incongruity' (Wilson, pp. 96–7)? Wilson suggests textual revision introducing inconsistent afterthoughts. This is possible, yet that an unstable character should be braced into resolution by the hazards of conspiracy

His countenance, like richest alchemy,
Will change to virtue and to worthiness.   160
CASSIUS
Him and his worth and our great need of him
You have right well conceited. Let us go,
For it is after midnight, and ere day
We will awake him and be sure of him.   *Exeunt*

2.1   *Enter Brutus in his orchard*
BRUTUS   What, Lucius, ho!
I cannot by the progress of the stars
Give guess how near to day. – Lucius, I say! –
I would it were my fault to sleep so soundly. –
When, Lucius, when? Awake, I say! What, Lucius!
         Enter Lucius
LUCIUS   Called you, my lord?
BRUTUS
Get me a taper in my study, Lucius.
When it is lighted, come and call me here.
LUCIUS   I will, my lord.   *Exit*
BRUTUS
It must be by his death; and, for my part,   10

2.1] F (*Actus Secundus.*)

and the inspiration of Brutus is entirely
acceptable. The very impressive tribute to
Brutus needs to stand out against Brutus'
well-meant errors and later self-
righteousness: 'when Cassius felt his
friends and did stir them up against
Caesar, they all agreed . . . to take part
with him, so Brutus were the chief of their
conspiracy. For . . . so high an enterprise
. . . did not so much require men of manhood and courage . . . as . . . to have a man
of such estimation as Brutus, to make
every man boldly think that by his only
presence the fact were holy and just'
(*Brutus*, p. 111).

159 **countenance** (a) demeanour (b) support
alchemy Alchemy sought to transmute
base metals into 'noble' ones.

160 **virtue** high, precious moral value. *Virtue* has its direct literal sense but also,
symbolically, that of the rich treasure
which alchemy (l. 159) produces (*OED* 9).
worthiness nobility (a strong sense)

162 **conceited** (a) conceived, understood (b)
expressed in poetic figures

2.1 'a scene remarkable for its gentle prelude
and its sensitive close. The vigour of the
political argument is mitigated by his
[Brutus'] courteous treatment of the boy
Lucius, and its humanity heightened by
his affection for his wife Portia' (Styan,
p. 209).

0.1 *orchard* garden. In *Much Ado* the 'orchard' where Hero and Ursula gull
Beatrice has a 'pleachèd bower' of honey-
suckles and is clearly a pleasure garden
(3.1.7–9).

1 **Lucius** Shakespeare invents Lucius (not
in Plutarch) to bring out Brutus' con-
siderateness; see 4.2.290–1.

7 **taper** candle

10–34 **It must be . . . shell** This speech has
been much discussed. Coleridge was
puzzled about 'Shakespeare's motive, . . .
in what point he meant Brutus' character
to appear'. Hudson observed, 'Upon the
supposal that Shakespeare meant Brutus

I know no personal cause to spurn at him,
But for the general: he would be crowned.
How that might change his nature, there's the question.
It is the bright day that brings forth the adder,
And that craves wary walking. Crown him that,
And then, I grant, we put a sting in him
That at his will he may do danger with.
Th'abuse of greatness is when it disjoins
Remorse from power, and, to speak truth of Caesar,
I have not known when his affections swayed   20
More than his reason. But 'tis a common proof
That lowliness is young ambition's ladder,
Whereto the climber-upward turns his face;
But when he once attains the upmost round
He then unto the ladder turns his back,
Looks in the clouds, scorning the base degrees

15 him that,] F; him – that – ROWE   23 climber-upward] F (*not hyphenated*)

for a wise and good man, the speech seems . . . unintelligible'. It is not, in fact, difficult to follow Brutus' train of thought, though his moral logic is shaky: Caesar, so far temperate, may become tyrannical. The moral dubiety lies in the fact that (a) Brutus theorizes not by his experience of his friend and benefactor but by generalizations about ambition (ll. 21 ff.), and having argued that such men can prove dangerous he resolves to act as if Caesar will be so; and (b) since Caesar has given no *colour* for his death (l. 29) a hypothesis must be dressed up as a certainty (ll. 32–4). 'Irony there is, but tender, deep, and unavoidable in this dramatic exploration of a mind that thinks of its own and others' acts in high heroic abstractions, rising tranquilly above the petty and the particular' (Brower, p. 225).

11 **spurn at** kick against (a strong sense, involving violent rejection, as at 3.1.46 – 'I spurn thee like a cur')

12 **general** common weal, public good

14–17 **It is . . . danger with** A fact of natural history is taken to prove a political law – Brutus prefers concepts to actualities. Such analogies are common in Elizabethan writing, especially that of Lyly.

15 **craves** calls urgently for

15 **Crown him that,** i.e. crown him king. Some editors (with varied punctuation) follow Rowe's 'Crown him – that –'; i.e. 'Crown him *?* – if *that* were to happen –'. The subconscious train of idea is, perhaps, 'Crown him [as a being dangerous as] an adder'. Fortunately the image remains too subliminal to conjure up an actual vision of a crowned adder.

19 **Remorse** The primary sense here (the normal Shakespearian one) is 'compassion' (*OED* 3 marks it *Obs.*). But 'conscience' may be meant, too.

20 **affections swayed** passions ruled

21–7 **But 'tis . . . ascend** Henry IV's account of how he 'stole all courtesy from heaven | And dressed [himself] in such humility | That [he] did pluck allegiance from men's hearts' (*1 Henry IV* 3.2.50–2) vividly describes the process. Caesar in his early career, Plutarch reports, attracted many by his courtesies, beyond the point at which his opponents could hold him back: 'the people loved him marvellously also, because of the courteous manner he had . . . His enemies judging that this favour of the common people would soon quail . . . suffered him to run on, till by little and little he was grown to be of great strength' (*Caesar*, p. 23).

24 **round** rung

26 **base degrees** (a) lower rungs (b) ignoble ranks (c) humble folk

By which he did ascend. So Caesar may.
Then, lest he may, prevent. And since the quarrel
Will bear no colour for the thing he is,
Fashion it thus: that what he is, augmented,   30
Would run to these and these extremities;
And therefore think him as a serpent's egg,
Which, hatched, would as his kind grow mischievous,
And kill him in the shell.

    Enter Lucius

LUCIUS

The taper burneth in your closet, sir.
Searching the window for a flint, I found
This paper, thus sealed up; and I am sure
It did not lie there when I went to bed.

    He gives him the letter

BRUTUS

Get you to bed again, it is not day.
Is not tomorrow, boy, the Ides of March?   40
LUCIUS I know not, sir.

BRUTUS

Look in the calendar and bring me word.
LUCIUS I will, sir.   *Exit*

38.1 *He] not in* F   40 Ides] THEOBALD; first F

28 **prevent** forestall, take preventive measures
    quarrel cause of complaint
29 **bear no colour** *Colour* often means 'plausible or convincing reason' as in 2 *Henry IV* 1.2.235 ('I have the wars for my colour'), but with an element of dubiety which implies disguise or pretext.
30 **Fashion it** put the matter (Brutus means his way of putting things to be entirely justified: by a law of nature harmless beginnings may lead to harmful ends. But though not wilfully specious he unwittingly reveals the rationalization inherent in his thinking.)
31 **extremities** (a) conclusions (b) severities
33 **as his kind** 'according to his nature' (Johnson)
    mischievous dangerous (a strong sense)
34 **kill him in the shell** Kittredge quotes a close parallel, from Gabriel Harvey's *Trimming of Thomas Nashe*, 1597 (ed. Grosart, iii. 37) – 'Had I but known this cockatrice whilst 'twas in the shell, I would have broken it, it never should have been hatched by my patronage.' The idea of killing the cockatrice in the shell was proverbial (Tilley C496).
35 **closet** study, private room
40 **Ides** fifteenth day (see l. 59). F's 'first' is either a misreading, a Shakespearian slip, or the result of possible incomplete revision: see the Introduction, p. 80, note 1. Plutarch says that the Senate was to offer Caesar a crown on 'the first day . . . of March' (*Brutus*, p. 112) but also that it met on the day of the assassination 'on the fifteenth day of . . . March, which the Romans call *Idus Martias*' (*Brutus*, p. 120).

BRUTUS

The exhalations whizzing in the air
Give so much light that I may read by them.
    He opens the letter and reads
'Brutus, thou sleep'st. Awake, and see thyself!
Shall Rome, et cetera. Speak, strike, redress!'
'Brutus, thou sleep'st. Awake!'
Such instigations have been often dropped
Where I have took them up.   50
'Shall Rome, et cetera.' Thus must I piece it out:
Shall Rome stand under one man's awe? What, Rome?
My ancestors did from the streets of Rome
The Tarquin drive, when he was called a king.
'Speak, strike, redress!' Am I entreated
To speak, and strike? O Rome, I make thee promise,
If the redress will follow, thou receivest
Thy full petition at the hand of Brutus.
    Enter Lucius

45.1 *He*] *not in* F   46–8 'Brutus . . . Awake!'] (*italic, with no quotation marks, in* F)   51 'Shall . . . cetera.'] (*italic, with no quotation marks, in* F)   52 What, Rome?] ROWE (*after* F, 'What Rome?')   55 'Speak . . . redress!'] (*italic, with no quotation marks, in* F)

44 **exhalations** meteors, 'fires in the element' (*Caesar*, p. 86), supposedly the incandescence of 'vapours drawn up into the Middle Region of the Air' (Florio, *A World of Words*, 1598) – that is, 'exhaled' from earth by the sun. In *Henry VIII* 3.2.226 Wolsey will fall 'Like a bright exhalation in the evening'.

46 **Brutus . . . Awake** 'Under the image of his ancestor Junius Brutus, that drave the kings out of Rome, they wrote: "Oh that it pleased the gods thou wert now alive, Brutus." . . . His tribunal, or chair, where he gave audience during the time he was Praetor, was full of such bills: "Brutus, thou art asleep, and art not Brutus indeed"' (*Brutus*, p. 110; similarly *Caesar*, pp. 84–5).

47 **et cetera** Why Shakespeare preferred this cryptic hint to the undisguised instigations in Plutarch is not clear.

51 **Thus . . . out** 'Brutus fills out the blank in strict accordance with the words of Cassius in 1.2.151–61, which have made a powerful impression on him' (Kittredge).

52 **Shall Rome . . . awe** 'This certainly has somewhat of the republican ring. It breathes the same spirit as Cassius' own avowal [1.2.93–9]. But . . . of the positive essence of republicanism, . . . in which all the lawful authority is derived from the whole body of fully qualified citizens, there is . . . no trace whatever in any of his utterances' (MacCallum, p. 203).

53–4 **My ancestors . . . king** See Commentary, 1.2.159.

54 **The Tarquin** Presumably the use (now archaic) distinguished by *OED* ('the' 10c) 'Before names and titles of men', instancing 1 *Henry VI* 3.3.37: 'Who craves a parley with the Burgundy'.

56–8 **I make thee promise . . . Brutus** Having theorized himself into believing that Caesar must die (ll. 28–34) Brutus feels absolutely confirmed by the 'instigations' Cassius has forged. In Plutarch, Brutus' ambition is 'stirred up the more by these seditious bills' (*Caesar*, p. 85) but Shakespeare rejects any such motive, as also he rejects Caesar's distrust of Brutus – see Commentary, 1.2.192–5.

LUCIUS Sir, March is wasted fifteen days.
  Knock within

BRUTUS

 'Tis good. Go to the gate; somebody knocks. *Exit Lucius*   60
 Since Cassius first did whet me against Caesar
 I have not slept.
 Between the acting of a dreadful thing
 And the first motion, all the interim is
 Like a phantasma or a hideous dream.
 The genius and the mortal instruments
 Are then in council, and the state of man,

60 *Exit Lucius*] not in F   67 man] F2;   a man F1

59 **fifteen days** i.e. it is now early morning on the Ides of March.

61–2 **Since . . . slept** Though in the play's strict time-scale Cassius' urgings took place only the previous evening (at 1.2.305–19 and 1.3.151 the forged papers are to be sent; at 1.3.153–4 Casca and Cassius are to call on Brutus), a more protracted period is suggested (ll. 49–50). It can readily be taken for the 'double time' which allows far longer to elapse off stage than on. But it may instead be a sign of the possible rewriting discussed in the Introduction, pp. 78–9. The result, in any case, is a sense simultaneously of tight consecutiveness and of extended perspectives.

61 **did whet me** incited me (like the sharpening of a knife). The metaphor subconsciously recognizes that (a) Brutus has been brought to the fatal point by Cassius' pressure, not by his own deliberations, and (b) he is turning into a lethal agent of vengeance rather than the autonomous rationalist he aims at being.

63–9 **Between . . . insurrection** This is the acutest analysis of a tormented mind before the great tragedies, to be paralleled later in *Macbeth* 1.3.138–41 – 'My thought, whose murder yet is but fantastical, | Shakes so my single state of man that function | Is smothered in surmise, and nothing is | But what is not.' Plutarch gave a lead: 'either care did wake him against his will when he would have slept, or else oftentimes of himself he fell into such deep thoughts of this enterprise, casting in his mind all the dangers that might happen, that his wife . . . found

that there was some marvellous great matter that troubled his mind' (*Brutus*, pp. 116–17).

63 **acting** This, *OED*'s first occurrence as a verbal substantive, is antedated by Nashe's *The Unfortunate Traveller* (1594; McKerrow ii. 324. 28).

64 **motion** impulse, proposal

65 **phantasma** hallucination, wild vision

66–9 **The genius . . . insurrection** What this process is has been much discussed, though the general tenor is evident: the ruling or guardian spirit which conceives action (*genius*), and the human functions, mental and physical, which effect action (*mortal instruments*), interact so disturbedly that the human frame is shaken as with civil war. Thomson comments that according to psychology apparently taken by Plato from the Pythagoreans the ruling element of the psyche was reason or pure intelligence, the soul's only immortal part. It is absolutely sovereign and the *mortal instruments* should obey. So for them to be *in council* with it (arguing what should be done) is 'a rising of the governed against the governor' (p. 146). Several passages offer parallels: e.g. ll. 176–8 below; *Troilus* 2.3.169–70 ('"twixt his mental and his active parts | Kingdomed Achilles in commotion rages'); *Macbeth* 1.3.138–41 (see Commentary, ll. 63–9 above).

67 **state of man** human realm (the frequent analogy between the commonwealth and the individual, political macrocosm and microcosm). Theodore Spencer in *Shakespeare and the Nature of Man* (1942), p. 17, comments on 'the universal use of

Like to a little kingdom, suffers then
The nature of an insurrection.
    Enter Lucius

LUCIUS

Sir, 'tis your brother Cassius at the door,   70
Who doth desire to see you.

BRUTUS   Is he alone?

LUCIUS

No, sir, there are more with him.

BRUTUS   Do you know them?

LUCIUS

No, sir, their hats are plucked about their ears,
And half their faces buried in their cloaks,
That by no means I may discover them
By any mark of favour.

BRUTUS   Let 'em enter.   *Exit Lucius*

They are the faction. O conspiracy,
Sham'st thou to show thy dang'rous brow by night,
When evils are most free? O then, by day
Where wilt thou find a cavern dark enough   80
To mask thy monstrous visage? Seek none, conspiracy;
Hide it in smiles and affability;

76 *Exit Lucius*] *not in* F

analogy' in sixteenth-century literature – 'the cosmos is explained by the body, and the body is explained by the state; all three hierarchies are parallel – as they had been for centuries.' Some editors follow F's 'state of a man', but the metrical drive demands regularity and Brutus means the human state generally, not individually.

70 **brother** brother-in-law. 'Cassius had married Junia, Brutus' sister' (*Brutus*, p. 108).

72 **more** In F, 'moe' ('mo' at 5.3.101); in Elizabethan usage it is used for a larger number, *more* for a larger degree (though the distinction was fading by Shakespeare's time).

73–4 **hats . . . cloaks** These are not necessarily unRoman anachronisms; see Introduction, pp. 50–1, on Roman dress in the drama. Pope decided that *hats* did not fit a Roman context but, uncertain what to substitute, left a ludicrous blank,

reading 'their ——— are pluckt about their ears'. The Romans did in fact have various headgear, as Dorsch indicates at this point.

75 **discover them** tell who they are

76 **mark of favour** indication of features

77–82 **O conspiracy . . . affability** Brutus knows that his course is treacherous, dark, and gravely hypocritical; he also voices 'the abhorrence of an Elizabethan audience for conspiracy in general' (Wilson).

79 **are most free** roam unrestrained

82 **Hide . . . affability** As do Brutus himself, and Decius and Ligarius (both trusted beneficiaries of Caesar; see Commentary, 1.3.148, 2.1.216), and others (except Cassius), professing friendship for Caesar while veiling their threats (2.2.124–5, 128–9). Tilley F3 illustrates the proverb, 'Fair face, foul heart.' In public, Brutus 'did so . . . fashion his countenance . . . that no man could discern he had any-

For if thou path, thy native semblance on,
Not Erebus itself were dim enough
To hide thee from prevention.

> *Enter the conspirators – Cassius, Casca, Decius,*
> *Cinna, Metellus Cimber, and Trebonius*

CASSIUS

I think we are too bold upon your rest.
Good morrow, Brutus. Do we trouble you?

BRUTUS

I have been up this hour, awake all night.
Know I these men that come along with you?

CASSIUS

Yes, every man of them; and no man here   90
But honours you; and every one doth wish
You had but that opinion of yourself
Which every noble Roman bears of you.
This is Trebonius.

BRUTUS   He is welcome hither.

CASSIUS

This, Decius Brutus.

BRUTUS   He is welcome too.

CASSIUS

This, Casca; this, Cinna; and this, Metellus Cimber.

BRUTUS They are all welcome.
What watchful cares do interpose themselves
Betwixt your eyes and night?

---

83 path,] F2; path F1; march, POPE; put DYCE 1866 (*conj.* Coleridge)   85.2 *Cimber*] *not in* F

thing to trouble his mind' (*Brutus*, p. 116). Lady Macbeth gives similar advice: 'To beguile the time, | Look like the time; bear welcome in your eye, | Your hand, your tongue; look like the innocent flower, | But be the serpent under't' (*Macbeth* 1.5.60–3).

83 **path** pursue thy way. F has no comma, as if *path* were transitive and *semblance* its object. This, and its unusualness, have prompted emendations; Coleridge's 'put' may be supported by l. 226. Yet would a scribe or compositor, faced with an ill-written 'put', jump to so unusual a verb as 'path'? *OED* gives *path* as a verb ('to go along or tread (a way)') though only as

transitive, but Kittredge adduces an intransitive use from *A Gorgeous Gallery of Gallant Inventions* (1578) – 'Their pleasant course strange traces hath, | On tops of trees that groundless path' (= they take their course strangely on tree tops without setting foot to ground).

83 **thy native semblance on** in your natural, true, appearance

84 **Erebus** The dark underworld through which the shades of the dead pass to Hades, as in *Merchant* 5.1.87 – 'his affections dark as Erebus'.

85 **prevention** being forestalled (as also in 3.1.19)

85.1 *Decius* See Commentary, 1.3.148.

86 **are too bold** intrude too presumptuously

CASSIUS Shall I entreat a word?   100
    Brutus and Cassius whisper aside

DECIUS

Here lies the east. Doth not the day break here?

CASCA No.

CINNA

O, pardon, sir, it doth; and yon grey lines
That fret the clouds are messengers of day.

CASCA

You shall confess that you are both deceived.
Here, as I point my sword, the sun arises,
Which is a great way growing on the south,
Weighing the youthful season of the year.
Some two months hence, up higher toward the north
He first presents his fire, and the high east   110
Stands as the Capitol, directly here.

BRUTUS (*coming forward*)

Give me your hands all over, one by one.

CASSIUS

And let us swear our resolution.

BRUTUS

No, not an oath. If not the face of men,

100.1 *Brutus and Cassius*] F (*They*)   *aside*] not in F   112 *coming forward*] not in F

101–11 **Here ... here** This brief intermission relieves the tension, creates the local atmosphere, marks the significant progress of the hours, and fixes attention on the Capitol.

104 **fret** interlace (as, in *Much Ado* 5.3.27, dawn 'Dapples the drowsy east')

105 **deceived** mistaken

107 **a great way growing on** encroaching far upon. Were Shakespeare caring about small details he might have reflected that (a) in mid-March dawn breaks actually in the east, but (b) it does not do so before 3 a.m.; see l. 193. Such atmospheric colouring enlivens the scene, and minor inconsistencies pass unremarked on the stage. For possible revision occasioning this time discrepancy see the Introduction, pp. 78–80.

108 **Weighing** taking into account

112 **all over** one and all

114 **No, not an oath** Brutus speaks with an ethical passion very different from Cassius' high-charged prejudice. In Shakespeare, he vetoes oaths on principle: in Plutarch, no plotter raises the matter at all, 'who having never taken oaths together ... nor binding themselves one to another by any religious oaths, they all kept the matter so secret . . .' (*Brutus*, p. 115). This is the first time Brutus overrules Cassius.

114–16 **If not . . . weak** The negative formulation turns suddenly to the positive but the sense is clear.

114 **the face of men** 'the *countenance*, the *regard*, the *esteem* of the publick; or, *the face of men* may mean, the dejected look of the people' (Johnson). Emendations have been proposed for *face*, e.g. 'fate', 'faith' (Plutarch glosses the episode, 'The wonderful faith and secrecy of the conspirators'), but seem unnecessary.

The sufferance of our souls, the time's abuse –
If these be motives weak, break off betimes,
And every man hence to his idle bed.
So let high-sighted tyranny range on
Till each man drop by lottery. But if these –
As I am sure they do – bear fire enough   120
To kindle cowards, and to steel with valour
The melting spirits of women, then, countrymen,
What need we any spur but our own cause
To prick us to redress? What other bond
Than secret Romans that have spoke the word
And will not palter? And what other oath
Than honesty to honesty engaged,
That this shall be, or we will fall for it?
Swear priests, and cowards, and men cautelous,
Old feeble carrions, and such suffering souls   130
That welcome wrongs; unto bad causes swear
Such creatures as men doubt; but do not stain
The even virtue of our enterprise,
Nor th'insuppressive mettle of our spirits,
To think that or our cause or our performance
Did need an oath, when every drop of blood
That every Roman bears, and nobly bears,
Is guilty of a several bastardy

118 high-sighted tyranny] F (high-sighted-Tyranny)   122 women, then] F (women. Then)
136 oath, when] F (Oath. When)

115 **sufferance** suffering, distress
    abuse misdeeds
116 **betimes** without delay
117 **idle** (a) unoccupied (b) lazy, inactive
118 **high-sighted tyranny** Either, or both,
    tyranny which (a) imposes itself from on
    high (b) strikes even the highest placed.
    The image is of the soaring bird of prey;
    see Commentary, 1.1.72–3, and, for the
    punctuation, Commentary, 1.3.10.
119 **lottery** i.e. the tyrant's caprice
126 **palter** equivocate, play fast and loose
129 **cautelous** (a) crafty (b) cautious, canny.
    Both senses are apt here.
130 **carrions** wretches (literally, corpses);
    'still in midland dialect ... used contemp-
    tuously of a living person, as being no
    better than carrion' (Onions).

133 **even virtue** flawless honour
134 **insuppressive mettle** indomitable spirit.
    (On adjectives with both active and, as
    here, passive meaning see Abbott 3.)
    insuppressive (*OED*'s first occurrence)
136 **oath, when** F's 'Oath. When' does not
    signify a division between two finite sen-
    tences. By Elizabethan practice, if colons
    or semicolons had already been used to
    structure an extended sentence, and a
    stronger pause was required, 'a full stop
    could be used even for an unfinished
    sentence. In such cases the sense was a
    sufficient guide' (Percy Simpson, *Shake-
    spearian Punctuation*, 1911, p. 79).
138 **guilty ... bastardy** individually guilty of
    proving itself not truly Roman

If he do break the smallest particle
Of any promise that hath passed from him.   140
CASSIUS

But what of Cicero? Shall we sound him?
I think he will stand very strong with us.
CASCA

Let us not leave him out.
CINNA   No, by no means.
METELLUS

O, let us have him, for his silver hairs
Will purchase us a good opinion,
And buy men's voices to commend our deeds.
It shall be said his judgement ruled our hands.
Our youths and wildness shall no whit appear,
But all be buried in his gravity.
BRUTUS

O, name him not. Let us not break with him,   150
For he will never follow anything
That other men begin.
CASSIUS Then leave him out.
CASCA Indeed he is not fit.
DECIUS

Shall no man else be touched but only Caesar?
CASSIUS

Decius, well urged. I think it is not meet
Mark Antony, so well beloved of Caesar,
Should outlive Caesar. We shall find of him

143–54 **Let us . . . not fit** Contradictory decisivenesses from the variable Casca.
145–6 **purchase . . . buy** *Silver* (l. 144) prompts these metaphors.
148 **youths and wildness** Unexpected traits suggested perhaps by Plutarch's reference to conspirators 'stout enough to attempt any desperate matter [which] specially required hot and earnest execution' (*Brutus*, p. 114).
149 **gravity** The word combines Cicero's sober nature and weighty authority.
150–2 **O . . . begin** In Plutarch they 'durst not' include Cicero as too timid and elderly (*Brutus*, p. 114). Shakespeare instead (a) gives Cassius an initiative to include him which others support but Brutus

characteristically rejects, and (b) has Brutus specify Cicero's dislike of subordination, a trait perhaps drawn from Plutarch's *Cicero*, where the Delphic oracle tells Cicero 'to make his own nature, and not the opinion of the multitude, his guide in life' (*Life of Cicero*, Loeb edition, p. 93).
150 **break with** broach it to
156–66 **Decius . . . Caesar** In Plutarch, Antony's fate is discussed only after Caesar's death, and Brutus saves him not because of his unimportance (l. 166) but because killing him 'was not honest' and because Antony 'being a noble-minded and courageous man, . . . would willingly help his country to recover her liberty'

A shrewd contriver; and, you know, his means,
If he improve them, may well stretch so far   160
As to annoy us all; which to prevent,
Let Antony and Caesar fall together.

BRUTUS

Our course will seem too bloody, Caius Cassius,
To cut the head off and then hack the limbs,
Like wrath in death and envy afterwards,
For Antony is but a limb of Caesar.
Let us be sacrificers, but not butchers, Caius.
We all stand up against the spirit of Caesar,
And in the spirit of men there is no blood.
O that we then could come by Caesar's spirit   170
And not dismember Caesar! But, alas,
Caesar must bleed for it. And, gentle friends,
Let's kill him boldly, but not wrathfully;
Let's carve him as a dish fit for the gods,
Not hew him as a carcase fit for hounds.
And let our hearts, as subtle masters do,

167 Let us] POPE; Let's F

(*Brutus*, pp. 124–5). In *Antonius* (p. 188) Brutus vetoes the proposal for his death since, acting for justice, they 'ought to be clear from all villainy'.

159 **shrewd contriver** (a) astute and able strategist (b) dangerous schemer

160 **improve** make the most of

161 **annoy** harm, hurt (a stronger sense than the modern one)

165 **wrath . . . afterwards** fury in the act of murder and malignity after it. *Envy* (originally from Latin *invidia*) strongly implies ill will, as in *Merchant* 4.1.9–10 – 'No lawful means can carry me | Out of his [Shylock's] envy's reach'.

166 **limb** dependent part (as in ll. 183–4)

167 **sacrificers, but not butchers** Brutus' high-minded aim (not mentioned in Plutarch) wholly fails: the conspirators become the 'butchers' Antony calls them (3.1.255, 5.1.40–1). In Plutarch the murder is horrible: Caesar 'was hacked and mangled among them, as a wild beast taken of hunters. . . . Brutus himself gave him one wound about his privities. . . . divers of the conspirators did hurt

themselves, striking one body with so many blows' (*Caesar*, pp. 94–5; similarly *Brutus*, p. 124).

168–71 **We all . . . Caesar** A wish ironically thwarted: Caesar's spirit dominates later events as his person does earlier ones.

168–70 **spirit of Caesar . . . Caesar's spirit** A slight word-play, from *spirit* as 'influence of Caesar' ('Caesarism') to *spirit* as 'soul'.

172 **gentle** noble, magnanimous

174 **Let's . . . gods** This extraordinary notion of punctilious and ceremonial murder, a sign of blinkered idealism, is violently refuted by events. The image of Caesar as the supreme dish at a divine banquet is grotesque.

175 **Not hew . . . hounds** Brutus proposes the proper and honourable way of formally carving up the hart which, unlike such ignobler prey as the fox or marten, should be not rudely hacked (cf. *hew*) for the pack but 'reverently disposed of' (D. H. Madden, *The Diary of Master William Silence*, 1897, p. 63); see Commentary, l. 167, and 3.1.204–10.

176–8 **And let . . . chide 'em** These lines seem to recommend gross hypocrisy and were

Stir up their servants to an act of rage
And after seem to chide 'em. This shall make
Our purpose necessary, and not envious;
Which so appearing to the common eyes,   180
We shall be called purgers, not murderers.
And for Mark Antony, think not of him,
For he can do no more than Caesar's arm
When Caesar's head is off.

CASSIUS   Yet I fear him,

For in the engrafted love he bears to Caesar –

BRUTUS

Alas, good Cassius, do not think of him.
If he love Caesar, all that he can do
Is to himself – take thought, and die for Caesar:
And that were much he should, for he is given
To sports, to wildness, and much company.   190

TREBONIUS

There is no fear in him. Let him not die,
For he will live and laugh at this hereafter.

        Clock strikes

BRUTUS

Peace! Count the clock.

CASSIUS   The clock hath stricken three.

generally cut on the stage, from Bell's acting edition (1777) to the early twentieth century. Modern directors, less concerned to idealize Brutus, often retain them; see W. P. Halstead, *Shakespeare as Spoken* (Ann Arbor, 1979), vol. 10. The conspirators, 'subtle masters' of their actions, are to kill Caesar and then profess regrets for their hands' actions. Tilley K64 gives many examples of the proverbial idea that 'A king (prince) loves the treason but hates the traitor'. Idealize though he may, Brutus recurrently shows a half-suppressed awareness of the hypocrisies the plot calls for (ll. 28–30).

179 **envious** spiteful; see Commentary, l. 165.

181 **purgers** purifiers, healers

185 **engrafted** infixed, implanted (*OED*'s first example, but antedated by Nashe's Preface to Greene's *Menaphon* (1589; McKerrow 3.311.30))

186 **do not think of him** '... the first fault he

did was when he would not consent ... that Antonius should be slain; and therefore he was justly accused that thereby he had saved and strengthened a ... grievous enemy' (*Brutus*, pp. 127–8).

188 **Is to himself ... die** concerns himself only (and cannot harm us), by his dying of grief; as in *Antony* 3.13.1 – '*Cleopatra.* What shall we do, Enobarbus? | *Enobarbus.* Think, and die.' 'Thought for "deep melancholy" is very common' (Kittredge). Pope read 'to himself take thought' (i.e. think of his own position), but this is less decisive.

189 **much he should** more than is to be expected of him

190 **sports ... company** Plutarch dwells on Antony's wasteful feasts, insobriety, and lasciviousness (*Antonius*, pp. 183–4).

191 **no fear** nothing to fear

193 **The clock ... three** The striking clock was a medieval invention. The play stresses the inexorable drive of time towards the climax.

TREBONIUS

 'Tis time to part.

CASSIUS   But it is doubtful yet

 Whether Caesar will come forth today or no;

 For he is superstitious grown of late,

 Quite from the main opinion he held once

 Of fantasy, of dreams, and ceremonies.

 It may be these apparent prodigies,

 The unaccustomed terror of this night,   200

 And the persuasion of his augurers

 May hold him from the Capitol today.

DECIUS

 Never fear that. If he be so resolved,

 I can o'ersway him; for he loves to hear

 That unicorns may be betrayed with trees,

 And bears with glasses, elephants with holes,

 Lions with toils, and men with flatterers.

 But when I tell him he hates flatterers,

 He says he does, being then most flatterèd.

 Let me work;   210

 For I can give his humour the true bent,

 And I will bring him to the Capitol.

---

195 **Whether** Slurred as a monosyllable – 'whe'er'; see 1.1.61.

196 **superstitious** This trait is not specifically mentioned in Plutarch (where it is Calpurnia's superstitious fears that hold Caesar back: *Caesar*, pp. 88–9; *Brutus*, p. 120), but it accords with his role of father-figure-to-the-Roman-masses, as in 1.2.7–9; see Commentary. His earlier rationalism is vanishing.

197 **main** basic

198 **ceremonies** prescribed rites

199 **apparent** manifest (not mere 'seeming')

205 **unicorns . . . trees** The legendary way of capturing this legendary beast was to tempt it to charge and then dodge behind a tree, into which its horn would stick. Spenser, *Faerie Queene*, II. v. 10, describes a lion which acts so: 'And when him running in full course he spies, | He slips aside; the whiles that furious beast | His precious horn . . . | Strikes in the stock' – whereupon the lion devours him.

206 **glasses** mirrors to dazzle and bewilder them

206 **elephants with holes** Pliny, *Natural History*, viii. 8, relates that elephants in Africa are trapped in pits (into which their fellow-elephants considerately throw earth and branches to help them out again).

207 **toils** snares, nets. Elyot in *The Governor*, illustrating flatterers 'which more covertly lay their snares to take the hearts of princes', cites traps set for 'the fierce and mighty lion', making him 'suddenly tumble into the net' (II. xiv). Though no Shakespearian debt is provable, the concurrence in both texts of flattery and ensnared lions is interesting.

211 **give . . . true bent** direct his inclinations the right way

212 **the Capitol** See Commentary, 1.1.63, 1.3.126. After the murder Brutus and his supporters 'went straight to the Capitol' to address the people, and 'certain of the Senators . . . went to the Capitol unto them' (*Brutus*, p. 125). Here he delivered a first oration before descending to the market-place for a second.

CASSIUS

Nay, we will all of us be there to fetch him.

BRUTUS

By the eighth hour. Is that the uttermost?

CINNA

Be that the uttermost, and fail not then.

METELLUS

Caius Ligarius doth bear Caesar hard,

Who rated him for speaking well of Pompey.

I wonder none of you have thought of him.

BRUTUS

Now, good Metellus, go along by him.

He loves me well, and I have given him reasons.   220

Send him but hither and I'll fashion him.

CASSIUS

The morning comes upon's. We'll leave you, Brutus.

And, friends, disperse yourselves – but all remember

What you have said, and show yourselves true Romans.

BRUTUS

Good gentlemen, look fresh and merrily.

Let not our looks put on our purposes,

But bear it as our Roman actors do,

With untired spirits and formal constancy.

And so good morrow to you every one.

Exeunt all but Brutus

Boy! Lucius! Fast asleep? It is no matter.   230

222 The . . . Brutus] ROWE; *as two lines, breaking after* 'vpon's' F   229.1 *all but*] F (*Manet*)

213 **all of us** In fact Cassius is absent, without explanation (see entry direction at 2.2.107.1). For the possible substitution of Publius for him see the Introduction, pp. 80–1.

216 **bear Caesar hard** In Plutarch, Ligarius (like Decius and Brutus too) had been generously treated by Caesar (forgiven for supporting Pompey). Yet he 'thanked not Caesar so much for his discharge, as he was offended with him for . . . his tyrannical power. And therefore in his heart he was alway his mortal enemy' (*Brutus*, p. 113).

217 **rated** scolded

219 **by him** to his house

221 **fashion** work upon, mould, shape

225–6 **Good gentlemen . . . purposes** A shrewd precaution, certainly, yet further evidence that Brutus realizes the duplicity involved, very evident in the treacherous friendliness the conspirators have to show at 2.2.108 ff. Tilley F16 illustrates the proverbial idea, 'To laugh (smile) in one's face and cut one's throat'; compare 2.1.81–2.

226 **put on** give any outward show of

227 **as our Roman actors do** Roman actors in fact wore masks; Shakespeare has his own time in mind.

228 **formal** (a) of merely external appearance (*OED a.* 2c) (b) precise, rigorously observant of form

constancy steadfastness

Enjoy the honey-heavy dew of slumber.
Thou hast no figures, nor no fantasies,
Which busy care draws in the brains of men;
Therefore thou sleep'st so sound.
    Enter Portia

PORTIA   Brutus, my lord.

BRUTUS

Portia! What mean you? Wherefore rise you now?
It is not for your health thus to commit
Your weak condition to the raw cold morning.

PORTIA

Nor for yours neither. You've ungently, Brutus,
Stole from my bed; and yesternight at supper
You suddenly arose, and walked about,   240
Musing, and sighing, with your arms across;
And when I asked you what the matter was,
You stared upon me with ungentle looks.
I urged you further; then you scratched your head,
And too impatiently stamped with your foot.
Yet I insisted; yet you answered not,
But with an angry wafture of your hand
Gave sign for me to leave you. So I did,
Fearing to strengthen that impatience
Which seemed too much enkindled, and withal   250
Hoping it was but an effect of humour,

---

231 honey-heavy dew] F (hony heauy-Dew)   247 wafture] F (wafter)

231 **honey-heavy dew** See Commentary,
    1.3.10, for punctuation.
232 **figures . . . fantasies** imaginings, phan-
    tasms
234–310 *Enter . . . Exit Portia* This episode
    closely follows Plutarch (*Brutus*, pp.
    117–19), one of many examples of
    Shakespeare's reworking of a prose origi-
    nal into living poetry while retaining its
    exact details; see Appendix A. In its lucid,
    ordered style the episode captures the
    most sympathetic tone of 'classical'
    decorum. It parallels, and contrasts with,
    the scene between Hotspur and Lady
    Percy in *1 Henry IV* (2.3.33 ff.), its deeply
    troubled devotion differing widely from
    the earlier comic boisterousness.
237 **weak condition** Brutus does not yet
    know of Portia's wound, but in Plutarch

she is brave in principle yet physically
and emotionally vulnerable – 'too weak
to away with so great . . . grief of mind',
with a 'weak constitution of her body'
(*Brutus*, pp. 121, 133).
238, 243 **ungently . . . ungentle** unkind(ly),
    discourteous(ly)
241 **your arms across** The traditional pos-
    ture of one sunk in thought.
246 **Yet . . . yet** still . . . still
247 **wafture** gesture, wave of the hand. *OED*
    records F's form 'wafter' as a verb *c*.1450,
    'to wave', and suggests that Shake-
    speare's use here may reflect a Warwick-
    shire survival. Rowe changed it to 'waf-
    ture', of which *OED* has no earlier but
    several later examples.
251 **effect of humour** outcome of a mood

Which sometime hath his hour with every man.
It will not let you eat, nor talk, nor sleep,
And could it work so much upon your shape
As it hath much prevailed on your condition,
I should not know you Brutus. Dear my lord,
Make me acquainted with your cause of grief.
BRUTUS
I am not well in health, and that is all.
PORTIA
Brutus is wise, and were he not in health
He would embrace the means to come by it.   260
BRUTUS
Why, so I do. Good Portia, go to bed.
PORTIA
Is Brutus sick, and is it physical
To walk unbracèd and suck up the humours
Of the dank morning? What, is Brutus sick,
And will he steal out of his wholesome bed
To dare the vile contagion of the night,
And tempt the rheumy and unpurgèd air
To add unto his sickness? No, my Brutus.
You have some sick offence within your mind,
Which by the right and virtue of my place   270
I ought to know of; and upon my knees
        She kneels
I charm you, by my once commended beauty,

268 his] F2; hit F1   271.1 *She kneels*] *not in* F

252 **his** its; see Commentary, 1.2.124.
255 **condition** cast of mind. *OED, sb.* II. 11,
     marks as obsolete this and similar uses for
     personal qualities.
256 **know you Brutus** recognize you as
     Brutus. A comma after 'you', as
     introduced in F4, weakens the effect.
259 **Brutus is wise** That the third-person,
     proper-name address in the play is not
     solely for grandiose status is evident here.
     Portia's use of it presents in the tenderest
     way Brutus' role-playing – living up to
     what being 'Brutus' signifies, as in ll.
     256, 294.
262 **physical** healthful

263 **unbracèd** with unloosed dress
     humours dampness
267 **rheumy and unpurgèd** damp and im-
     pure (*OED*'s earliest example of *rheumy*).
     Dekker's *The Gull's Horn-book* (1609), has
     'It is not good to trust the air with our
     bodies till the sun . . . hath fanned away
     the misty smoke of the morning, and
     refined that thick tobacco-breath which
     the rheumatic night throws abroad' (in
     Thomas Dekker, ed. E. D. Pendry, 1967, p.
     81).
269 **sick offence** painful disturbance
272 **charm** conjure

By all your vows of love, and that great vow
Which did incorporate and make us one,
That you unfold to me, your self, your half,
Why you are heavy, and what men tonight
Have had resort to you; for here have been
Some six or seven, who did hide their faces
Even from darkness.

BRUTUS   Kneel not, gentle Portia.

He raises her

PORTIA

I should not need, if you were gentle Brutus.   280
Within the bond of marriage, tell me, Brutus,
Is it excepted I should know no secrets
That appertain to you? Am I your self
But as it were in sort or limitation,
To keep with you at meals, comfort your bed,
And talk to you sometimes? Dwell I but in the suburbs
Of your good pleasure? If it be no more,
Portia is Brutus' harlot, not his wife.

BRUTUS

You are my true and honourable wife,

279.1 *He raises her*] *not in* F   281 the] F2;   tho F1

273–4 **that great vow … one** Wilson comments that *that great vow* and *incorporate* suggest the Christian marriage service (as in Matthew 19: 5, 'they twain shall be one flesh').

275 **your self, your half** That one's marriage partner is one's (other) self or (better) half is, of course, proverbial (Tilley F696, H49).

276 **heavy** sad, heavy-hearted

281–4 **bond … excepted … limitation** Legal terms of land tenure, for a binding agreement with exceptions and time limits (Wilson).

284 **in sort** after a fashion

285 **keep** stay, lodge (a frequent Elizabethan sense)
comfort gladden (*OED*, *v.* 5, marks it obsolete in this sense, its latest examples being this and one in Drayton's *Polyolbion*, 1612.)

286–8 **suburbs … harlot** The idea of living in the outskirts, not the city centre, leads to that of the brothels which Tudor ordinances restricted to Southwark, outside London city. ' "I being, O Brutus," said she, "the daughter of Cato, was married unto thee, not to be thy bedfellow and companion in bed and at board only, like a harlot, but to be partaker also with thee of thy good and evil fortune' (*Brutus*, p. 118; see Appendix A).

289 **You are … wife** 'This absolute communion of souls is in designed contrast to the shallow relation of Caesar and Calpurnia. The dictator treats his wife as a child to be humoured … Portia assumes that … she is entitled to share her husband's inmost thoughts' (F. S. Boas, *Shakespeare and his Predecessors*, 1896; repr. 1940, p. 467).

As dear to me as are the ruddy drops 290
That visit my sad heart.
PORTIA
If this were true, then should I know this secret.
I grant I am a woman; but withal
A woman that Lord Brutus took to wife.
I grant I am a woman; but withal
A woman well-reputed, Cato's daughter.
Think you I am no stronger than my sex,
Being so fathered and so husbanded?
Tell me your counsels, I will not disclose 'em.
I have made strong proof of my constancy, 300
Giving myself a voluntary wound
Here, in the thigh. Can I bear that with patience,
And not my husband's secrets?
BRUTUS   O ye gods,
Render me worthy of this noble wife!
     Knocking heard
Hark, hark! One knocks. Portia, go in awhile,
And by and by thy bosom shall partake
The secrets of my heart.
All my engagements I will construe to thee,
All the charactery of my sad brows.

304.1 *Knocking heard*] F (*Knocke*)

290–1 **ruddy drops . . . heart** These words have been taken to prove that Shakespeare knew how the blood circulated before William Harvey announced his famous discovery in *De Motu Cordis* (1628). A long note in Furness, however, concludes that, while associating the heart with blood made by the liver and furnished to the lungs, he was ignorant of its general circulation.
296 **Cato's daughter** Marcus Porcius Cato (95–46 BC), noted for inflexible integrity, was an ally of Pompey and antagonist of Caesar. Facing defeat after Pompey's cause was lost he took his life; see 5.1.102.
298 **fathered** (*OED*'s first occurrence as participial adjective)
     husbanded (*OED*'s first occurrence as participial adjective in the sense of 'having a husband')
301–4 **Giving myself . . . wife** Having given herself 'a great gash withal in her thigh, that she was straight all of a gore-blood', Portia showed it to Brutus, and, 'lifting up his hands to heaven, he besought the gods . . . that he might be found a husband worthy of so noble a wife' (*Brutus*, pp. 118–19; see Appendix A).
308 **All my engagements** all I am pledged to do
     engagements *OED*'s first occurrence (1624) is antedated by this example.
     construe explain (accented on the first syllable)
309 **All the charactery of** everything expressed (as if by shorthand) in. Quoting this line *OED* defines *charactery* as 'Expression of thought by symbols or characters'. The accent is on the second syllable.

Leave me with haste.   *Exit Portia*
    Enter Lucius and Caius Ligarius
                Lucius, who's that knocks?   310
LUCIUS
Here is a sick man that would speak with you.
BRUTUS
Caius Ligarius, that Metellus spake of.
Boy, stand aside. Caius Ligarius, how?
LIGARIUS
Vouchsafe good morrow from a feeble tongue.
BRUTUS
O, what a time have you chose out, brave Caius,
To wear a kerchief! Would you were not sick!
LIGARIUS
I am not sick if Brutus have in hand
Any exploit worthy the name of honour.
BRUTUS
Such an exploit have I in hand, Ligarius,
Had you a healthful ear to hear of it.   320
LIGARIUS
By all the gods that Romans bow before,
I here discard my sickness.
       ⌈*He throws off his kerchief*⌉
                Soul of Rome,
Brave son, derived from honourable loins,

310 *Caius*] not in F   314 LIGARIUS] F (*Cai.*), *so throughout the scene*   322 *He . . . kerchief*] *not in* F

310 **Lucius, who's that** Some editors, thinking this line defective, have read, for
example, 'Lucius, who's that that'
(Capell), 'Lucius, who is that' (Steevens
1773), or 'Lucius, who is't that' (Rann).
But 'Lucius', even if usually counting as
two syllables, must be 'Luc-i-us' (not
'Looshus'), and can well be trisyllabic
here. ('Cassius', too, has sometimes two
syllables, sometimes three.)

312 **Caius Ligarius** Historically Quintus, but
Caius in Plutarch. Shakespeare shifts his
meeting with Brutus from its place in
Plutarch, before the dialogue with Portia,
so as to change from the poignant
intimacy just seen back to practical plot
urgencies. In Plutarch, it is Brutus who
visits the ailing Ligarius but Shakespeare
reverses this so as to end on a note of high

anticipation the scene begun with
Brutus' resolve on action: even the in-
valid is spurred into health. 'The incident
of Ligarius . . . skilfully concludes a long
and solemn scene on a note of vigour and
hope' (Wilson).

313 **how** how are you

314 **Vouchsafe** deign to receive (not the normal 'deign to grant')

315 **brave** noble (as often; e.g. l. 323); 'an
indeterminate word used to express the
superabundance of any valuable quality'
(Johnson's *Dictionary*).

316 **kerchief** shawl (often referred to as
bound round invalids' heads)

323 **derived . . . loins** Again Brutus'
ancestry: he embodies a whole tradition
of republican autonomy.

146

Thou like an exorcist hast conjured up
My mortifièd spirit. Now bid me run,
And I will strive with things impossible,
Yea, get the better of them. What's to do?

BRUTUS

A piece of work that will make sick men whole.

LIGARIUS

But are not some whole that we must make sick?

BRUTUS

That must we also. What it is, my Caius,   330
I shall unfold to thee, as we are going,
To whom it must be done.

LIGARIUS   Set on your foot,
And with a heart new-fired I follow you,
To do I know not what; but it sufficeth
That Brutus leads me on.
      Thunder

BRUTUS   Follow me, then.   *Exeunt*

2.2   *Thunder and lightning. Enter Julius Caesar*
     in his nightgown

CAESAR

Nor heaven nor earth have been at peace tonight.
Thrice hath Calpurnia in her sleep cried out
'Help, ho! They murder Caesar!' – Who's within?
    Enter a Servant

SERVANT My lord?

328 A . . . whole] ROWE; *as two lines, breaking after* 'worke' F   331–2 going, | To] F; going
| To CAPELL
   2.2.1 Nor heaven . . . tonight] ROWE; *as two lines, breaking after* 'Earth' F

324–5 **Thou . . . spirit** Either (a) as an exorcist revives those succumbing (to demonic
   possession), so you have restored my
   dying spirit (by banishing hurtful influences), or (b) as an exorcist calls to life
   phantoms of the dead, so you have done
   my dying spirit.
325 **mortifièd** deadened, made insensible
328 **make . . . whole** restore to health those
   ailing (under tyranny)
330–2 **What it is . . . done** Flexible syntax
   which the insertion of 'And' before 'To
   whom' would stiffen. 'Mixed construc-
   tions are especially common in the
   spoken language' (Brook, p. 70).

332 **Set . . . foot** press forward
335 *Thunder* Except as preliminary
   atmospherics for what is to follow (a
   sophistication rather unlikely on Shakespeare's stage) thunder is out of place
   here, and Brutus and Ligarius show no
   signs of noticing it. It may be a prompter's
   cue for its use as the next scene opens.
2.2.0.2 *nightgown* dressing gown
2–3 **Thrice . . . Caesar** 'he heard his wife
   Calpurnia, being fast asleep, weep and
   sigh and put forth many fumbling
   lamentable speeches. For she dreamed
   that Caesar was slain' (*Caesar*, p. 88).

CAESAR

Go bid the priests do present sacrifice,
And bring me their opinions of success.

SERVANT I will, my lord.   *Exit*

    Enter Calpurnia

CALPURNIA

What mean you, Caesar? Think you to walk forth?
You shall not stir out of your house today.

CAESAR

Caesar shall forth. The things that threatened me   10
Ne'er looked but on my back. When they shall see
The face of Caesar, they are vanishèd.

CALPURNIA

Caesar, I never stood on ceremonies,
Yet now they fright me. There is one within,
Besides the things that we have heard and seen,
Recounts most horrid sights seen by the watch.
A lioness hath whelpèd in the streets,
And graves have yawned and yielded up their dead.
Fierce fiery warriors fight upon the clouds
In ranks and squadrons and right form of war,   20

---

19 fight] F; fought WHITE

---

5 **do present sacrifice** seek at once for auguries (good or ill) in the entrails of the sacrificed animals

6 **success** the result (whether good or bad)

9 **You shall ... today** 'she prayed him if it were possible not to go out of the doors that day' (*Caesar*, p. 89).

10 **Caesar shall forth** Abbott 41 illustrates the omission of verbs of motion with 'forth', 'hence', 'hither'. The phrase (see Commentary, l. 28) brings to a head Caesar's suprapersonal pomp.

13 **stood on ceremonies** set store by external shows. 'Calpurnia until that time was never given to any fear or superstition' (*Caesar*, p. 89).

16–24 **horrid sights ... streets** These portents, not all from Plutarch, are Shakespeare's inventions or gatherings from various sources including, probably, his favourite Ovid; see Introduction, p. 28. Elizabethan writers often took these over, as Marlowe did in *2 Tamburlaine* 4.1.141–3 ('meteors | . . . | [Which] pour

down blood and fire on thy head') and 202–3 ('meteors that, like armèd men, | Are seen to march upon the towers of heaven'). Similar omens, 'precurse of feared events', are described in *Hamlet* 1.1.113–21, 'A little ere the mightiest Julius fell' – ghosts, meteors, 'dews of blood', 'disasters in the sun', and a lunar eclipse.

18 **yawned** gaped (used often of astonishment; not necessarily suggesting drowsiness). An almost identical line occurs in *Much Ado*, 'Graves, yawn and yield your dead' (5.3.19).

19 **fight** Some editors change to 'fought', but 'have yawned' and 'have yielded' include present effects and justify the present tense, despite 'drizzled' in l. 21. The hurry of Shakespeare's mind often results in discrepant tenses. F's 'do neigh' at l. 23, however, seems wrong; by then the past tense is established.

20 **right form of war** regular battle order

Which drizzled blood upon the Capitol.
The noise of battle hurtled in the air,
Horses did neigh, and dying men did groan,
And ghosts did shriek and squeal about the streets.
O Caesar, these things are beyond all use,
And I do fear them.

CAESAR   What can be avoided
Whose end is purposed by the mighty gods?
Yet Caesar shall go forth; for these predictions
Are to the world in general as to Caesar.

CALPURNIA

When beggars die there are no comets seen;   30
The heavens themselves blaze forth the death of princes.

CAESAR

Cowards die many times before their deaths;
The valiant never taste of death but once.
Of all the wonders that I yet have heard,
It seems to me most strange that men should fear,

---

23 did neigh] F2; do neigh F1

---

22 **hurtled** gave sound of collision

24 **shriek and squeal** Homer (*Odyssey*, xxiv.
. 6–7), Horace (*Satires*, I. viii. 41), and Virgil (*Aeneid*, vi. 491) describe the thin batlike squealings of ghosts. In *Hamlet* 1.1.115–16, before Caesar's murder 'the sheeted dead | Did squeak and gibber in the Roman streets'.

25 **all use** anything usual

26–7 **What . . . mighty gods** proverbial: Tilley F83

28 **Caesar shall go forth** The imperious words are anticipated (or perhaps echoed) in Marlowe's *Massacre at Paris* (acted 1593); since this was printed at an unknown date in memorially reported form the borrowing may be either way, or both plays may be repeating an accepted stage tag. The haughty Guise, facing death, cries, 'Yet Caesar shall go forth. | Let mean conceits and baser men fear death: | . . . I am the Duke of Guise; | And princes with their looks engender fear', and, when dying, 'Thus Caesar did go forth, and thus he died' (Revels edn., ed. H. J. Oliver, 1968, Scene 21, ll. 67–70, 87).

30–1 **When beggars die . . . death of princes** In popular belief celestial bodies symbolized princely rank and their falling marked the death of great ones. In Plutarch, 'the great comet, which seven nights together was seen very bright after Caesar's death, the eighth night after was never seen more' (*Caesar*, p. 99). On Henry V's death, 'Comets, importing change of times and states, | Brandish [their] crystal tresses in the sky' (*1 Henry VI* 1.1.2–3); and Cardinal Wolsey will fall 'Like a bright exhalation [comet] in the evening' (*Henry VIII* 3.2.226).

31 **blaze** (a) flame (b) proclaim

32 **Cowards . . . deaths** 'when some of his friends did counsel him to have a guard . . . he would never consent to it, but said, it was better to die once than always to be afraid of death' (*Caesar*, p. 78). Similarly Caesar in Kyd's *Cornelia* – 'That death that comes unsent for or unseen | And suddenly doth take us at unware | Methinks is sweetest' (4.2.162–4). The idea was proverbial (Tilley C774, D27).

33 **taste of death** The phrase is biblical (Matthew 16: 28, etc.).

Seeing that death, a necessary end,
Will come when it will come.
> *Enter Servant*

                                        What say the augurers?

SERVANT

They would not have you to stir forth today.
Plucking the entrails of an offering forth
They could not find a heart within the beast.   40

CAESAR

The gods do this in shame of cowardice.
Caesar should be a beast without a heart
If he should stay at home today for fear.
No, Caesar shall not. Danger knows full well
That Caesar is more dangerous than he.
We are two lions littered in one day,
And I the elder and more terrible,
And Caesar shall go forth.

CALPURNIA   Alas, my lord,
Your wisdom is consumed in confidence.
Do not go forth today. Call it my fear   50
That keeps you in the house, and not your own.
We'll send Mark Antony to the Senate House,
And he shall say you are not well today.
Let me upon my knee prevail in this.
> *She kneels*

---

37 *Servant*] F (*a Seruant*)   46 are] CAPELL (*conj.* Upton); heare F; heard ROWE; were THEO-
BALD   54.1 *She kneels*] *not in* F

36–7 **Seeing . . . it will come** A proverbial
sentiment; Tilley N311. Similarly *Hamlet*
5.2.212–13 – 'if it be not to come, it will
be now; if it be not now, yet it will come
– the readiness is all.'

39–40 **Plucking . . . beast** 'Caesar self also,
doing sacrifice unto the gods, found that
one of the beasts . . . had no heart; and
that was a strange thing in nature – how
a beast could live without a heart. . . . the
soothsayers, having sacrificed many
beasts . . . told him that none did like
them' (*Caesar*, pp. 87, 89).

42 **should** would indeed. Abbott 322 and
Brook, p. 114, illustrate *should* for
modern 'would'.

46 **We are** F reads 'We heare'. In special

cases 'hear' could mean 'be styled' or 'be
reputed' but that does not help in this
instance. Perhaps 'he' of l. 45 was
erroneously repeated, corrected to 'We'
but not deleted, and in printing joined
with 'are' (H. F. Brooks's suggestion in
Dorsch). Theobald read 'We were', which
Sisson (*New Readings*, ii. 186) defends
since secretary 'w' could be misread as
italic 'h' in the mixed hand common in
1620. Yet for Caesar Danger and himself
are present rivals, and a flashback to the
past seems unlikely.

47–8 **And I . . . forth** A high point of arrogance; see l. 28, Commentary.

49 **confidence** i.e. over-confidence

CAESAR

Mark Antony shall say I am not well,

And for thy humour I will stay at home.

He raises her.

Enter Decius

Here's Decius Brutus, he shall tell them so.

DECIUS

Caesar, all hail! Good morrow, worthy Caesar.

I come to fetch you to the Senate House.

CAESAR

And you are come in very happy time   60

To bear my greeting to the senators

And tell them that I will not come today.

Cannot, is false; and that I dare not, falser.

I will not come today – tell them so, Decius.

CALPURNIA

Say he is sick.

CAESAR   Shall Caesar send a lie?

Have I in conquest stretched mine arm so far

To be afeard to tell greybeards the truth?

Decius, go tell them Caesar will not come.

DECIUS

Most mighty Caesar, let me know some cause,

Lest I be laughed at when I tell them so.   70

CAESAR

The cause is in my will: I will not come.

That is enough to satisfy the Senate.

But for your private satisfaction,

Because I love you, I will let you know.

Calpurnia here, my wife, stays me at home.

56.1 *He raises her*] *not in* F

55–6 **Mark Antony . . . home** 'for that he saw her [Calpurnia] so troubled in mind with this dream she had . . . he determined to send Antonius to adjourn the session of the Senate' (*Caesar*, p. 89).
56 **for thy humour** because of your whim
60 **happy** opportune
65 **sick . . . lie** A drastic change from l. 55,

from one who professes such constancy.
74 **Because I love you** The recurrent theme of warm affection is, amid all Caesar's hauteur, particularly touching as addressed to one about to betray him. For Caesar's goodness to Decius see Commentary, 1.3.148.

She dreamt tonight she saw my statue,
Which, like a fountain with an hundred spouts,
Did run pure blood; and many lusty Romans
Came smiling, and did bathe their hands in it.
And these does she apply for warnings and portents   80
And evils imminent, and on her knee
Hath begged that I will stay at home today.

DECIUS

This dream is all amiss interpreted.
It was a vision fair and fortunate:
Your statue spouting blood in many pipes,
In which so many smiling Romans bathed,
Signifies that from you great Rome shall suck
Reviving blood, and that great men shall press
For tinctures, stains, relics, and cognizance.
This by Calpurnia's dream is signified.   90

CAESAR

And this way have you well expounded it.

DECIUS

I have, when you have heard what I can say;
And know it now – the Senate have concluded
To give this day a crown to mighty Caesar.
If you shall send them word you will not come,
Their minds may change. Besides, it were a mock
Apt to be rendered, for someone to say
'Break up the Senate till another time,
When Caesar's wife shall meet with better dreams.'
If Caesar hide himself, shall they not whisper   100
'Lo, Caesar is afraid'?

76–9 **She dreamt . . . in it** This combines
(a) Plutarch's details that Calpurnia
'dreamed that Caesar was slain', and that
at the murder Pompey's statue 'ran all
of a gore-blood' (*Caesar*, pp. 88, 95), and
(b) Shakespeare's own anticipations as to
how the assassins will celebrate the murder (3.1.105–10).

76 **tonight** this past night
statue A trisyllable here and at 3.2.185
(though a disyllable at l. 85), in some
editions indicated by the spelling 'statua'.

80 **apply for** take for, interpret as
portents Accented in Shakespeare on

-*tents*. The line is a regular hexameter.

89 **tinctures . . . relics** sacred tokens coloured
and stained with the blood of martyrs
cognizance emblems worn by a lord's
retainers. 'The Romans, says Decius, all
come to you, as to a saint, for reliques; as
to a prince, for honours' (Johnson).

91 **this way . . . it** 'Caesar, taken with the
notion of his blood being sacred, doesn't
notice that it implies his death no less
than Calpurnia's interpretation' (Wilson).

96–7 **were . . . rendered** would be a likely jibe

Pardon me, Caesar, for my dear dear love
To your proceeding bids me tell you this,
And reason to my love is liable.

CAESAR

How foolish do your fears seem now, Calpurnia!
I am ashamèd I did yield to them.
Give me my robe, for I will go.

> *Enter Brutus, Caius Ligarius, Metellus Cimber,*
> *Casca, Trebonius, Cinna, and Publius*

And look where Publius is come to fetch me.

PUBLIUS

Good morrow, Caesar.

CAESAR   Welcome, Publius.
What, Brutus, are you stirred so early too?   110
Good morrow, Casca. Caius Ligarius,
Caesar was ne'er so much your enemy
As that same ague which hath made you lean.
What is't o'clock?

BRUTUS   Caesar, 'tis strucken eight.

CAESAR

I thank you for your pains and courtesy.

> *Enter Antony*

See, Antony, that revels long a-nights,
Is notwithstanding up. Good morrow, Antony.

ANTONY

So to most noble Caesar.

CAESAR ⌈*to Calpurnia*⌉   Bid them prepare within.
I am to blame to be thus waited for.   ⌈*Exit Calpurnia*⌉

107.1 *Caius*] *not in* F   *Cimber*] *not in* F   118 *to Calpurnia*] WILSON; *not in* F; *to an Att⟨endant⟩.*
CAPELL   119 to blame] F3; too blame F1   *Exit Calpurnia*] WILSON (*subs.*); *not in* F

---

102 **dear dear love** A blatantly hypocritical
profession.

103 **proceeding** advancement

104 **reason . . . liable** my sense of propriety
is overruled by my love

107.1 *Enter . . . Publius* On the possibility
that Cassius was originally included here
see the Introduction, pp. 81–2.

112 **ne'er so much your enemy** For their
relationship see Commentary, 2.1.216.
In private, Caesar is urbanely friendly to
his fellows, and the conspirators show up
badly by comparison.

116 **revels long** Plutarch mentions Antony's
'banquets and drunken feasts' (*Antonius*,
p. 183). Shakespeare is milder.

118 *to Calpurnia* This may alternatively be
addressed to someone else on stage, or
may be called off stage.
   prepare i.e. to set out for the Capitol

119 **to blame** F's 'too blame' may be right;
blame could mean blameworthy (*OED* 6).
But the metre needs a light stress, and
Caesar has no cause to emphasize his
fault, if any.

Now, Cinna. Now, Metellus. What, Trebonius!   120
I have an hour's talk in store for you;
Remember that you call on me today.
Be near me, that I may remember you.

TREBONIUS

Caesar, I will. (*Aside*) And so near will I be
That your best friends shall wish I had been further.

CAESAR

Good friends, go in, and taste some wine with me,
And we, like friends, will straightway go together.

BRUTUS (*aside*)

That every like is not the same, O Caesar,
The heart of Brutus yearns to think upon.   *Exeunt*

2.3   *Enter Artemidorus, reading a paper*

ARTEMIDORUS 'Caesar, beware of Brutus. Take heed of
Cassius. Come not near Casca. Have an eye to Cinna. Trust
not Trebonius. Mark well Metellus Cimber. Decius Brutus
loves thee not. Thou hast wronged Caius Ligarius. There is
but one mind in all these men, and it is bent against Caesar.   5
If thou beest not immortal, look about you. Security gives
way to conspiracy. The mighty gods defend thee!
                              Thy lover,
                                  Artemidorus.'

2.3.0.1 *reading a paper*] *not in* F   1 ARTEMIDORUS] *not in* F   1–9 'Caesar . . . Artemidorus.']
(*italic, with no quotation marks, in* F)

121 **hour's** (two syllables)

124–5 **so near . . . further** Trebonius in fact
  leads Antony away before the murder
  (3.1.25–6).

129 **yearns** grieves (F's 'earnes' is an obsolete variant: *OED v.* 3). Shakespeare
  never uses 'yearn' to mean 'earnestly
  desire'.

2.3.0.1 *Artemidorus* 'one Artemidorus also,
  . . . a doctor of rhetoric in the Greek tongue, who by means of his profession was
  very familiar with certain of Brutus' confederates and therefore knew the most
  part of all their practices against Caesar,
  came and brought him a little bill . . . of
  all that he meant to tell him' (*Caesar*, p.

91). This 'bill' is not said to have named
  names, a detail Shakespeare could add
  himself, though he may have drawn it
  from 'Caius Julius Caesar' (*Parts Added to
  'The Mirror for Magistrates*' [in 1587], ed.
  L. B. Campbell, 1946, p. 301), where
  Caesar meets a well-wisher 'presenting
  me a scroll of every name', or from
  Caesar's Revenge (see the Introduction, p.
  26), where names are mentioned.

6–7 **Security gives way** overconfidence,
  heedlessness (Latin *securitas*) opens the
  way; also in *Macbeth* 3.5.32–3, 'Security
  | Is mortals' chiefest enemy'.

8 **lover** devoted friend

Here will I stand till Caesar pass along,   10
And as a suitor will I give him this.
My heart laments that virtue cannot live
Out of the teeth of emulation.
If thou read this, O Caesar, thou mayst live;
If not, the Fates with traitors do contrive.   *Exit*

2.4   *Enter Portia and Lucius*

PORTIA

I prithee, boy, run to the Senate House.
Stay not to answer me, but get thee gone.
Why dost thou stay?

LUCIUS   To know my errand, madam.

PORTIA

I would have had thee there and here again
Ere I can tell thee what thou shouldst do there.
(*Aside*) O constancy, be strong upon my side;
Set a huge mountain 'tween my heart and tongue!
I have a man's mind, but a woman's might.
How hard it is for women to keep counsel!
(*To Lucius*) Art thou here yet?

LUCIUS   Madam, what should I do?   10
Run to the Capitol, and nothing else?
And so return to you, and nothing else?

PORTIA

Yes, bring me word, boy, if thy lord look well,
For he went sickly forth; and take good note
What Caesar doth, what suitors press to him.
Hark, boy! What noise is that?

LUCIUS

I hear none, madam.

---

14 mayst] ROWE (may'st);   mayest F

13 **Out . . . emulation** beyond the bite of
envious rivalry
15 **contrive** conspire. Elizabethan pronunciation made this 'almost certainly' a
rhyme for 'live' (Cercignani, pp. 256–7).
2.4.4–9 **I would . . . counsel** 'Portia being
very . . . pensive for that which was to
come . . . could hardly keep within, . . .
asking every man that came from the
market-place what Brutus did, and still

sent messenger after messenger, to know
what news. At length, . . . she suddenly
swooned [and] her speech and senses
failed her' (*Brutus*, p. 121).
6 **constancy** self-control, resolution
9 **keep counsel** Brutus has evidently told
his secret, though between his leaving
with Caesar in 2.2 and the opening of 3.1
there is no chance to do so – an instance
of double time.

PORTIA   Prithee listen well.
 I heard a bustling rumour like a fray,
 And the wind brings it from the Capitol.
LUCIUS Sooth, madam, I hear nothing.   20
   Enter the Soothsayer
PORTIA
 Come hither, fellow. Which way hast thou been?
SOOTHSAYER At mine own house, good lady.
PORTIA
 What is't o'clock?
SOOTHSAYER   About the ninth hour, lady.
PORTIA
 Is Caesar yet gone to the Capitol?
SOOTHSAYER
 Madam, not yet – I go to take my stand,
 To see him pass on to the Capitol.
PORTIA
 Thou hast some suit to Caesar, hast thou not?
SOOTHSAYER
 That I have, lady, if it will please Caesar
 To be so good to Caesar as to hear me:
 I shall beseech him to befriend himself.   30
PORTIA
 Why, know'st thou any harm's intended towards him?
SOOTHSAYER
 None that I know will be, much that I fear may chance.
 Good morrow to you. Here the street is narrow.
 The throng that follows Caesar at the heels,
 Of senators, of praetors, common suitors,
 Will crowd a feeble man almost to death.
 I'll get me to a place more void, and there
 Speak to great Caesar as he comes along.   *Exit*

2.4.32 None . . . chance] POPE (*omitting* 'may chance'), CAPELL; *as two lines, breaking after* 'be' F

18 **bustling rumour** confused outcry
20 **Sooth** truly
23 **the ninth hour** Again the theme of critical time.

35 **praetors** judges. Both Brutus (chief justice, *praetor urbanus*) and Cassius held this
 rank.

PORTIA

I must go in. Ay me, how weak a thing
The heart of woman is! O Brutus, 40
The heavens speed thee in thine enterprise! –
Sure the boy heard me. – Brutus hath a suit
That Caesar will not grant. – O, I grow faint. –
Run, Lucius, and commend me to my lord;
Say I am merry. Come to me again,
And bring me word what he doth say to thee.

Exeunt severally

3.1 *Flourish. Enter Caesar, Brutus, Cassius, Casca, Decius,
Metellus Cimber, Trebonius, Cinna, Antony, Lepidus,
⌈Popilius Lena,⌉ Publius⌈, and other senators⌉;
⌈meeting them,⌉ the Soothsayer and Artemidorus⌈;
citizens following⌉*

CAESAR *(to the Soothsayer)* The Ides of March are come.
SOOTHSAYER Ay, Caesar, but not gone.
ARTEMIDORUS Hail, Caesar! Read this schedule.

---

39 I . . . thing] ROWE; *as two lines, breaking after* 'in' F   46.1 *severally*] *not in* F
3.1] F (*Actus Tertius.*)   0.2 *Cimber*] *not in* F   0.3 *Popilius Lena*] F2; *not in* F1   0.3–5 *Publius
. . . following*] *Artimedorus, Publius, and the Soothsayer.* F

46.1 *severally* separately
3.1.0.1–5 **Lepidus** The presence of the un-
heralded Lepidus is odd, as is the absence
of the Ligarius who at 2.1.332–5 was so
keen to take part and at 3.3.38 is a subject of the mob's vengeance. Perhaps an
abbreviated '*Li.*' or '*Lig.*' was misread as
'*Le.*' or '*Lep.*' (Ringler, p. 116). Ringler's
chart of role-doubling (p. 122) shows
that one actor could play both parts, and
confusion might arise as to whom he
represented here.
0.3 **Popilius Lena . . . other senators** Their
entry could be delayed till l. 12, when it
would help to suggest the change of location.
0.4 **meeting them** Alternatively, the Soothsayer and Artemidorus could precede the
procession, and Caesar could approach
the Soothsayer.
0.5 **citizens following** Attending citizens
seem likely but are not certainly required.

1–2 **The Ides . . . gone** 'That day being come,
Caesar going into the Senate-house and
speaking merrily unto the soothsayer,
told him: "The Ides of March be come."
"So be they," softly answered the soothsayer, "but yet they are not past" '
(*Caesar*, p. 88). In the play Caesar may
perhaps speak 'merrily' but one would
think his manner more imperious. The
soothsayer in 'Caius Julius Caesar', *Parts
Added to 'The Mirror for Magistrates'* (ed. L.
B. Campbell, p. 304, l. 374), has the same
antithesis as Shakespeare and may have
influenced him ('The Ides of March be
come, yet th'are not gone'), though the
come–gone contrast is too obvious to need
specific prompting. For other possible
Mirror for Magistrates echoes see the
Commentary on 2.3.0.1, and 3.1.6–10
and 149.
3 **schedule** note or scroll (*OED* 1)

DECIUS

Trebonius doth desire you to o'er-read,

At your best leisure, this his humble suit.

ARTEMIDORUS

O Caesar, read mine first, for mine's a suit

That touches Caesar nearer. Read it, great Caesar!

CAESAR

What touches us ourself shall be last served.

ARTEMIDORUS

Delay not, Caesar, read it instantly!

CAESAR

What, is the fellow mad?

PUBLIUS   Sirrah, give place.   10

CASSIUS

What, urge you your petitions in the street?

Come to the Capitol.

     ⌐*Caesar and his followers move on. He sits to preside*⌐

POPILIUS (*to Cassius*)

I wish your enterprise today may thrive.

CASSIUS

What enterprise, Popilius?

12.1 *Caesar . . . preside*] *not in* F

4–5 **Trebonius . . . suit** Nothing is said in Plutarch of this suit, or heard further of it in the play. Decius is trying a diversionary tactic.

6–10 **O Caesar . . . place** 'Artemidorus, . . . marking how Caesar received all the supplications . . . and that he gave them straight to his men . . ., pressed nearer to him and said: "Caesar, read this memorial to yourself, and that quickly, for they be matters of great weight, and touch you nearly." Caesar took it of him, but could never read it, though he many times attempted it, for the number of people that did salute him' (*Caesar*, p. 91). For Plutarch's 'little bill' or 'memorial' *The Mirror for Magistrates* ('Caius Julius Caesar') has 'suit' (l. 364), which Shakespeare perhaps caught up in ll. 5, 6.

8 **What . . . served** A brilliant combination of magnanimity and royal-plural vainglory.

   served In Shakespeare's time, as now, used in the sense 'legally delivered (of a writ, etc.)'.

10 **Sirrah** Fellow – a variant of 'Sir' used to inferiors, contemptuously (as here and at 4.2.184) or familiarly (as at 5.3.25, 36).

12 **the Capitol** In Plutarch the Senate meeting and the assassination take place in Pompey's Theatre, but from the Middle Ages popular tradition assigned them to the Capitol; see Commentary, 1.1.63 and 1.3.126.

12.1 *Caesar . . . preside* At this point the location becomes the Capitol. Such flexibility of staging was permitted by the conventions of Shakespeare's theatre. A chair is needed for Caesar; he need not immediately occupy it, though his doing so will assist the sense that we are now in the Capitol. The Soothsayer, Artemidorus, and citizens group themselves on each side of the stage. A statue of Pompey should figure prominently.

POPILIUS (*to Cassius*)   Fare you well.

BRUTUS What said Popilius Lena?

CASSIUS

He wished today our enterprise might thrive.

I fear our purpose is discoverèd.

BRUTUS

Look how he makes to Caesar. Mark him.

Popilius speaks apart to Caesar

CASSIUS   Casca,

Be sudden, for we fear prevention.

Brutus, what shall be done? If this be known,   20

Cassius or Caesar never shall turn back,

For I will slay myself.

BRUTUS   Cassius, be constant.

Popilius Lena speaks not of our purposes,

For look, he smiles, and Caesar doth not change.

CASSIUS

Trebonius knows his time; for look you, Brutus,

He draws Mark Antony out of the way.

                              Exit Trebonius with Antony

DECIUS

Where is Metellus Cimber? Let him go

And presently prefer his suit to Caesar.

BRUTUS

He is addressed. Press near and second him.

CINNA

Casca, you are the first that rears your hand.   30

CAESAR

Are we all ready? What is now amiss

That Caesar and his Senate must redress?

---

18 *Popilius . . . Caesar*] *not in* F   18–19 Casca . . . prevention] DYCE 1866 (*conj.* Walker, *Crit.*); *as one line* F   26.1 *Exit . . . Antony*] *not in* F

19 **sudden** swift in action (*OED a.* 4)
  prevention being forestalled (four syllables)
22 **I will slay myself** i.e. if Caesar is not slain.
  In Plutarch Cassius is distraught with the
  sense of danger which 'made him like a
  man half beside himself' (*Caesar*, p. 92).
25 **Trebonius** So in *Brutus*, p. 123; Decius in
  Caesar, p. 92.

28 **presently** at once. The common modern
  sense ('soon') developed gradually and
  examples before *c.*1650 'are doubtful'
  (*OED adv.* 4).
  prefer present
29 **addressed** prepared
32 **his Senate** A signal touch of Caesarism.

METELLUS (*kneeling*)
   Most high, most mighty, and most puissant Caesar,
   Metellus Cimber throws before thy seat
   An humble heart –
CAESAR   I must prevent thee, Cimber.
   These couchings and these lowly courtesies
   Might fire the blood of ordinary men,
   And turn pre-ordinance and first decree
   Into the law of children. Be not fond
   To think that Caesar bears such rebel blood   40
   That will be thawed from the true quality
   With that which melteth fools – I mean sweet words,
   Low-crookèd curtsies, and base spaniel fawning.
   Thy brother by decree is banishèd.
   If thou dost bend, and pray, and fawn for him,
   I spurn thee like a cur out of my way.
   Know, Caesar doth not wrong, nor without cause
   Will he be satisfied.

---

33 *kneeling*] *not in* F   39 law] MALONE (*conj.* Johnson); lane F   Low-crookèd curtsies] F (Low-crooked-curtsies)

---

35 **prevent** forestall
36 **couchings** prostrations (virtually, crouchings, implying ignominious abasement)
   lowly courtesies Both (a) humble civilities (courtesies) and (b) low obeisances (curtsies).
37 **fire the blood of** incite (to reckless action)
38 **pre-ordinance . . . decree** what has been ordained by prior fiat. 'Caesar speaks as if his ordinances were those of a deity' (Wright).
39 **law of children** childish caprice (i.e. children know nothing of fixed or rational decisions). *Law* is Johnson's proposal for F's 'lane' and is much likelier than such alternatives as 'lune', 'play', or 'vane'. 'Lane' has been supported as meaning 'path', 'track' (i.e. 'narrow idea'), or alternatively (Hulme, p. 210) as a variant of 'line', in the sense of 'Rule, canon, precept', but any such interpretation is very forced, and *OED*, Line, 5, marks this sense as obsolete and rare.
39–40 **fond | To** so foolish as to
40 **rebel blood** blood acting against its true duty
41 **thawed** (implying that Caesar regards *the*

true quality as cold-bloodedness)
41 **quality** (a) character, property (b) excellence
42 **With that . . . fools** Tilley W794 illustrates the proverb, 'Fair words make fools fain'.
43 **Low-crookèd curtsies** curtsies with body and knee low-bent. The phrase has figurative as well as literal sense, implying 'ignoble and disingenuous'. For the punctuation see Commentary, 1.3.10.
   spaniel fawning That spaniels fawn is proverbial (Tilley S704). The association of fawning dogs with flattery (ll. 45–6, and 5.1.42) and with melting (often of sweetmeats) is a recurrent image-cluster in Shakespeare, first noted by Whiter (pp. 123–4, footnote). See also Spurgeon, pp. 195–9.
45 **bend, and pray** The words suggest prostration before a god.
46 **spurn thee like a cur** 'Caesar at the first simply refused their . . . entreaties. But afterwards . . . he violently thrust them from him' (*Brutus*, pp. 123–4).
47–8 **Know . . . satisfied** For apparent revision of these lines see the Introduction, pp. 4–5, 82.

METELLUS

Is there no voice more worthy than my own,
To sound more sweetly in great Caesar's ear   50
For the repealing of my banished brother?

BRUTUS (*kneeling*)

I kiss thy hand, but not in flattery, Caesar,
Desiring thee that Publius Cimber may
Have an immediate freedom of repeal.

CAESAR

What, Brutus?

CASSIUS (*kneeling*) Pardon, Caesar! Caesar, pardon!

As low as to thy foot doth Cassius fall
To beg enfranchisement for Publius Cimber.

CAESAR

I could be well moved, if I were as you;
If I could pray to move, prayers would move me.
But I am constant as the northern star,   60
Of whose true-fixed and resting quality
There is no fellow in the firmament.
The skies are painted with unnumbered sparks,
They are all fire, and every one doth shine;
But there's but one in all doth hold his place.
So in the world: 'tis furnished well with men,
And men are flesh and blood, and apprehensive;
Yet in the number I do know but one
That unassailable holds on his rank,

52, 55 *kneeling*] *not in* F

49–57 **Is there ... Cimber** 'They all made as
though they were intercessors for him,
and took him by the hands and kissed his
head and breast' (*Brutus*, p. 123).

53 **Publius Cimber** Plutarch (*Caesar*, p. 92)
simply mentions him, unnamed, as
brother to Metellus (in *Brutus*, p. 123,
Tullius) Cimber. The name is Shakespeare's addition.

54 **of repeal** to return from banishment

55–7 **Pardon . . . Cimber** 'The servility of
Metellus and Cassius is important in that
it provokes Caesar into such extravagant
expressions of arrogance that all sympathy for him is alienated, and the action
of the assassins is for the moment almost
accepted as justifiable' (Dorsch).

59 **If I . . . move me** Caesar's pose raises him
virtually above godhead, since the gods
are moved by prayer.
pray to move beg for concessions

60 **northern star** Pole star

61 **resting quality** constant and immovable
nature. (*OED*, ppl.a. 2, defines *resting* as
'remaining stationary', citing this as its
only example.)

62 **fellow** equal

63 **The skies . . . sparks** The line perhaps
implies a gesture towards the stage canopy, or 'heavens', painted with stars.

67 **apprehensive** capable of perception,
physical and mental

69 **holds on his rank** continues unvaried in
his position

Unshaked of motion; and that I am he,   70
Let me a little show it, even in this –
That I was constant Cimber should be banished,
And constant do remain to keep him so.

CINNA (*kneeling*)

O Caesar –

CAESAR   Hence! Wilt thou lift up Olympus?

DECIUS (*kneeling*)

Great Caesar –

CAESAR   Doth not Brutus bootless kneel?

CASCA Speak, hands, for me!

They stab Caesar, Casca first, Brutus last

CAESAR *Et tu, Brute?* – Then fall, Caesar!   *He dies*

CINNA

Liberty! Freedom! Tyranny is dead!
Run hence, proclaim, cry it about the streets!

CASSIUS

Some to the common pulpits, and cry out   80
'Liberty, freedom, and enfranchisement!'

⌈*The onlookers show signs of panic*⌉

74, 75 *kneeling*] *not in* F   76.1 *Casca . . . last*] *not in* F   77 *He*] *not in* F   81.1 *The onlookers
. . . panic*] *not in* F

74 **Olympus** In Greek mythology the mountain (in Thessaly) of the gods, with whom
Caesar ranges himself.

76 **Speak, hands** The staging of this crucial
moment depends on how these words are
interpreted – as a prayer (hands raised,
instead of knees bent), or as a call (to
himself and others) to act instead of
speaking. The raised hands could reveal
the drawn dagger.

76.1 **Casca first, Brutus last** 'Casca behind
him strake him in the neck with his
sword. . . . Caesar, turning straight unto
him, caught hold of his sword and held it
hard; and they both cried out, Caesar in
Latin: "O vile traitor Casca, what doest
thou?" And Casca in Greek to his
brother: "Brother, help me." . . . They . . .
compassed him in on every side with
their swords drawn in their hands, that
Caesar turned him nowhere but he was
stricken at by some . . . And then Brutus
himself gave him one wound about his
privities' (*Caesar*, pp. 93–4; similarly
Brutus, p. 124).

77 *Et tu, Brute* Even thou, Brutus. On the
origin of the phrase see the Introduction,
pp. 24–5. *Brute* (printed *Brutè* in the
Folio) has two syllables.

78–81 **Liberty . . . enfranchisement** 'Brutus
and his confederates . . . came all in a
troop together out of the Senate, and
went into the market-place, . . . boldly
holding up their heads like men of
courage, and called to the people to
defend their liberty' (*Caesar*, p. 96;
similarly *Brutus*, p. 125).

80 **pulpits** platforms (for orations); though it
would be difficult for an Elizabethan to
suppress the standard English sense. At
3.2.63 is a reference (echoing Plutarch)
to 'the public chair', and even if Shakespeare did not expect Brutus or Antony to
be seated while delivering their orations,
he seems to have expected a chair to be
provided.

81 **enfranchisement** Synonymous with
'Liberty, freedom'; it does not imply
voting rights.

BRUTUS

People and Senators, be not affrighted.

Fly not; stand still. Ambition's debt is paid.

CASCA

Go to the pulpit, Brutus.

DECIUS   And Cassius too.

BRUTUS Where's Publius?

CINNA

Here, quite confounded with this mutiny.

METELLUS

Stand fast together, lest some friend of Caesar's

Should chance –

BRUTUS

Talk not of standing. Publius, good cheer;

There is no harm intended to your person,   90

Nor to no Roman else. So tell them, Publius.

CASSIUS

And leave us, Publius, lest that the people,

Rushing on us, should do your age some mischief.

BRUTUS

Do so; and let no man abide this deed

But we the doers.   ⌜*Exeunt all but the conspirators*⌝

    Enter Trebonius

95 *Exeunt . . . conspirators*] *not in* F

82–3 **People and Senators . . . Fly not** 'the Senate . . . presently ran out of the house, and flying filled all the city with marvellous fear and tumult' (*Caesar*, p. 96; similarly *Brutus*, p. 124). What Plutarch describes should be reflected in the stage action.

83 **Ambition's debt is paid** Caesar's ambition has received its due.

86 **mutiny** tumult. On the seeming difference between the conspiratorial Publius earlier and the stupefied Publius here see the Introduction, pp. 81–2.

91 **Nor to no Roman** Abbott 406 illustrates the frequent double negative arising from 'the desire of emphasis which suggests repetition'.

92–5 **leave us . . . doers** 'Brutus . . . sent back again the noblemen that came thither

with him, thinking it no reason that they, which were no partakers of the murder, should be partakers of the danger' (*Brutus*, p. 126). Shakespeare turns Plutarch's general description into individual compassionate concern; Brutus and Cassius intend Caesar's murder to lead to personal safety. Cinna's lynching (3.3) shows up their delusion and the difference between their hopes and Antony's ruthlessness.

94 **abide** suffer the consequences of (as at 3.2.114 also); and, perhaps, also 'stay with', 'stand by' (Hulme, pp. 312–13).

95 *Exeunt . . . conspirators* Some of the bystanders – or all but Publius – may leave earlier.

CASSIUS

Where is Antony?

TREBONIUS   Fled to his house amazed.

Men, wives, and children stare, cry out, and run,

As it were doomsday.

BRUTUS   Fates, we will know your pleasures.

That we shall die we know; 'tis but the time,

And drawing days out, that men stand upon.   100

CASCA

Why, he that cuts off twenty years of life

Cuts off so many years of fearing death.

BRUTUS

Grant that, and then is death a benefit.

So are we Caesar's friends, that have abridged

His time of fearing death. Stoop, Romans, stoop,

And let us bathe our hands in Caesar's blood

Up to the elbows, and besmear our swords.

Then walk we forth, even to the market-place,

And waving our red weapons o'er our heads,

Let's all cry 'Peace, freedom, and liberty!'   110

CASSIUS

Stoop, then, and wash. How many ages hence

---

101 CASCA] F (*Cask.*);   *Cassius* POPE

96–8 **Where is Antony . . . doomsday** 'some
did shut-to their doors, others forsook
their shops and warehouses, and others
. . . ran home to their houses again. But
Antonius and Lepidus, which were two of
Caesar's chiefest friends, . . . fled into
other men's houses' (*Caesar*, p. 96).

96 **amazed** in consternation

98–118 **Fates . . . liberty** The self-gratulation
is theatrical and extravagant, a hubris
inviting nemesis.

99–100 **That . . . stand upon** A proverbial
sentiment (Tilley N311). *Stand upon* =
set store by (as at 2.2.13).

105–10 **Stoop . . . liberty** 'By this solemn
action Brutus gives the assassination of
Caesar a religious air and turn' (Upton,
p. 90): in reality he half-disguises a
sensationally gruesome action. Plutarch
says nothing about this ritual of blooding,
merely that the confederates, with bloody

swords, went to the Capitol 'persuading
the Romans . . . to take their liberty again'
(*Brutus*, p. 125). Leo Kirschbaum in
'Shakespeare's Stage Blood' (*PMLA*, 64,
1949) makes five points about it: (i) its
shocking brutality; (ii) its contrast with
the conspirators' lofty aims; (iii) in particular its contrast with our idea of
Brutus, illustrating his moral disorder, a
contrast such that Pope transferred the
lines to Casca as unfitting Brutus' 'mild
and philosophical character'; (iv) its
evidence of the conspirators' violence just
before Antony's servant heralds the
countermovement; (v) its inauguration
of the theme of Caesar's blood as 'the
symbol and mark of destruction which is
to flow through the rest of the play'.

108 **the market-place** the Forum, centre of
public life

111–16 **How many ages . . . the dust** 'What

Shall this our lofty scene be acted over
In states unborn and accents yet unknown!
BRUTUS
How many times shall Caesar bleed in sport,
That now on Pompey's basis lies along,
No worthier than the dust!
CASSIUS   So oft as that shall be,
So often shall the knot of us be called
The men that gave their country liberty.
DECIUS
What, shall we forth?
CASSIUS   Ay, every man away.
Brutus shall lead, and we will grace his heels   120
With the most boldest and best hearts of Rome.
        Enter Antony's Servant
BRUTUS
Soft! Who comes here? A friend of Antony's.

---

113 states] F2; State F1   115 lies] F2; lye F1   121.1 *Antony's*] This edition; *a* F

---

a strange effect these words are apt to produce . . ! "How true!" we say, "The prophecy is fulfilled." . . . And then the reflection comes that . . . the whole thing is being enacted "in sport". We experience a kind of vertigo, in which we cannot distinguish the real and the illusory, and yet are conscious of both in their highest potence' (MacCallum, p. 280): similarly *Antony* 5.2.215–20 ('the quick comedians | Extemporally will stage us . . . | . . . Antony | Shall be brought drunken .forth, and I shall see | Some squeaking Cleopatra boy my greatness | I'th' posture of a whore'). Shakespeare may be echoing Daniel's *Musophilus* (1599) on the future fame of English poetry; this wonders 'to what strange shores | This gain of our best glory shall be sent, | T'enrich unknowing nations with our stores? | What worlds in th'yet unformèd Occident | May come refined with th'accents that are ours?'

113 **accents** languages
114 **in sport** for entertainment. In *3 Henry VI* 2.3.27–8 Warwick exhorts his fellows to fight seriously, not 'as if the tragedy | Were played in jest by counterfeiting actors' –

again the stage/life double-focus effect.
115 **on Pompey's basis** In Plutarch Caesar falls 'against the base whereupon Pompey's image stood' as if 'the image took just revenge of Pompey's enemy' (*Caesar*, p. 95).
       along at full length
117 **knot** 'small group . . . or company [of associates]' (*OED*, Knot, *sb.*¹ 18).
120–1 **Brutus . . . Rome** 'Brutus went foremost, very honourably compassed in round about with the noblest men of the city' (*Brutus*, p. 126).
121 **most boldest** Abbott 11 illustrates the double superlative, as also 'most unkindest' at 3.2.180.
121.1 *Enter Antony's Servant* This entrance is the hinge of the whole action, though this becomes apparent only as the hitherto insignificant Antony reveals his virtuosity.
122 **friend of Antony's** In Plutarch, Antony as consul, inviting the conspirators down from the Capitol, 'sent them his son for a pledge' (*Brutus*, p. 127; similarly *Antonius*, p. 188). This was the day after the murder, during Senate negotiations. Shakespeare allows no gap, and dramatically polarizes the two sides.

SERVANT

    Thus, Brutus, did my master bid me kneel;
    Thus did Mark Antony bid me fall down,
    And being prostrate, thus he bade me say:
    'Brutus is noble, wise, valiant, and honest;
    Caesar was mighty, bold, royal, and loving.
    Say I love Brutus and I honour him;
    Say I feared Caesar, honoured him, and loved him.
    If Brutus will vouchsafe that Antony   130
    May safely come to him and be resolved
    How Caesar hath deserved to lie in death,
    Mark Antony shall not love Caesar dead
    So well as Brutus living, but will follow
    The fortunes and affairs of noble Brutus
    Thorough the hazards of this untrod state
    With all true faith.' So says my master Antony.

BRUTUS

    Thy master is a wise and valiant Roman;
    I never thought him worse.
    Tell him, so please him come unto this place,   140
    He shall be satisfied, and, by my honour,
    Depart untouched.

SERVANT   I'll fetch him presently.   *Exit*

BRUTUS

    I know that we shall have him well to friend.

CASSIUS

    I wish we may; but yet have I a mind

---

142 *Exit*] F (*Exit Seruant.*)

---

127 **royal** princely (in munificence, benevolence, grandeur, and so on)

129 **feared** 'Antony politicly places this word with "Caesar" and thus half aligns himself with the conspirators; its equally skilfully chosen counterpoise is "love Brutus"' (Sanders). It was (and generally is) accepted doctrine that the political leader needs to be feared and loved; as in *Henry V* 2.2.25–6, 'Never was monarch better feared and loved | Than is your majesty.'

131 **be resolved** learn for certain

136 **Thorough ... state** through the dangers of this unprecedented course
untrod poetic, metrical variant of 'untrodden', first recorded in Marlowe's translation of Lucan's *Pharsalia*, i. 567 (c.1584, published 1600).

140 **so please him come** if it please him to come. For *so* with subjunctive to express a condition see Abbott 133.

142 **presently** at once (as elsewhere)

143 **well to friend** as a good friend. For *to* so used see Abbott 189.

That fears him much, and my misgiving still
Falls shrewdly to the purpose.
      Enter Antony
BRUTUS
But here comes Antony. Welcome, Mark Antony!
ANTONY
O mighty Caesar! Dost thou lie so low?
Are all thy conquests, glories, triumphs, spoils,
Shrunk to this little measure? Fare thee well.   150
I know not, gentlemen, what you intend,
Who else must be let blood, who else is rank.
If I myself, there is no hour so fit
As Caesar's death's hour, nor no instrument
Of half that worth as those your swords, made rich
With the most noble blood of all this world.
I do beseech ye, if you bear me hard,
Now, whilst your purpled hands do reek and smoke,

---

147 But . . . Mark Antony] POPE; *as two lines, breaking after* 'comes Antony' F

145 **misgiving** (*OED*'s first occurrence as verbal substantive)

145–6 **still . . . purpose** continues acutely relevant. *Shrewdly* combines the senses of 'severely', 'seriously', and 'astutely' (*OED*, 2, 5, and 7 respectively).

148–63 **O . . . age** Antony stresses Caesar's supreme value to Rome (l. 156), a fact so far obscured by the conspirators' propaganda but henceforth dominant. The speech masterfully combines exaltation of Caesar, passionate grief, and strategic flattery. Parallels abound in Antony's reflections on worldly might eclipsed by death: e.g. Ovid, *Amores* III. ix. 33, 40; Juvenal, *Satires* x. 147–8; Nashe, *Christ's Tears Over Jerusalem* (McKerrow, ii. 82; on Caesar's ambition) – 'he . . . had the dust of his bones in a brazen urn (no bigger than a bowl) barrelled up, whom (if he had lived) all the sea and earth and air would have been too little for. Let the ambitious man stretch out his limbs never so, he taketh up no more ground (being dead) than the beggar.' It occurs already in Shakespeare, in *Richard II* 3.3.153 – 'my large kingdom for a little grave' – and *1 Henry IV*

5.4.87–92, as Hal addresses the dead Hotspur.

149 **conquests, glories, triumphs, spoils** A possible echo of *A Mirror for Magistrates* (ed. L. B. Campbell, 1938, p. 378; 'Shore's Wife', ll. 155–6) – 'Duke Hannibal in all his conquest great, | Or Caesar yet, whose triumphs did exceed, | Of all their spoils'.

152 **rank** overblown, swollen (and ripe for blood-letting)

153–6 **If I . . . world** Brutus having promised him safety (ll. 140–2), this gesture incurs no danger; yet it still rings with genuine feeling.

157 **bear me hard** bear me ill will (as at 1.2.310)

158 **purpled** According to *OED*, the fashion for describing blood as 'purple' arose in the 1590s and is a purely poetic usage (*a*. 2d). More traditionally, purple was the 'distinguishing colour of emperors, kings, etc. . . . hence imperial, royal' (*a*. 1), and also 'the hue of mourning' (*a*. 2c).
reek steam (the sense 'stink' arose much later)
smoke steam (synonymous with *reek* in Elizabethan usage)

Fulfil your pleasure. Live a thousand years,
I shall not find myself so apt to die.   160
No place will please me so, no mean of death,
As here by Caesar, and by you cut off,
The choice and master spirits of this age.
BRUTUS
O Antony, beg not your death of us!
Though now we must appear bloody and cruel,
As by our hands and this our present act
You see we do, yet see you but our hands
And this the bleeding business they have done.
Our hearts you see not; they are pitiful;
And pity to the general wrong of Rome –   170
As fire drives out fire, so pity pity –
Hath done this deed on Caesar. For your part,
To you our swords have leaden points, Mark Antony.
Our arms in strength of malice, and our hearts
Of brothers' temper, do receive you in
With all kind love, good thoughts, and reverence.
CASSIUS
Your voice shall be as strong as any man's
In the disposing of new dignities.

174 in strength of malice] F; exempt from malice POPE; no strength of malice CAPELL; in strength of welcome COLLIER 1858; in strength of manhood COLLIER 1877; in strength of amity HUDSON 1879 (*conj.* Singer, *N. & Q.*, 24 Jan. 1857, p. 61)

161 **mean** means. The singular occurs often in Elizabethan English.
169 **pitiful** full of pity
171 **fire . . . fire** Proverbial (Tilley F277). It means that the heat of a fire will ease the smart of a burn. The first *fire* is disyllabic. **so pity pity** so pity for Rome drives out pity for Caesar
173 **leaden** (a) blunt, since lead is malleable (b) heavy, suggesting swords that have been lowered, or cannot be lifted, against Antony. *OED* lists 'leaden sword' as a type of an ineffectual weapon.
174 **in strength of malice** Much discussed. 'Unstrengthed' is not impossible (i.e. 'our malice has lost its strength'): *OED* records it, but only *c.*1225, and it would seem too odd for the play's lucid style. 'Unstrengthed' might mean 'relaxed' (as of instrumental strings: see *Richard II* 1.3.162 – 'an un-

stringèd viol or a harp') but would be a forced metaphor. S. W. Singer suggested (*N. & Q.*, 24 January 1857, p. 61) that *malice* could be a misread 'amitie'. But F may well be right. While their hands, Brutus says, are bloody, their hearts are compassionate (ll. 165–9); their arms, though strongly hostile to Caesar (see *Merchant* 4.1.18 – 'this fashion of thy malice'), or, perhaps, strong in power to harm (see *OED*, Malice, 5, and *K. John* 2.1.251 – 'our cannons' malice'), go along with hearts of brothers to Antony.
177–8 **Your voice . . . dignities** In Plutarch the Senate 'gave certain provinces also and convenient [i.e. appropriate] honours unto Brutus and his confederates' (*Caesar*, p. 97; similarly *Brutus*, p. 125). Cassius sees Antony as an ambitious politician.

BRUTUS

    Only be patient till we have appeased

    The multitude, beside themselves with fear,   180

    And then we will deliver you the cause

    Why I, that did love Caesar when I struck him,

    Have thus proceeded.

ANTONY   I doubt not of your wisdom.

    Let each man render me his bloody hand.

    First, Marcus Brutus, will I shake with you;

    Next, Caius Cassius, do I take your hand;

    Now, Decius Brutus, yours; now yours, Metellus;

    Yours, Cinna; and, my valiant Casca, yours;

    Though last, not least in love, yours, good Trebonius.

    Gentlemen all – Alas, what shall I say?   190

    My credit now stands on such slippery ground

    That one of two bad ways you must conceit me,

    Either a coward or a flatterer.

    That I did love thee, Caesar, O, 'tis true!

    If then thy spirit look upon us now,

    Shall it not grieve thee dearer than thy death

    To see thy Antony making his peace,

    Shaking the bloody fingers of thy foes,

    Most noble! in the presence of thy corpse?

    Had I as many eyes as thou hast wounds,   200

    Weeping as fast as they stream forth thy blood,

    It would become me better than to close

    In terms of friendship with thine enemies.

198–9 foes, | . . . corpse?] ROWE (*subs.*); Foes? | . . . Coarse, F

180 **beside . . . fear** In Plutarch the senators 'filled all the city with marvellous fear and tumult' (*Caesar*, p. 96; *Brutus*, p. 121).

183 **I doubt not of your wisdom** Diplomatic irony.

188–9 **my valiant Casca . . . not least in love** Further covert irony. For Antony's real feelings see 5.1.44 – 'damnèd Casca, like a cur'.

189 **good Trebonius** Again covertly ironical: it was Trebonius who lured him away before the assassination.

191 **My credit . . . ground** my credibility is so precariously poised (perhaps implying the ground slippery with blood)

192 **conceit** conceive (first example in *OED* of this sense and construction)

195 **thy spirit** The first invocation of Caesar's spirit, soon to dominate the action; see ll. 270–3.

196 **dearer** more keenly, deeply

197 **thy Antony** A revealing touch of intimacy.

199 **Most noble** Probably addressed to Caesar rather than ironically to the conspirators.

202 **close** unite

Pardon me, Julius! Here wast thou bayed, brave hart;
Here didst thou fall; and here thy hunters stand,
Signed in thy spoil, and crimsoned in thy lethe.
O world, thou wast the forest to this hart,
And this indeed, O world, the heart of thee!
How like a deer, strucken by many princes,
Dost thou here lie!   210
CASSIUS
    Mark Antony –
ANTONY   Pardon me, Caius Cassius.
    The enemies of Caesar shall say this;
    Then, in a friend, it is cold modesty.
CASSIUS·
    I blame you not for praising Caesar so,
    But what compact mean you to have with us?
    Will you be pricked in number of our friends,
    Or shall we on, and not depend on you?
ANTONY
    Therefore I took your hands, but was indeed
    Swayed from the point by looking down on Caesar.
    Friends am I with you all, and love you all,   220
    Upon this hope, that you shall give me reasons
    Why and wherein Caesar was dangerous.
BRUTUS
    Or else were this a savage spectacle.

208 heart] F (Hart)

204 **bayed, brave hart** brought to bay like a
    noble stag. The image of the great animal
    hunted to death may derive from
    Plutarch, where Caesar is 'mangled
    among them as a wild beast taken of hun-
    ters' (*Caesar*, p. 94). Puns on 'hart'/
    'heart' are frequent, as in ll. 207–8.
206 **Signed in thy spoil** 'bearing the bloody
    tokens of thy slaughter' (Onions). 'Spoil'
    was a hunting term for the cutting up of
    the quarry, from Old French *espoille*, Latin
    spolium, the skin stripped from the dead
    animal.
    crimsoned (first recorded occurrence)
    lethe Much discussed since Capell's un-
    confirmed definition of it (in *Notes*) as a
    hunting term for the quarry's blood used
    to anoint its killers (Furness, p. 151).

Elsewhere in Shakespeare it means the
river in Hades causing oblivion of the
past; here, presumably, 'stream of death',
implying also 'blood-stream', i.e. 'crimsoned in the stream which bears thee to
oblivion' (White). Shakespeare may, as
others did, have assumed an origin in
Latin *letum* (death), often spelt *lethum* by
association with Lethe.
213 **cold modesty** sober moderation
215 **compact** Accented on the second syl-
    lable.
216 **pricked** marked (originally with a pin-
    prick), ticked, as at 4.1.1, 3, 16.
221 **Upon this hope** An apparently reason-
    able yet potentially explosive proviso, like
    that also at ll. 227–30.
223 **were this** this would be

Our reasons are so full of good regard
That were you, Antony, the son of Caesar,
You should be satisfied.
ANTONY   That's all I seek;
And am moreover suitor that I may
Produce his body to the market-place,
And in the pulpit, as becomes a friend,
Speak in the order of his funeral.   230
BRUTUS
You shall, Mark Antony.
CASSIUS   Brutus, a word with you.
    (*Aside to Brutus*) You know not what you do. Do not
            consent
    That Antony speak in his funeral.
    Know you how much the people may be moved
    By that which he will utter?
BRUTUS (*aside to Cassius*)   By your pardon:
    I will myself into the pulpit first,
    And show the reason of our Caesar's death.
    What Antony shall speak, I will protest
    He speaks by leave and by permission;
    And that we are contented Caesar shall   240
    Have all true rites, and lawful ceremonies,
    It shall advantage more than do us wrong.
CASSIUS (*aside to Brutus*)
    I know not what may fall. I like it not.
BRUTUS
    Mark Antony, here, take you Caesar's body.
    You shall not in your funeral speech blame us,
    But speak all good you can devise of Caesar,

---

224 **regard** consideration, heed (but playing
    on the literal sense, 'sight', after *spectacle*)
228 **Produce** bring forth
230 **order** ceremony
231 **Brutus, a word** 'Antonius thinking good
    his [Caesar's] testament should be read
    openly [3.2.128 ff.], and also that his
    body should be honourably buried . . .,
    Cassius stoutly spake against it. But
    Brutus went with the motion, . . .
    Wherein . . . he committed a second fault'
    (the first being in sparing Antony; *Brutus*,
    pp. 127–8).

237 **our Caesar's death** 'In his [Brutus']
    opinion, all the conspirators in striking at
    Caesar did so regretfully. . . . He does not
    admit to himself that any of them were
    other than Caesar's personal friends'
    (Kittredge).
238 **protest** proclaim
239, 247 **permission** (four syllables)
240–2 **And . . . wrong** The flexible syntax
    allows ll. 240–1 to be both the object of
    'will protest' (l. 238) and the subject of
    'shall advantage' (l. 242).

And say you do't by our permission;
Else shall you not have any hand at all
About his funeral. And you shall speak
In the same pulpit whereto I am going,   250
After my speech is ended.

ANTONY   Be it so.
    I do desire no more.

BRUTUS
    Prepare the body, then, and follow us.

Exeunt all but Antony

ANTONY
    O, pardon me, thou bleeding piece of earth,
    That I am meek and gentle with these butchers!
    Thou art the ruins of the noblest man
    That ever livèd in the tide of times.
    Woe to the hand that shed this costly blood!
    Over thy wounds now do I prophesy –
    Which like dumb mouths do ope their ruby lips   260
    To beg the voice and utterance of my tongue –
    A curse shall light upon the limbs of men.
    Domestic fury and fierce civil strife
    Shall cumber all the parts of Italy.
    Blood and destruction shall be so in use,
    And dreadful objects so familiar,
    That mothers shall but smile when they behold
    Their infants quartered with the hands of war,

253.1 *all but*] F (*Manet*)   254 ANTONY] *not in* F

257 **tide of times** course, stream of history
260 **mouths . . . lips** See also 3.2.218,
    and 'mouthèd wounds' in *1 Henry IV*
    1.3.97. Wounds, gaping red, are often
    imaged as *mouths* accusing their in-
    flicters. For a parallel idea (though not
    necessarily Shakespeare's source) in *A
    Warning for Fair Women* see the Introduc-
    tion, p. 2, n. 3.
261 **utterance** (a) speech (b) vehemence.
    OED's last example of this second sense is
    in Greene's *Royal Exchange*, 1590.
262 **limbs** Much emended, but un-
    necessarily. The sense in l. 258 of the
    murderer's 'hand' extends its
    consequences to the 'limbs' to be woun-

ded in civil war. Rather than the modern
'arms and legs' it covers 'any organ or
part of the body' (*OED*, Limb, *sb.*[1] 1). In
Timon 4.1.23–6 diseases are to strike the
'limbs . . . minds and marrows' of young
and old. Hulme (p. 311) thinks that
Antony also means the organs of the
body politic but, although these do in fact
suffer, the sense here is direct and un-
metaphorical – actual human bodies.
263 **Domestic** indigenous, national (the
    sense 'pertaining to the home,
    household' is of later development)
264 **cumber** Two senses are possible: (a)
    distress, harass (b) encumber, choke up
    (*OED v.* 4).

All pity choked with custom of fell deeds.
And Caesar's spirit, ranging for revenge,   270
With Ate by his side, come hot from hell,
Shall in these confines, with a monarch's voice,
Cry 'Havoc!' and let slip the dogs of war,
That this foul deed shall smell above the earth
With carrion men, groaning for burial.
    Enter Octavius' Servant
You serve Octavius Caesar, do you not?
SERVANT I do, Mark Antony.
ANTONY
Caesar did write for him to come to Rome.
SERVANT
He did receive his letters and is coming,
And bid me say to you by word of mouth –   280
O Caesar!
ANTONY
Thy heart is big. Get thee apart and weep.
Passion, I see, is catching, for mine eyes,
Seeing those beads of sorrow stand in thine,
Began to water. Is thy master coming?
SERVANT
He lies tonight within seven leagues of Rome.
ANTONY
Post back with speed and tell him what hath chanced.

269 deeds.] F4; deeds, F1   275.1 *Octavius*'] ROWE (Octavius's); *Octavio's* F   283 catching,
for] F2; catching from F1   287 Post ... chanced] ROWE; *as two lines, breaking after* 'speede' F

269 **custom of fell** familiarity with cruel
271 **Ate** Greek goddess of discord, daughter
of Zeus (in Homer), of Strife (in Hesiod).
Shakespeare repeatedly mentions her as
the spirit of destruction, as in *K. John*
2.1.63, *LLL* 5.3.676–7 and *Much Ado*
2.1.227.
272 **confines** 'regions'; but playing on the
sense 'confined space, enclosure' (*OED sb.*[2]
5), where escape is impossible. A contemporary parallel would be the loosing of
dogs to attack a bear, in the London bear-
pits.
  monarch's Emphatic; in a battle the
monarch (or his representative) was the
only one qualified to cry 'Havoc!', as in
K. John 2.1.357 – 'Cry havoc! kings'.
273 **Havoc** kill without mercy

273 **the dogs of war** Similarly *Henry V*,
Prologue 7–8, where, 'Leashed in like
hounds', famine, sword, and fire attend
on the King.
275 **carrion men** (a) human corpses (b) men
who are no better than corpses
275.1 **Octavius'** F *Octavio's* (*Octavius* at
ll. 276, 296); see the Introduction, p. 74.
282 **big** swollen with grief
283 **Passion** sorrow. Similarly *Twelfth Night*
3.4.196–7 – 'With the same haviour that
your passion bears | Goes on my master's
griefs'.
285 **Began** Perhaps a slip for the expected
'Begin', which some editors read, following Hanmer; or the sense may be 'Have
begun'.

Here is a mourning Rome, a dangerous Rome,
No Rome of safety for Octavius yet.
Hie hence and tell him so. Yet stay awhile –   290
Thou shalt not back till I have borne this corpse
Into the market-place. There shall I try,
In my oration, how the people take
The cruel issue of these bloody men;
According to the which thou shalt discourse
To young Octavius of the state of things.
Lend me your hand.   *Exeunt with Caesar's body*

3.2   *Enter Brutus and Cassius, with the Plebeians*
PLEBEIANS

We will be satisfied! Let us be satisfied!
BRUTUS

Then follow me and give me audience, friends.
Cassius, go you into the other street
And part the numbers.
Those that will hear me speak, let 'em stay here;   5
Those that will follow Cassius, go with him;
And public reasons shall be renderèd
Of Caesar's death.
        ⌜*Brutus goes up into the pulpit*⌝
FIRST PLEBEIAN   I will hear Brutus speak.

297 with Caesar's body] *not in* F
    3.2.0.1 *Enter . . . Plebeians*] CAPELL (*subs.*);   *Enter Brutus and goes into the Pulpit, and Cassius,*
with the Plebeians F   7 renderèd] F (rendred)   8 *Brutus . . . pulpit*] This edition; *direction at*
3.2.0.1 F;   *direction at* 3.2.10 CAPELL

288–9 **Rome . . . No Rome** Puns on 'Rome'/
    'room'; cf. 1.2.156.
294 **issue** action, deed (*OED sb.* 8b). *OED*
    marks this sense as rare, its only other
    example being *Cymbeline* 2.1.51. The
    more normal sense, which may be used
    figuratively here, is 'outcome, product'
    (*sb.* 8a).
296 **young Octavius** He was twenty-one.
    Plutarch refers to 'young Caesar' (*Caesar*,
    p. 100) and 'the young man Octavius
    Caesar . . . a stripling . . . of twenty year
    old' (*Brutus*, pp. 131, 136), and remarks
    that Antony at first underrated him
    'because he was very young' (*Antonius*,
    p. 190). This is repeatedly stressed, gener-
    ally in scorn, in this play (4.1.18,
    5.1.60–1) and *Antony and Cleopatra*

(3.13.17, 'To the boy Caesar send this
    grizzled head'; 4.1.1, 'He calls me boy';
    and 4.12.48, 'To the young Roman boy
    she hath sold me').˙
3.2.7 **public** reasons (a) reasons given in
    public (b) reasons of public policy
    8 *Brutus goes up* Brutus and Antony
    probably did not give their orations from
    the Globe's upper (gallery) stage:
    dialogue and action hardly suffice here
    and at ll. 66–71 for their ascents, and at
    ll. 48–52 and 161–3 for their descents.
    Moreover, were they to leave the one
    stage level for the other one would expect
    exit and re-entry directions, and, since
    these are lacking, the 'pulpit' or 'public
    chair' (l. 63) may rather have been some
    kind of rostrum (Saunders, p. 252).

SECOND PLEBEIAN

I will hear Cassius, and compare their reasons,

When severally we hear them renderèd.   10

             Exit Cassius with some of the Plebeians

THIRD PLEBEIAN

The noble Brutus is ascended. Silence!

BRUTUS Be patient till the last.

Romans, countrymen, and lovers, hear me for my cause,
and be silent, that you may hear. Believe me for mine
honour, and have respect to mine honour, that you may
believe. Censure me in your wisdom, and awake your
senses, that you may the better judge. If there be any in
this assembly, any dear friend of Caesar's, to him I say
that Brutus' love to Caesar was no less than his. If then
that friend demand why Brutus rose against Caesar, this   20
is my answer – not that I loved Caesar less, but that I loved
Rome more. Had you rather Caesar were living, and die
all slaves, than that Caesar were dead, to live all free men?
As Caesar loved me, I weep for him; as he was fortunate,
I rejoice at it; as he was valiant, I honour him; but as he
was ambitious, I slew him. There is tears for his love; joy
for his fortune; honour for his valour; and death for his
ambition. Who is here so base that would be a bondman?

---

10 renderèd] F (rendred)   10.1 *Exit . . . Plebeians*] *not in* F   23 free men] F (Free-men)

---

10 **severally** separately
13–33 **Romans . . . reply** In Plutarch,
Brutus, when writing letters, imitated the
'brief compendious manner' of the
Lacedaemonians (Spartans); for example, 'I understand you have given
Dolabella money: if you have done it
willingly, you confess you have offended
me; if against your wills, show it then by
giving me willingly' (*Brutus*, p. 104). The
clipped formality is foreshadowed in
1.2.162–70. The oration is in sober prose
yet its parallelisms suggest measured
verse. Conceding little to emotionalism, it
is impressive, and it wins its audience.
Plutarch (who does not give its contents)
relates that Brutus' hearers listened
dubiously, 'For by their great silence they
showed that they were sorry for Caesar's
death, and also that they did reverence

Brutus' (*Caesar*, p. 97). Elsewhere, they
respected Brutus' first address but at a
second 'showed that they were not all
contented with the murder' (*Brutus*,
pp. 125, 126). Shakespeare shapes all
this into the bold simplicity of noble justifi-
cation and ready approval.
13 **lovers** dear friends
    cause (a) position I advocate (b) business,
matter of concern (c) case at law, matter
in dispute (d) good grounds for action
15 **have respect to mine honour** bear in
mind that I am a man of honour
16 **Censure** judge (though the sense 'blame'
was also current)
17 **senses** reason (*OED*, Sense, *sb.* I. 10)
26 **There is tears** Abbott 335 illustrates the
frequent 'quasi-singular verb' (especially
in 'There is') preceding a plural subject.

If any, speak, for him have I offended. Who is here so rude
that would not be a Roman? If any, speak, for him have   30
I offended. Who is here so vile that will not love his
country? If any, speak, for him have I offended. I pause for
a reply.

ALL THE PLEBEIANS None, Brutus, none.

BRUTUS Then none have I offended. I have done no more to
Caesar than you shall do to Brutus. The question of his
death is enrolled in the Capitol; his glory not extenuated,
wherein he was worthy; nor his offences enforced, for
which he suffered death.

Enter Mark Antony and others, with Caesar's body
Here comes his body, mourned by Mark Antony, who,   40
though he had no hand in his death, shall receive the
benefit of his dying, a place in the commonwealth, as
which of you shall not? With this I depart, that as I slew
my best lover for the good of Rome, I have the same
dagger for myself, when it shall please my country to need
my death.

ALL THE PLEBEIANS Live, Brutus! Live! Live!

⌈*Brutus comes down*⌉

FIRST PLEBEIAN
Bring him with triumph home unto his house.

FOURTH PLEBEIAN
Give him a statue with his ancestors.

THIRD PLEBEIAN
Let him be Caesar.

34 THE PLEBEIANS] *not in* F; *so to l. 238 inclusive*   39.1 *and others*] *not in* F   47.1 *Brutus comes down*] *not in* F   49 FOURTH PLEBEIAN] This edition; 2. (*or* 2 Ple.) F; *so to l. 250 inclusive*

29 **rude** barbarous
36 **question** subject
37 **enrolled** recorded
     extenuated diminished
38 **enforced** insisted upon
42 **in the commonwealth** with all the rights
     of a free Roman. What they are Brutus
     leaves quite unspecific – perhaps a vague
     'freedom from servitude' or 'citizenship in
     the republic'.
44–5 **the same dagger** No interval having
     elapsed since the scene before, it would be
     dramatically effective for Brutus to
     flourish his bloodstained dagger over
     Caesar's body.

49 FOURTH PLEBEIAN Other editions follow F
     in designating the speaker Second
     Plebeian, and this edition's FIFTH
     PLEBEIAN (see l. 50) 'Fourth Plebeian'. But
     the actual Second Plebeian has left at l.
     10 and it seems logical to renumber these
     new speakers.
     his ancestors This is the recurrent invok-
     ing of Lucius Junius Brutus; see Com-
     mentary, 1.2.159.
50–1 **Let him . . . Brutus** Bitter if uncon-
     scious ironies to one who slew his best
     friend to avert the crowning of Caesarism
     – a measure of Brutus' inability to judge
     the popular mood. Plutarch refers to

FIFTH PLEBEIAN   Caesar's better parts   50
  Shall be crowned in Brutus.
FIRST PLEBEIAN
  We'll bring him to his house with shouts and clamours.
BRUTUS
  My countrymen –
FOURTH PLEBEIAN   Peace! Silence! Brutus speaks!
FIRST PLEBEIAN Peace, ho!
BRUTUS
  Good countrymen, let me depart alone,
  And, for my sake, stay here with Antony.
  Do grace to Caesar's corpse, and grace his speech
  Tending to Caesar's glories, which Mark Antony,
  By our permission, is allowed to make.
  I do entreat you, not a man depart,   60
  Save I alone, till Antony have spoke.   *Exit*
FIRST PLEBEIAN
  Stay, ho! and let us hear Mark Antony.
THIRD PLEBEIAN
  Let him go up into the public chair.
  We'll hear him. Noble Antony, go up.
ANTONY
  For Brutus' sake I am beholden to you.
        He goes into the pulpit
FIFTH PLEBEIAN
  What does he say of Brutus?
THIRD PLEBEIAN   He says, for Brutus' sake
  He finds himself beholden to us all.
FIFTH PLEBEIAN
  'Twere best he speak no harm of Brutus here.
FIRST PLEBEIAN
  This Caesar was a tyrant.
THIRD PLEBEIAN   Nay, that's certain.
  We are blest that Rome is rid of him.   70

50 FIFTH PLEBEIAN] This edition; 4. (*or* 4 *Ple.*) F; *so to l. 252 inclusive*   52 We'll ... clamours]
CAPELL; *as two lines, breaking after* 'House' F   65 beholden] F (beholding)   65.1 *He ... pulpit*]
not in F   67 beholden] F (beholding)

some 'that desired change and wished   body and hear Antony courteously
Brutus only their prince and governor'   58 **Tending to** dealing with
(*Caesar*, p. 84).   63 **the public chair** 'the chair or pulpit for
                                                    orations' (*Brutus*, p. 136).
57 **Do grace . . . speech** honour Caesar's

FOURTH PLEBEIAN

Peace! Let us hear what Antony can say.

ANTONY

You gentle Romans –

ALL THE PLEBEIANS   Peace, ho! Let us hear him.

ANTONY

Friends, Romans, countrymen, lend me your ears.
I come to bury Caesar, not to praise him.
The evil that men do lives after them;
The good is oft interrèd with their bones –
So let it be with Caesar. The noble Brutus
Hath told you Caesar was ambitious.
If it were so, it was a grievous fault,
And grievously hath Caesar answered it.   80
Here, under leave of Brutus and the rest –
For Brutus is an honourable man;
So are they all, all honourable men –
Come I to speak in Caesar's funeral.
He was my friend, faithful and just to me;

71 **Peace . . . say** *Caesar* mentions no oration
by Antony, and the will is read by an
unspecified 'they', Antony playing no
part in this or in the subsequent riot
(*Caesar*, p. 97). In *Brutus* (pp. 127–8)
Antony proposes that the will be read:
Brutus approves the move, overruling
Cassius (see Commentary, 3.1.231): the
will is read in the Senate, though not
specifically by Antony, and wins popular
acclaim: only later does Antony make his
funeral oration and excite the crowd (see
Commentary, ll. 73–254). Plutarch
observes that Antony's style was 'called
Asiatic, which carried the best grace and
estimation at that time' (*Antonius*, p. 175),
though he then disparages it as osten-
tatious. Shakespeare may have noted this
difference from Brutus' 'brief compendious manner' (see Commentary, ll.
13–33), but he does not make Antony
too florid.

72 **gentle Romans** Virtually, 'good citizens',
gentle here being used in general commendation. Plutarch calls them 'a multitude of rakehells' (*Brutus*, p. 126).

73–254 **Friends . . . wilt** 'perceiving that his
words moved the common people to compassion, he framed his eloquence to make

their hearts yearn the more; and, taking
Caesar's gown all bloody in his hand, he
laid it open to the sight of them all, showing what a number of cuts and holes it
had upon it. Therewithal the people fell
presently into such a rage and mutiny
that there was no more order kept'
(*Brutus*, pp. 188–9). In *Antonius* (pp. 188–9)
similarly 'he mingled his oration with
lamentable words, and by amplifying of
matters did greatly move their hearts and
affections unto pity and compassion,'
unfolding the bloodstained robe and in-
furiating the people. For possible
influence of Appian's *Chronicle* see the
Introduction, pp. 25–6. The general
spirit of Antony's oration derives from the
sources, but its brilliantly developed contents are virtually Shakespeare's alone.

75–6 **The evil . . . bones** A proverbial sentiment: Tilley (T619) quotes G. Whet-
stone's 1 *Promos and Cassandra* 3.4 ('The
proverb says, that ten good turns lie dead,
| And one ill deed . . . report abroad doth
spread').

78 **ambitious** (four syllables)

79 **If it were so** The subjunctive 'implies a
distinct doubt' (Kittredge).

80 **answered** paid the penalty for

But Brutus says he was ambitious,
And Brutus is an honourable man.
He hath brought many captives home to Rome,
Whose ransoms did the general coffers fill.
Did this in Caesar seem ambitious?   90
When that the poor have cried, Caesar hath wept;
Ambition should be made of sterner stuff;
Yet Brutus says he was ambitious,
And Brutus is an honourable man.
You all did see that on the Lupercal
I thrice presented him a kingly crown,
Which he did thrice refuse. Was this ambition?
Yet Brutus says he was ambitious,
And sure he is an honourable man.
I speak not to disprove what Brutus spoke,   100
But here I am to speak what I do know.
You all did love him once, not without cause;
What cause withholds you then to mourn for him?
O judgement, thou art fled to brutish beasts,
And men have lost their reason! Bear with me;
My heart is in the coffin there with Caesar,
And I must pause till it come back to me.
FIRST PLEBEIAN
Methinks there is much reason in his sayings.
FOURTH PLEBEIAN
If thou consider rightly of the matter,
Caesar has had great wrong.
THIRD PLEBEIAN   Has he, masters?   110
I fear there will a worse come in his place.

---

104 art] F2; are FI   110–11 Has ... place] CAPELL; *as one line* F   110 Has he,] F (Ha's hee);
Has he, my CAPELL; Has he not, DYCE 1866 (*conj.* Craik); Ha! has he, ANON. *conj. in*
Cambridge; That he has, HUNTER; That has he, MACMILLAN *conj.*

95 **the Lupercal** the occasion of the Luper-
    calia.
96–7 **thrice** . . . **thrice** See Commentary,
    1.2.225.
104–5 **O judgement . . . reason** For a likely
    Jonson parody see the Introduction, p. 3.
107 **I must pause . . . to me** 'His pause is a test
    of the strength of his position, fortified by
    a show of emotion. . . . Antony may now

proceed with a confidence he has earned'
(Styan, p. 190). Still, his grief is genuine,
however ingeniously deployed; he is acting and not acting simultaneously.
111 **I fear** . . . **place** A proverbial notion
(Tilley B332), as in *Richard III* 2.3.4 ('Ill
news, by'r lady: seldom comes the
better').

FIFTH PLEBEIAN

Marked ye his words? He would not take the crown;
Therefore 'tis certain he was not ambitious.

FIRST PLEBEIAN

If it be found so, some will dear abide it.

FOURTH PLEBEIAN

Poor soul, his eyes are red as fire with weeping.

THIRD PLEBEIAN

There's not a nobler man in Rome than Antony.

FIFTH PLEBEIAN

Now mark him, he begins again to speak.

ANTONY

But yesterday the word of Caesar might
Have stood against the world. Now lies he there,
And none so poor to do him reverence.   120
O masters, if I were disposed to stir
Your hearts and minds to mutiny and rage,
I should do Brutus wrong, and Cassius wrong,
Who – you all know – are honourable men.
I will not do them wrong. I rather choose
To wrong the dead, to wrong myself and you,
Than I will wrong such honourable men.
But here's a parchment, with the seal of Caesar;
I found it in his closet – 'tis his will.
Let but the commons hear this testament –   130
Which, pardon me, I do not mean to read –
And they would go and kiss dead Caesar's wounds,
And dip their napkins in his sacred blood,
Yea, beg a hair of him for memory,
And dying, mention it within their wills,
Bequeathing it as a rich legacy
Unto their issue.

---

114 **abide** suffer the consequences of (as at 3.1.94)

115 **red as fire** A popular tag (Tilley F248).

122 **mutiny and rage** 'The people fell presently into such a rage and mutiny' (*Brutus*, p. 129).

128 **here's a parchment** In Plutarch the will is read earlier, in quite different circumstances; see Commentary, l. 71.

129 **closet** private room, study (as at 2.1.35)

130 **commons** common people

133 **napkins . . . sacred blood** handkerchiefs (like cloths dipped in martyrs' blood and cherished as saving relics). In Plutarch the Senate ordains that 'Caesar's funerals should be honoured as a god' (*Caesar*, p. 97).

FIFTH PLEBEIAN

We'll hear the will! Read it, Mark Antony.

ALL THE PLEBEIANS

The will! The will! We will hear Caesar's will!

ANTONY

Have patience, gentle friends; I must not read it.   140
It is not meet you know how Caesar loved you.
You are not wood, you are not stones, but men;
And being men, hearing the will of Caesar,
It will inflame you, it will make you mad.
'Tis good you know not that you are his heirs,
For if you should, O, what would come of it?

FIFTH PLEBEIAN

Read the will! We'll hear it, Antony!
You shall read us the will, Caesar's will!

ANTONY

Will you be patient? Will you stay awhile?
I have o'ershot myself to tell you of it.   150
I fear I wrong the honourable men
Whose daggers have stabbed Caesar; I do fear it.

FIFTH PLEBEIAN

They were traitors. 'Honourable men'!

ALL THE PLEBEIANS The will! The testament!

FOURTH PLEBEIAN

They were villains, murderers! The will! Read the will!

ANTONY

You will compel me, then, to read the will?
Then make a ring about the corpse of Caesar,
And let me show you him that made the will.
Shall I descend? And will you give me leave?   160

ALL THE PLEBEIANS

Come down.

FOURTH PLEBEIAN Descend.

THIRD PLEBEIAN   You shall have leave.

Antony comes down

161.1 *Antony comes down*] not in F

140 **gentle friends** See Commentary, l. 72.
148 **shall** must
150 **o'ershot myself** gone further than I
should

151–2 **honourable men . . . stabbed Caesar**
Specious praise suddenly undercut by
shocking reality: Antony dramatically
abandons his pose.

FIFTH PLEBEIAN   A ring.
    Stand round.
FIRST PLEBEIAN Stand from the hearse, stand from the body.
FOURTH PLEBEIAN
    Room for Antony, most noble Antony!
ANTONY
    Nay, press not so upon me. Stand far off.
ALL THE PLEBEIANS Stand back! Room! Bear back!
ANTONY
    If you have tears, prepare to shed them now.
    You all do know this mantle. I remember
    The first time ever Caesar put it on.
    'Twas on a summer's evening in his tent,
    That day he overcame the Nervii.   170
    Look, in this place ran Cassius' dagger through.
    See what a rent the envious Casca made.
    Through this, the well-belovèd Brutus stabbed,
    And as he plucked his cursèd steel away,
    Mark how the blood of Caesar followed it,
    As rushing out of doors to be resolved
    If Brutus so unkindly knocked or no –
    For Brutus, as you know, was Caesar's angel.

---

164 **far off** *Far* often means 'farther', as at
5.3.11 (probably), and *Winter's Tale*
4.4.423 ('Farre than Deucalion off'); see
Abbott 478. In all three places F reads
'farre'.

167 **mantle** cloak, toga; see Commentary,
ll. 73–254.

170 **the Nervii** Plutarch describes these as
'the stoutest warriors of all the Belgae',
whose onset (in 57 BC) all but destroyed
the Roman army. 'Had not Caesar self
taken his shield on his arm and, flying in
amongst the barbarous people, made a
lane through them . . . there had not a
Roman escaped alive'. Consequently the
Senate decreed thanksgivings to the gods
and solemn processions 'because they
saw the danger had been marvellous
great, . . . and further the love of the
people unto him made his victory much
more famous' (*Caesar*, pp. 41–2): the
reference is a potent reminder. Not until
three years later did Antony join Caesar
in Gaul, so 'I remember' is poetic licence
as, of course, are his identifications of the

conspirators' hole-stabbings done while
he was off the scene.

172 **envious** rancorous, malevolent (a
strong sense; see Commentary, 2.1.165)

175–7 **Mark . . . knocked** A far-fetched conceit (of a kind abnormal in the play) such
as Shakespeare evolves at moments of
emotional extravagance; as in *Lucrece*,
1734–6, when an earlier Brutus, Lucius
Junius, pulls out the 'murd'rous knife' of
Lucrece's suicide, and, following it, 'Her
blood, in poor revenge, held it in chase';
and *Macbeth* 2.3.110–15 ('Here lay Dun-
can, | His silver skin laced with his golden
blood, | And his gashed stabs looked like
a breach in nature | For ruin's wasteful
entrance: there, the murderers, | . . . their
daggers | Unmannerly breeched with
gore').

176 **be resolved** learn for certain (as at
3.1.131)

177 **unkindly** both 'cruelly', and 'unnaturally' (i.e. against 'kind', or nature);
similarly at l. 180.

178 **angel** dearest friend, darling

Judge, O you gods, how dearly Caesar loved him!
This was the most unkindest cut of all;   180
For when the noble Caesar saw him stab,
Ingratitude, more strong than traitors' arms,
Quite vanquished him. Then burst his mighty heart,
And in his mantle muffling up his face,
Even at the base of Pompey's statue,
Which all the while ran blood, great Caesar fell.
O, what a fall was there, my countrymen!
Then I, and you, and all of us fell down,
Whilst bloody treason flourished over us.
O, now you weep, and I perceive you feel   190
The dint of pity. These are gracious drops.
Kind souls, what weep you when you but behold
Our Caesar's vesture wounded? Look you here!
      He removes the mantle
Here is himself, marred as you see with traitors.

FIRST PLEBEIAN

O piteous spectacle!

FOURTH PLEBEIAN   O noble Caesar!

THIRD PLEBEIAN   O woeful day!

FIFTH PLEBEIAN

O traitors! Villains!

FIRST PLEBEIAN   O most bloody sight!

FOURTH PLEBEIAN   We will be revenged.

193.1 *He . . . mantle*] *not in* F   198–9 revenged. | ALL THE PLEBEIANS Revenge! About!] GLOBE
(*subs.; conj.* White *and* Delius);   reueng'd: Reuenge | About, F

180 **most unkindest** For the double sense of
  unkindest see Commentary, l. 177; for the
  double superlative see Abbott 11.
184–6 **in his mantle . . . fell** 'When he saw
  Brutus with his sword drawn in his hand,
  then he pulled his gown over his head
  and made no more resistance, and was
  driven . . . against the base whereupon
  Pompey's image stood, which ran all of a
  gore-blood' (*Caesar*, pp. 94–5).
185 **statue** Trisyllabic, as at 2.2.76.
186 **which . . . blood** Sometimes explained as
  the old belief that a corpse bleeds afresh in
  its murderer's presence (as Henry VI's
  does before Richard in *Richard III* 1.2.55–6),
  and indeed Plutarch imagines the statue
  (*Caesar*, p. 95) avenging Pompey (killed
  in Egypt after defeat by Caesar). But

Antony, swaying the crowd to Caesar's
  cause, would be unlikely to depict him as
  a murderer, and the phrase is best taken
  as graphic detail for its own sake.
189 **flourished** The word combines multiple
  senses, e.g. 'grew rampant', 'triumphed',
  and 'brandished its sword'.
191 **dint** 'mark or impression made by a
  blow' (*OED*)
192 **what weep you** how much do you weep
194 **Here is himself** In Plutarch the citizens
  'saw his body . . . all bemangled with
  gashes of swords' (*Caesar*, p. 97; in *Brutus*
  and *Antonius* their attention is confined to
  his rent and bloody gown), but this is not
  presented as the dramatic climax Shakespeare makes it, for whom it is the clinch-
  ing of Antony's case.

ALL THE PLEBEIANS

    Revenge! About! Seek! Burn! Fire! Kill! Slay!

    Let not a traitor live!

ANTONY   Stay, countrymen.   200

FIRST PLEBEIAN

    Peace there! Hear the noble Antony.

FOURTH PLEBEIAN

    We'll hear him, we'll follow him, we'll die with him!

ANTONY

    Good friends, sweet friends, let me not stir you up

    To such a sudden flood of mutiny.

    They that have done this deed are honourable.

    What private griefs they have, alas, I know not,

    That made them do it. They are wise and honourable,

    And will no doubt with reasons answer you.

    I come not, friends, to steal away your hearts.

    I am no orator, as Brutus is,   210

    But, as you know me all, a plain blunt man

    That love my friend, and that they know full well

    That gave me public leave to speak of him.

    For I have neither wit, nor words, nor worth,

    Action, nor utterance, nor the power of speech

    To stir men's blood; I only speak right on.

    I tell you that which you yourselves do know,

    Show you sweet Caesar's wounds, poor poor dumb mouths,

---

214 wit] F2;   writ F1

199–200 **Revenge . . . live** 'Some of them cried out: "Kill the murderers". Others plucked up forms, tables, and stalls, . . . and having laid them all on a heap together, they set them on fire' (*Brutus*, p. 129).

199 **About** set about it

203–23 **Good friends . . . mutiny** Antony, in his 'honest-simple-plain-blunt-man' role, as against Brutus' alleged sophistication, flagrantly reverses the true state of things; his version is superbly designed to win the plebeians.

206 **private griefs** Antony reduces Brutus' open public principles to private grudges too obscure to be guessed at.
    griefs grievances

208 **And will . . . answer you** This implies that no reasons have yet been given, and

that any to come will be mere window-dressing.

214–16 **For I . . . blood** Kittredge comments that these qualities constitute the whole technique of good oratory – 'intellectual cleverness (*wit*); fluency (*words*); *auctoritas*, the weight that comes from character . . . (*worth*); gesture and bearing (*action*); skilful elocution (*utterance*); and "the power of speech to stir men's blood"'.

214 **wit** F's 'writ', though kept by a few editors as meaning 'script', reads awkwardly and F2's 'wit' is surely right. The 'w' alliteration through the line is part of the oratorical swing.

218 **dumb mouths** See Commentary, 3.1.260.

And bid them speak for me. But were I Brutus,
And Brutus Antony, there were an Antony   220
Would ruffle up your spirits, and put a tongue
In every wound of Caesar that should move
The stones of Rome to rise and mutiny.

ALL THE PLEBEIANS
We'll mutiny!

FIRST PLEBEIAN   We'll burn the house of Brutus!

THIRD PLEBEIAN
Away then! Come, seek the conspirators.

ANTONY
Yet hear me, countrymen, yet hear me speak.

ALL THE PLEBEIANS
Peace, ho! Hear Antony, most noble Antony.

ANTONY
Why, friends, you go to do you know not what.
Wherein hath Caesar thus deserved your loves?
Alas, you know not. I must tell you then –   230
You have forgot the will I told you of.

ALL THE PLEBEIANS
Most true! The will! Let's stay and hear the will.

ANTONY
Here is the will, and under Caesar's seal.
To every Roman citizen he gives,
To every several man, seventy-five drachmas.

FOURTH PLEBEIAN
Most noble Caesar! We'll revenge his death!

221 **ruffle up** stir to rage (a strong sense of the words, as in *Lear* 2.4.299–300 – 'the high winds | Do sorely ruffle').

221–2 **put a tongue . . . wound** Similarly *Coriolanus* 2.3.6–8 ('if he show us his wounds . . . we are to put our tongues into those wounds and speak for them').

222–3 **move | The stones** An echo of Luke 19: 40, 'If these [the disciples praising Jesus] should hold their peace, the stones would immediately cry out'.

231 **You have forgot the will** As already in stressing the display of Caesar's body (not dramatized in Plutarch; see Commentary, l. 194), Shakespeare brilliantly exploits his source, in which the reading of the will is merely a precipitating incident (*Caesar*, p. 97; *Brutus*, p. 128).

Here it becomes the climactic sign of (a) Caesar's nobility, (b) the mob's fickleness (in needing to be reminded), and (c) Antony's virtuosity.

234–42 **To every Roman citizen . . . Tiber** 'He bequeathed unto every citizen of Rome seventy-five drachmas a man, and . . . his gardens and arbours . . . on this side of the river of Tiber . . . The people then loved him and were marvellously sorry for him' (*Brutus*, p. 128). *Antonius* (p. 190) merely mentions 'three-score and fifteen silver drachmas . . . to every man'. Currencies fluctuate and no modern equivalent will long be valid but this was, as *Caesar* (p. 97) has it, 'a liberal legacy'.

THIRD PLEBEIAN O royal Caesar!

ANTONY Hear me with patience.

ALL THE PLEBEIANS Peace, ho!

ANTONY

Moreover, he hath left you all his walks,   240
His private arbours, and new-planted orchards,
On this side Tiber. He hath left them you,
And to your heirs for ever – common pleasures
To walk abroad and recreate yourselves.
Here was a Caesar! When comes such another?

FIRST PLEBEIAN

Never, never! Come, away, away!
We'll burn his body in the holy place,
And with the brands fire the traitors' houses.
Take up the body.

FOURTH PLEBEIAN Go fetch fire!   250

THIRD PLEBEIAN Pluck down benches!

FIFTH PLEBEIAN Pluck down forms, windows, anything!

Exeunt Plebeians with Caesar's body

ANTONY

Now let it work! Mischief, thou art afoot,
Take thou what course thou wilt.

Enter Antony's Servant

How now, fellow?

SERVANT

Sir, Octavius is already come to Rome.

252.1 *Exeunt*] F (*Exit*)   *with . . . body*] *not in* F   254 Take . . . fellow?] POPE;   *as two lines, breaking after* 'wilt' F   254 *Enter Antony's Servant*] F (*Enter Seruant*; *after* 'Fellow?')

237 **royal** Both 'munificent' and (virtually) 'King'.

241 **orchards** gardens (see Commentary, 2.1.0.1)

243 **pleasures** pleasure grounds, parks (*OED* 3b, giving examples between 1485 and 1633)

247–52 **We'll burn . . . anything** In Plutarch the mob 'plucked up forms, tables, and stools, . . . and setting them afire burnt the corpse' (*Caesar*, p. 97). To these details *Brutus* (p. 129) adds that the cremation was 'in the middest of the most holy places' (i.e. the temples). Appian too refers to 'an holy place' (Bullough, v. 159). Both *Caesar* and *Brutus* mention attempts to lynch the conspirators, and the firing

of their houses.

252 **windows** *Window* in Shakespeare is not always an aperture (glazed or unglazed). It can mean 'shutter' (as here, of material for burning): see discussion by Kathleen Tillotson in Appendix I of Geoffrey Tillotson, *Essays in Criticism and Research* (1942).

255 **Octavius . . . Rome** In Plutarch (*Brutus*, p. 131 ff.), Octavius reaches Rome after an interval (historically, about six weeks); then for a considerable time he is bitterly at odds with Antony. Though indicating tensions between the two Shakespeare allows no delay and links them with Lepidus at once (4.1).

ANTONY Where is he?

SERVANT

He and Lepidus are at Caesar's house.

ANTONY

And thither will I straight to visit him.

He comes upon a wish. Fortune is merry,

And in this mood will give us anything.   260

SERVANT

I heard him say Brutus and Cassius

Are rid like madmen through the gates of Rome.

ANTONY

Belike they had some notice of the people,

How I had moved them. Bring me to Octavius.   *Exeunt*

3.3   *Enter Cinna the poet, and after him the Plebeians*

CINNA

I dreamt tonight that I did feast with Caesar,

And things unluckily charge my fantasy.

I have no will to wander forth of doors,

Yet something leads me forth.

FIRST PLEBEIAN What is your name?   5

SECOND PLEBEIAN Whither are you going?

3.3.2 unluckily] F; unlucky WARBURTON   5 FIRST PLEBEIAN] F (1); *so throughout the scene, and similarly for the other plebeians*

257 **Lepidus** He appears in Plutarch, along with Antony, as among 'Caesar's chiefest friends' (*Caesar*, p. 96). He was commanding an army outside Rome at the time of the murder, entered the city the next night, and exerted considerable authority.

259–60 **Fortune . . . anything** 'This conclusion . . . carries with it an estimate of Antony's limitations as a moral being. . . . The vision of chaos, far from appalling Antony, finally attracts him' (Traversi, p. 51).

261–2 **Brutus . . . gates of Rome** The tumult 'made Brutus and Cassius more afraid than of all that was past; and therefore within a few days after they departed out of Rome' (*Caesar*, p. 98: similarly *Brutus*, p. 130). In both *Lives* this happens after Cinna's death (3.3). Shakespeare intensifies the urgency by placing it immediately after Antony's incitements.

3.3.0.1. *Cinna the poet* 'a poet called Cinna,

who had been no partaker of the conspiracy but was always one of Caesar's chiefest friends' (*Brutus*, p. 129), i.e. Gaius Helvius Cinna, friend of Catullus and author of a reputedly learned and obscure epic now all but lost: 'Catullus predicted immortality for it, but only three lines remain' (*Oxford Companion to Classical Literature*).

2 **unluckily . . . fantasy** ominously oppress my imagination. A favourable dream boded ill, since dreams and moods were supposed to go by contraries – as in *2 Henry IV* 4.2.81–2, 'Against ill chances men are ever merry, | But heaviness foreruns the good event.' In Plutarch the dream is 'marvellous strange and terrible' and in it Cinna declines the invitation to dine with Caesar (*Caesar*, p. 98). Warburton's reading 'unlucky', adopted by several editors, makes good sense and regular metre.

THIRD PLEBEIAN Where do you dwell?

FOURTH PLEBEIAN Are you a married man or a bachelor?

SECOND PLEBEIAN Answer every man directly.

FIRST PLEBEIAN Ay, and briefly.   10

FOURTH PLEBEIAN Ay, and wisely.

THIRD PLEBEIAN Ay, and truly, you were best.

CINNA What is my name? Whither am I going? Where do
I dwell? Am I a married man or a bachelor? Then to
answer every man, directly and briefly, wisely and truly:
wisely I say, I am a bachelor.

SECOND PLEBEIAN That's as much as to say they are fools
that marry. You'll bear me a bang for that, I fear. Proceed,
directly.

CINNA Directly, I am going to Caesar's funeral.   20

FIRST PLEBEIAN As a friend, or an enemy?

CINNA As a friend.

SECOND PLEBEIAN That matter is answered directly.

FOURTH PLEBEIAN For your dwelling, briefly.

CINNA Briefly, I dwell by the Capitol.

THIRD PLEBEIAN Your name, sir, truly.

CINNA Truly, my name is Cinna.

FIRST PLEBEIAN Tear him to pieces, he's a conspirator!

CINNA I am Cinna the poet! I am Cinna the poet!

FOURTH PLEBEIAN Tear him for his bad verses, tear him for   30
his bad verses!

CINNA I am not Cinna the conspirator.

FOURTH PLEBEIAN It is no matter, his name's Cinna! Pluck
but his name out of his heart, and turn him going.

12 **you were best** it would be best for you. Abbott 230 illustrates this among 'Ungrammatical remnants of ancient usage'.

16 **wisely I say . . . bachelor** This implies the proverb 'They are fools that marry' (as in l. 17).

18 **bear me a bang** put up with a blow from me

20 **Directly** Innocent word-play; (a) answering directly (b) proceeding directly.

30 **Tear him** In Plutarch the mob has 'dispatched him' (*Caesar*, p. 98) or 'torn poor Cinna the poet in pieces' (*Brutus*, p. 130).

33 **It is no matter . . . Cinna** 'The first two casualties of Brutus' reasonable rebellion are the great Caesar, whose guilt is con-

testable, and the insignificant Cinna, whose innocence is incontestable. . . . The brief glimpse of mob violence . . . fix[es] some of the real meaning of what has passed' (Styan, pp. 204–5). Gareth Lloyd Evans (*Shakespeare III*, p. 113) adduces a modern parallel from William Shirer's *Rise and Fall of the Third Reich* (1960), chap. 3, where a minor musician in Germany, Willi Schmidt, because of his name and mistaken identity was seized by Nazi thugs during a family musical evening, thrust downstairs, and never seen again. On the scene's recent rise to stage prominence see the Introduction, p. 67.

34 **turn him going** send him packing

THIRD PLEBEIAN Tear him, tear him!

> *They set upon him*

Come, brands, ho! Firebrands! To Brutus', to Cassius'!
Burn all! Some to Decius' house, and some to Casca's;
some to Ligarius'! Away! Go!

> *Exeunt all the Plebeians, dragging off Cinna*

4.1 *Enter Antony, Octavius, and Lepidus*

ANTONY

These many, then, shall die; their names are pricked.

OCTAVIUS (*to Lepidus*)

Your brother too must die. Consent you, Lepidus?

LEPIDUS

I do consent –

OCTAVIUS   Prick him down, Antony.

LEPIDUS

Upon condition Publius shall not live,
Who is your sister's son, Mark Antony.   5

ANTONY

He shall not live. Look, with a spot I damn him.
But, Lepidus, go you to Caesar's house.
Fetch the will hither, and we shall determine

35.1 *They . . . him*] *not in* F   38.1 *dragging off Cinna*] *not in* F
4.1] F (*Actus Quartus.*)

4.1.0.1 *Enter . . . Lepidus* After bitter rivalry
and even armed conflict Antony and
Octavius, along with Lepidus, 'made an
agreement . . . and . . . divided the
provinces belonging to the Empire of
Rome among themselves' (*Brutus*,
p. 137; similarly *Antonius*, p. 194).

1 **These . . . die** This plunge into ruthlessness is startling, even though the end of
3.2 anticipates it. In Plutarch, the trium-
virate 'spurned all reverence of blood and
holiness of friendship . . . For Caesar left
Cicero to Antonius' will; Antonius also
forsook Lucius Caesar, who was his uncle
by his mother; and both of them together
suffered Lepidus to kill his own brother
Paulus. Yet some writers affirm that
Caesar and Antonius requested Paulus
might be slain, and that Lepidus was contented with it' (*Antonius*, p. 194; similarly,
though in less detail, *Brutus*, p. 137).
'Henceforth [Antony] and Octavius

interest us in so far only as they are the
instruments of Caesar's vengeance'
(Kittredge): sympathy for Brutus and
Cassius, dwindling during Act 3, is to
grow as their fortunes fail.

1 **pricked** marked down (as at 3.1.216)

2 **brother** Lucius Aemilius Paulus, once
consul, supporter of Brutus (though not
seen in the play), and political enemy of
Lepidus. According to Appian and Dio
Cassius he in fact escaped execution
(Furness, p. 191).

4 **Publius** This is hardly the elderly Publius
of 3.1.85–93. Antony had no recorded
nephew of that name, but Plutarch mentions a Publius Silicius who wept when
Brutus, in absence, was arraigned by
Octavius' servile judges, and who 'shortly
after was one of the proscripts or outlaws
appointed to be slain' (*Brutus*, p. 136–7).

6 **with a spot I damn him** i.e. I prick him
down and condemn him

189

How to cut off some charge in legacies.
LEPIDUS What, shall I find you here?   10
OCTAVIUS Or here, or at the Capitol.   *Exit Lepidus*
ANTONY
    This is a slight unmeritable man,
    Meet to be sent on errands. Is it fit,
    The threefold world divided, he should stand
    One of the three to share it?
OCTAVIUS   So you thought him,
    And took his voice who should be pricked to die
    In our black sentence and proscription.
ANTONY
    Octavius, I have seen more days than you;
    And though we lay these honours on this man
    To ease ourselves of divers sland'rous loads,   20
    He shall but bear them as the ass bears gold,
    To groan and sweat under the business,
    Either led or driven as we point the way;
    And having brought our treasure where we will,
    Then take we down his load, and turn him off,
    Like to the empty ass, to shake his ears
    And graze in commons.
OCTAVIUS   You may do your will;
    But he's a tried and valiant soldier.

---

9 **cut off . . . legacies** This cynically curtails Caesar's generosity so publicized in 3.2.128 ff.

12–15 **This is . . . share it** Plutarch records that Antony was the most feared of the triumvirs, 'being elder than Caesar and of more power . . . than Lepidus' (*Antonius*, p. 195). In *Antony and Cleopatra* Lepidus is an insignificant ally of the others, in 2.7.4 ff. foolishly drunk.

14 **The threefold world** Cf. *Antony* 4.6.6 – 'the three-nooked world'. The three great regions of the empire were Europe, Asia, and Africa.
    divided The triumvirate gave Antony Gaul, Lepidus Spain, and Octavius Africa with Sicily and Sardinia.

16 **took his voice** Either (a) asked his opinion, or (b) accepted his decision.

17 **black sentence** i.e. death sentence

18 **more days than you** For the contrast of ages see Commentary, 3.1.296.

20 **divers sland'rous loads** all sorts of burdensome accusations

21–7 **the ass . . . commons** This reflects the proverb, 'The ass, though laden with gold, still eats thistles' (Tilley A360) – i.e. he is no better off. The methodical exposition of the analogy, and of that in ll. 29–35, illustrates 'the peculiar amplifications and slow movement' of similes characteristic of the play's logical style (Spurgeon, p. 346).

22 **business** (three syllables)

26 **shake his ears** take himself aimlessly off (a proverbial phrase: Tilley E16)

27 **graze in commons** 'Common lands for pasturage were in Shakespeare's day adjacent to most villages, and the horse or donkey out . . . grazing was a familiar figure' (Kittredge).

28 **soldier** (three syllables)

ANTONY

So is my horse, Octavius, and for that
I do appoint him store of provender.   30
It is a creature that I teach to fight,
To wind, to stop, to run directly on,
His corporal motion governed by my spirit,
And, in some taste, is Lepidus but so.
He must be taught, and trained, and bid go forth:
A barren-spirited fellow; one that feeds
On objects, arts, and imitations,
Which, out of use and staled by other men,
Begin his fashion. Do not talk of him
But as a property. And now, Octavius,   40
Listen great things. Brutus and Cassius
Are levying powers. We must straight make head.
Therefore let our alliance be combined,
Our best friends made, our means stretched;
And let us presently go sit in council,
How covert matters may be best disclosed
And open perils surest answerèd.

OCTAVIUS

Let us do so; for we are at the stake

44 made. . . . stretched] F1 (*subs.*); made, and our best meanes stretcht out F2; made, our
means stretch'd to the utmost MALONE; made our means and our means stretched WILSON *conj.*

30 **appoint** assign, allot
32 **wind** wheel about (a term in horse riding)
34 **taste** degree
37 **objects, arts, and imitations** Finding the
line odd, most eighteenth-century editors
read 'abject orts', i.e. scraps thrown
away: 'abjects, orts' was a variation. But
the line is not really improved, and F's
words yield an adequately contemptuous
meaning. *Objects* are any kind of
curiosities (*OED*, 'a sight, spectacle,
gazing stock'). *LLL* 4.2.64 has 'A
foolish extravagant spirit, full of forms,
figures, shapes, objects, ideas', and in
Hamlet, 3.1.172, Hamlet's disturbed
mind may be soothed on his travels 'With
variable objects'. *Arts* and *imitations* are
derivative tricks, crafts, fashions, and the
like.
39 **Begin his fashion** i.e. he takes them to be
the latest thing
40 **property** 'mere means to an end' (Onions;
OED sb. 4); mere possession. The modern

theatrical sense was also available (*sb.* 3),
as were other contemptuous senses like
'personal possession' and 'adjunct, ap-
purtenance'.
41 **Listen** Abbott 199 illustrates this use
without 'to' as alternative to 'hear'.
41–2 **Brutus . . . powers** Brutus and Cassius
'were marvellous joyful, and no less
courageous, when they saw the great
armies together which they had both
levied' (*Brutus*, p. 138).
42 **make head** advance our forces
44 **stretched** i.e. extended to the utmost. F2
and some later editions add words to
mend F's defective metre, but any change
is guesswork. Wilson's suggested line,
'Our best friends made our means and
our means stretched', is bibliographically
the most plausible.
45 **presently** at once (as elsewhere)
48–9 **at the stake . . . enemies** A bear-baiting
metaphor, with the animals tied to a
stake and mastiffs baying around;

And bayed about with many enemies;
And some that smile have in their hearts, I fear,   50
Millions of mischiefs.   *Exeunt*

4.2   *Drum. Enter Brutus, Lucilius, and the army. Titinius
           and Pindarus meet them*
BRUTUS Stand, ho!
LUCILIUS Give the word, ho, and stand!
BRUTUS
     What now, Lucilius, is Cassius near?
LUCILIUS
     He is at hand, and Pindarus is come
     To do you salutation from his master.
BRUTUS
     He greets me well. Your master, Pindarus,
     In his own charge, or by ill officers,
     Hath given me some worthy cause to wish
     Things done undone; but if he be at hand
     I shall be satisfied.
PINDARUS   I do not doubt   10
     But that my noble master will appear
     Such as he is, full of regard and honour.
BRUTUS
     He is not doubted. (*Aside*) A word, Lucilius,

4.2.0.1 *Drum . . . them*] F; *Drum. LUCILIUS marches up at the head of troops; PINDARUS, the
bondman of Cassius, with them. BRUTUS comes from the tent with LUCIUS in attendance* WILSON
7 charge] WARBURTON; change F   13–14 Lucilius, | How … you: let] F (*subs.*); Lucillius
– | How … you, let ROWE

similarly *Macbeth* 5.7.1–2 – 'They have
tied me to a stake; I cannot fly, | But bear-
like I must fight the course.'

50–1 some . . . mischiefs This (like
2.1.225–6) echoes the proverb 'To smile
in one's face and cut one's throat': Tilley
F16.
4.2.0.1–2 Enter . . . them For discussion of
the entry direction see Appendix B.
0.1 *Lucilius* 'one of Brutus' friends' (*Brutus*,
p. 167)
   Titinius 'one of Cassius' chiefest friends'
   (*Brutus*, p. 159)
0.2 *Pindarus* 'one of his [Cassius'] freed
bondmen' (*Brutus*, p. 160)
2 Give the word repeat the command
3 is Cassius near 'Brutus sent to pray

Cassius to come to the city of Sardis; and
so he did. Brutus, understanding of his
coming, went to meet him with all his
friends' (*Brutus*, p. 145).
6 greets me well sends his greetings by an
excellent messenger ('Brutus is always
courteous to servants and subordinates';
Kittredge.)
7 In his own charge by his own command.
Warburton's alteration of F's 'change'
seems convincing. The error could easily
arise in a text based on a transcript.
8 worthy good (this sense now archaic)
8–9 to wish | . . . undone A proverbial
impossibility: 'Things done cannot be
undone' (Tilley T200).
10 be satisfied receive a full explanation
12 regard consideration, respect

How he received you : let me be resolved.
LUCILIUS
   With courtesy, and with respect enough,
   But not with such familiar instances
   Nor with such free and friendly conference
   As he hath used of old.
BRUTUS   Thou hast described
   A hot friend cooling. Ever note, Lucilius,
   When love begins to sicken and decay   20
   It useth an enforcèd ceremony.
   There are no tricks in plain and simple faith ;
   But hollow men, like horses hot at hand,
   Make gallant show and promise of their mettle ;
      Low march within
   But when they should endure the bloody spur,
   They fall their crests, and like deceitful jades
   Sink in the trial. Comes his army on?
LUCILIUS
   They mean this night in Sardis to be quartered.
   The greater part, the horse in general,
   Are come with Cassius.
BRUTUS   Hark, he is arrived.   30
      Enter Cassius and his powers
   March gently on to meet him.
CASSIUS Stand, ho!
BRUTUS Stand, ho! Speak the word along.
⌜FIRST SOLDIER⌝ Stand!
⌜SECOND SOLDIER⌝ Stand!
⌜THIRD SOLDIER⌝ Stand!

30.1 *Enter . . . powers*] F (*after* 'Are come with *Cassius.*')   34 FIRST SOLDIER] CAPELL (*subs.*);
not in F (*similarly at ll. 35, 36*)

14 **resolved** put out of doubt
16 **familiar instances** marks of friendship
17 **conference** conversation
20–1 **When love . . . ceremony** Compare
   Timon 1.2.15–18 – 'ceremony was but
   devised at first | To set a gloss on faint
   deeds, hollow welcomes, | . . . | But where
   there is true friendship there needs none.'
21 **enforcèd** constrained
23 **hot at hand** eager at the outset; *at hand* is
   'at the immediate moment, at the start'
   (*OED*, Hand, *sb.* 25c). 'Soon hot, soon
   cold' was proverbial: Tilley H732.

26 **fall** For the transitive use see Abbott 291.
   crests The crest is the ridge of a horse's
   neck ; a 'high crest' (as in *Venus* 297) was
   a sign of distinction.
28 **Sardis** In Asia Minor, east of modern
   Izmir, capital of the kingdom of Lydia.
29 **horse in general** main body of cavalry
31 **gently** slowly, quietly
34–6 FIRST . . . SOLDIER 'Speak the word
   along' (l. 33) clearly points to repetition
   along the line. F indicates no speakers;
   Lucilius might be one.

CASSIUS

Most noble brother, you have done me wrong.

BRUTUS

Judge me, you gods! Wrong I mine enemies?
And if not so, how should I wrong a brother?

CASSIUS

Brutus, this sober form of yours hides wrongs,   40
And when you do them –

BRUTUS   Cassius, be content.
Speak your griefs softly. I do know you well.
Before the eyes of both our armies here,
Which should perceive nothing but love from us,
Let us not wrangle. Bid them move away.
Then in my tent, Cassius, enlarge your griefs,
And I will give you audience.

CASSIUS   Pindarus,
Bid our commanders lead their charges off
A little from this ground.

BRUTUS

Lucilius, do you the like, and let no man   50
Come to our tent till we have done our conference.
Let Lucius and Titinius guard our door.

                    Exeunt all but Brutus and Cassius

---

50 Lucilius] F (*subs.*);   Lucius WHITE (*conj.* Craik)   52 Let Lucius] F;   Lucilius WHITE (*conj.*
Craik)   52.1 *all but*] F (*Manet*)

---

37 **brother** See Commentary, 2.1.70.
41 **content** 'calm, quiet, not uneasy' (*OED*, Content, I. 1b)
42, 46 **griefs** grievances (as elsewhere)
46 **enlarge** give free expression to
48 **charges** troops
50–2 **Lucilius . . . Lucius** Most recent editions, following White's adoption of G. L. Craik's suggestion in *The English of Shakespeare* (1851), read 'Lucius' for F's 'Lucillius' in l. 50 and 'Lucilius' for F's 'Let Lucius' in l. 52, since Lucius, a servant, is likelier as a messenger than Lucilius, an officer, and Lucilius likelier than Lucius as a fellow-guard with Titinius (Brutus addresses them jointly at l. 189). But change is unnecessary. Lucilius may well relay Brutus' order, and Lucius help

guard his door. True, it is Lucilius who struggles with the poet at ll. 174.1 and 177, and Lucius takes no part until Brutus orders wine at l. 192. But Lucilius is, after all, in general command of Brutus' guard (l. 51) and he may appropriately tackle the intruder. Shakespeare may still have been indefinite about the military functions of these minor characters. Plutarch never mentions Lucius; he names Titinius only later as Cassius' battle-companion and sharer in suicide (*Brutus*, pp. 159–60; see 5.3.1–90) and Lucilius only later still as impersonating Brutus in battle (*Brutus*, p. 167; see 5.4.7–25). The orders given here are not necessarily inconsistent with Lucilius' and Lucius' roles at ll. 174.1 ff.

CASSIUS

That you have wronged me doth appear in this:
You have condemned and noted Lucius Pella
For taking bribes here of the Sardians;
Wherein my letters, praying on his side
Because I knew the man, was slighted off.

BRUTUS

You wronged yourself to write in such a case.

CASSIUS

In such a time as this it is not meet
That every nice offence should bear his comment.   60

BRUTUS

Let me tell you, Cassius, you yourself
Are much condemned to have an itching palm,
To sell and mart your offices for gold

---

53 CASSIUS] F (*subs.*);   SCENE III. | *Cassius*. POPE

53 CASSIUS . . . this Editors since Pope have
followed his lead and introduced a new
scene (4.3), to mark the change from
outside Brutus' tent to inside, but a
specific change of scene and location is
no more necessary than at 3.1.12 when
the street becomes the Capitol; it is implied in the dialogue. The guards are
assumed to be stationed at the tent
entrance, off stage.

53–356 That you . . . my lord This edition
preserves the scene's unity, but to refer
to other editions 52 should be henceforth deducted from its line-numberings.
Of the scene itself Johnson remarked
that 'The contention and reconciliation
of *Brutus* and *Cassius* is universally
celebrated', and it has always been
admired; see the Introduction, pp. 4, 49.
'I know no part of Shakespeare that
more impresses on me the belief of his
genius being superhuman' (Coleridge,
Lectures and Notes upon Shakespeare;
'*Julius Caesar*'). It indicates that Caesar's
spirit is already active, it modifies our
sense of Brutus and Cassius, it adds poignancy after their quarrel, and in their
reconciliation it restores them to our
sympathy.

53 you have wronged me Shakespeare
follows Plutarch closely but
amalgamates two quarrels. In Plutarch,
after 'tales and complaints betwixt

them', the leaders 'went into a little
chamber together and bade every man
avoid, . . . grew hot and loud, earnestly
accusing one another, and at length fell
both a-weeping' (*Brutus*, p. 145),
whereon a crazy philosopher (in the play
a poet) bursts in as in ll. 175–88. Next
day Brutus renews the quarrel over
Lucius Pella's extortions and Cassius
retorts that they cannot be over-
scrupulous at such a time.

54 condemned . . . Pella 'Brutus . . . did
condemn and noted Lucius Pella for . . .
robbery and pilfery' (*Brutus*, p. 147).
noted stigmatized·

56–7 letters . . . was Elizabethan usage
abounds in plural subjects with singular
verbs; see Abbott 333.

57 slighted off disparagingly dismissed

59–60 In such a time . . . comment 'He
greatly reproved Brutus for that he
would show himself so strait and severe,
in such a time' (*Brutus*, p. 147).

60 nice trivial
   bear his comment be subject to criticism

61–4 Let me . . . undeservers Though
making no such accusation, Plutarch
contrasts Brutus' leniency with Cassius'
extortions from those he subjugated
(*Brutus*, p. 143). This is *OED*'s earliest
example of the phrase 'itching palm'.

62 condemned to have blamed for having

63 mart traffic in

To undeservers.

CASSIUS   I an itching palm!
You know that you are Brutus that speaks this,
Or, by the gods, this speech were else your last.

BRUTUS
The name of Cassius honours this corruption,
And chastisement doth therefore hide his head.

CASSIUS Chastisement?

BRUTUS
Remember March, the Ides of March remember.   70
Did not great Julius bleed for justice' sake?
What villain touched his body, that did stab
And not for justice? What, shall one of us,
That struck the foremost man of all this world
But for supporting robbers, shall we now
Contaminate our fingers with base bribes,
And sell the mighty space of our large honours
For so much trash as may be graspèd thus?
I had rather be a dog and bay the moon
Than such a Roman.

CASSIUS   Brutus, bait not me,   80
I'll not endure it. You forget yourself
To hedge me in. I am a soldier, I,
Older in practice, abler than yourself
To make conditions.

BRUTUS
Go to! You are not, Cassius.

CASSIUS   I am.

79–80 bay ... bait] F1 ; baite ... baite F2 ; bay ... bay THEOBALD   82 soldier, I,] F ; *construed as* 'soldier, ay,' STEEVENS

70–3 **Remember ... justice** 'Brutus ... answered that he should remember the Ides of March, at which time they slew Julius Caesar; who neither pilled nor polled the country, but only was a favourer ... of all them that did rob and spoil by his countenance and authority' (*Brutus*, p. 147). This fault was never mentioned while the conspiracy was being planned.

72–3 **What villain ... justice** i.e. which of us was so villainous as to stab for any cause but justice? (Naively ironic in view

of the motives of Cassius and the rest; compare 5.5.70–3)

75 **supporting robbers** This charge (see Commentary, ll. 70–3) is quite at odds with Brutus' exoneration of Caesar at 2.1.18–21 from any abuse of his power.

79 **a dog ... moon** A proverbial image (Tilley D449) for futile protests.

83 **Older in practice** 'Cassius ... was the elder man, and also ... he had the better experience' (*Brutus*, p. 156).

84 **make conditions** arrange matters

BRUTUS I say you are not.

CASSIUS

Urge me no more, I shall forget myself.

Have mind upon your health. Tempt me no farther.

BRUTUS Away, slight man!

CASSIUS

Is't possible?

BRUTUS   Hear me, for I will speak.   90

Must I give way and room to your rash choler?

Shall I be frighted when a madman stares?

CASSIUS

O ye gods, ye gods! Must I endure all this?

BRUTUS

All this? Ay, more! Fret till your proud heart break.

Go show your slaves how choleric you are,

And make your bondmen tremble. Must I budge?

Must I observe you? Must I stand and crouch

Under your testy humour? By the gods,

You shall digest the venom of your spleen

Though it do split you; for, from this day forth,   100

I'll use you for my mirth, yea, for my laughter,

When you are waspish.

CASSIUS   Is it come to this?

BRUTUS

You say you are a better soldier.

Let it appear so; make your vaunting true,

And it shall please me well. For mine own part,

I shall be glad to learn of noble men.

96 budge] F1 (bouge), F2–3 (boudge), F4

87 **Urge** coerce, harry
88 **Tempt** provoke
91 **your rash choler** In Plutarch Cassius is 'marvellous choleric and cruel, . . . a hot, choleric, and cruel man, that would oftentimes be carried away from justice for gain' (*Brutus*, p. 139).
94 **Fret . . . heart break** There is a submerged association between these words: *fret* as well as its modern sense 'chafe, be vexed' could mean to furnish a musical instrument with frets; a *heart* was imagined as having 'strings' (as in 'heart-strings'), which could *break* (like those of an instrument). Shakespeare often puns on the

musical image in *frets*.
96 **budge** *OED* (*v.* 1b) cites this as the first of a number of instances of a sense with the conjectural definition 'to wince, flinch, shirk (after Fr. *bouger*)'; see Collation.
97 **observe** humour, defer to
   stand and crouch stand cringing
99–100 **digest . . . split you** swallow your fits of passion even though you burst. The spleen was believed the source of explosive emotions, agreeable or not. In *Troilus* 1.3.177–8 Ulysses imagines Achilles, as Patroclus mimics the Greek chiefs, crowing with laughter and crying, 'I shall split all | In pleasure of my spleen'.

CASSIUS

   You wrong me every way, you wrong me, Brutus.

   I said an elder soldier, not a better.

   Did I say 'better'?

BRUTUS   If you did, I care not.

CASSIUS

   When Caesar lived he durst not thus have moved me.   110

BRUTUS

   Peace, peace, you durst not so have tempted him.

CASSIUS I durst not?

BRUTUS No.

CASSIUS

   What, durst not tempt him?

BRUTUS   For your life you durst not.

CASSIUS

   Do not presume too much upon my love,

   I may do that I shall be sorry for.

BRUTUS

   You have done that you should be sorry for.

   There is no terror, Cassius, in your threats;

   For I am armed so strong in honesty

   That they pass by me as the idle wind,   120

   Which I respect not. I did send to you

   For certain sums of gold, which you denied me;

   For I can raise no money by vile means.

   By heaven, I had rather coin my heart,

   And drop my blood for drachmas, than to wring

   From the hard hands of peasants their vile trash

   By any indirection. I did send

   To you for gold to pay my legions,

   Which you denied me. Was that done like Cassius?

107 You . . . Brutus] ROWE; *as two lines, breaking after* 'way' F

111 **tempted** provoked (as in l. 88)

119–29 **I am armed . . . denied me**
Elizabethan drama allows characters to
praise themselves without vanity. But the
way Brutus, after condemning Cassius
for countenancing Lucius Pella, demands
money gained by Cassius' extortions
since he himself cannot stoop to such
conduct is distasteful, a sign of the idealist
so at odds with practical necessities as to
have collapsed into moral chaos.

125–6 **wring . . . vile trash** Cassius raised
funds 'with great evil will of the people'
(*Brutus*, p. 141), but Brutus was extor-
tionate too; see the Commentary on ll.
131–6.

127 **indirection** crooked means (but the
literal sense, 'roundabout route', ironically implies the dubious logic Brutus uses
here)

128 **legions** (three syllables)

Should I have answered Caius Cassius so? 130
When Marcus Brutus grows so covetous,
To lock such rascal counters from his friends,
Be ready, gods, with all your thunderbolts,
Dash him to pieces!

CASSIUS   I denied you not.

BRUTUS

You did.

CASSIUS   I did not. He was but a fool
That brought my answer back. Brutus hath rived my heart.
A friend should bear his friend's infirmities,
But Brutus makes mine greater than they are.

BRUTUS

I do not, till you practise them on me.

CASSIUS

You love me not.

BRUTUS   I do not like your faults. 140

CASSIUS

A friendly eye could never see such faults.

BRUTUS

A flatterer's would not, though they do appear
As huge as high Olympus.

CASSIUS

Come, Antony, and young Octavius, come,
Revenge yourselves alone on Cassius,
For Cassius is aweary of the world:
Hated by one he loves; braved by his brother;
Checked like a bondman; all his faults observed,
Set in a notebook, learned and conned by rote
To cast into my teeth. O, I could weep 150

131–6 **When Marcus . . . answer back** This differs somewhat from Plutarch, where Brutus asks for money after spending on his navy 'all that he could rap and rend of his side', and Cassius, against his friends' advice, 'gave him the third part of his total sum' (*Brutus*, pp. 140–1).

132 **rascal counters** wretched coins (the 'vile trash' of l. 126)

136 **rived** split

147 **braved** defied

148 **Checked** rebuked

150–5 **O, I could weep . . . heart** ' "Being a

Roman" is not like being a nice, white, marble statue . . ., and such a passage predicts the emblematic use of the lover's bleeding heart in John Ford's *'Tis Pity She's a Whore* as well as the soft, eloquent emotionalism of [Beaumont and Fletcher's] *The Maid's Tragedy* . . . Cassius proposes a ceremony, a murder and a kind of *liebestod* all at once, and the proposition and its style are expressive of his highly-charged emotional state' (Ure, p. 21).

My spirit from mine eyes! There is my dagger,
And here my naked breast; within, a heart
Dearer than Pluto's mine, richer than gold.
If that thou be'st a Roman, take it forth;
I, that denied thee gold, will give my heart.
Strike as thou didst at Caesar; for I know,
When thou didst hate him worst, thou lov'dst him better
Than ever thou lov'dst Cassius.

BRUTUS   Sheathe your dagger.
Be angry when you will, it shall have scope.
Do what you will, dishonour shall be humour.   160
O Cassius, you are yokèd with a lamb
That carries anger as the flint bears fire,
Who, much enforcèd, shows a hasty spark,
And straight is cold again.

CASSIUS   Hath Cassius lived
To be but mirth and laughter to his Brutus,
When grief and blood ill-tempered vexeth him?

BRUTUS
When I spoke that, I was ill-tempered too.

CASSIUS
Do you confess so much? Give me your hand.

BRUTUS
And my heart too.

---

151 **spirit** As well as the whole range of abstract meanings, the use of the word may be influenced by two specific contemporary meanings: in reference to the 'vital spirits' which were supposed to permeate the blood and organs (*OED sb.* 16, especially Golding, 1587, 'A mans . . . eyes faile because the Spirites of them fayle'); and 'an essence or extract' (*sb.* 21, first example 1610).

153 **Dearer** fuller of treasure
Pluto The god of the nether world (also of gold and silver mines, and corn). Some editors change to 'Plutus' (the god of riches), but the two could be confused even in classical times; Liddell and Scott's *Greek-English Lexicon*, under 'Pluto', observes 'identified with Plutus and considered as the god of riches', citing Aristophanes' *Plutus*, l. 727, and Sophocles' *Fragmenta* 273 (ed. A. C. Pearson). *Troilus* 3.3.197 refers to 'every

grain of Pluto's [F 'Plutoes'] gold' and Webster's *The Duchess of Malfi* 3.2.283 to 'Pluto, the god of riches'.

155 **that denied** i.e. that *you say* denied (Cassius is not retracting his assertion at ll. 134-6).

160 **dishonour shall be humour** Either (a) we shall not demur even at dishonourable conduct, or (b) insults shall be excused as petulant whim or eccentricity.

162-4 **flint . . . again** Tilley F371 illustrates as proverbial 'In the coldest flint there is hot fire'. The stress here, however, is on the coldness, not the fire, as in *Troilus* 3.3.257 – '[Wit] lies as coldly in him as fire in a flint, which will not show without knocking.'

166 **blood ill-tempered** ill-balanced disposition (swayed by 'rash humour'; l. 171)

166, 167 **ill-tempered** (*OED*'s first occurrence)

CASSIUS   O Brutus!
BRUTUS   What's the matter?
CASSIUS

Have not you love enough to bear with me,   170
When that rash humour which my mother gave me
Makes me forgetful?
BRUTUS   Yes, Cassius, and from henceforth,
When you are over-earnest with your Brutus,
He'll think your mother chides, and leave you so.

Enter a Poet ⌜struggling with Lucilius and Titinius;
Lucius following⌝

POET

Let me go in to see the generals!
There is some grudge between 'em; 'tis not meet
They be alone.
LUCILIUS   You shall not come to them.
POET Nothing but death shall stay me.
CASSIUS How now? What's the matter?
POET

For shame, you generals! What do you mean?   180
Love and be friends, as two such men should be,
For I have seen more years, I'm sure, than ye.
CASSIUS

Ha, ha! How vilely doth this Cynic rhyme!
BRUTUS

Get you hence, sirrah! Saucy fellow, hence!

174.1–2 *struggling . . . following*] *not in* F

171 **rash humour** hasty temper
174.1 *Poet* In Plutarch he is a would-be
    Cynic philosopher, Marcus Phaonius,
    once a friend of Cato (*Brutus*, p. 146).
    Lucilius and Titinius Editors have
    sometimes had Lucilius and Titinius al-
    ready on stage, visibly guarding the door
    throughout the preceding scene; but this
    seems ruled out by the explicit Folio direc-
    tion at 52.1, and in any case unnecessary.
    Lucius might enter later, when he is
    specifically addressed (l. 192).
180–2 **For shame . . . ye** 'with a certain scof-
    fing and mocking gesture . . . he rehear-
    sed the verses which old Nestor said in
    Homer [*Iliad* i. 259]: "My lords, I pray

you hearken both to me, | For I have seen
moe years than suchie three." Cassius fell
a-laughing at him but Brutus thrust him
out of the chamber' (*Brutus*, p. 146).
183 **Cynic** i.e. one of 'the Cynic philosophers
    (as who should say "dogs")' (*Brutus*,
    p. 146); 'one of the same school of
    philosophy as Diogenes, who carried to
    an extreme of asceticism the principle of
    contempt for ease, wealth, and the enjoy-
    ments of life; (hence) surly, rude fellow'
    (Onions).
184 **sirrah** rascal; see Commentary, 3.1.10.
    Saucy impudent (a stronger sense than
    the modern one)

CASSIUS

Bear with him, Brutus, 'tis his fashion.

BRUTUS

I'll know his humour when he knows his time.

What should the wars do with these jigging fools?

Companion, hence!

CASSIUS   Away, away, be gone!   *Exit Poet*

BRUTUS

Lucilius and Titinius, bid the commanders

Prepare to lodge their companies tonight.   190

CASSIUS

And come yourselves, and bring Messala with you

Immediately to us.   *Exeunt Lucilius and Titinius*

BRUTUS   Lucius! A bowl of wine.   *Exit Lucius*

CASSIUS

I did not think you could have been so angry.

BRUTUS

O Cassius, I am sick of many griefs.

CASSIUS

Of your philosophy you make no use

If you give place to accidental evils.

BRUTUS

No man bears sorrow better. Portia is dead.

CASSIUS Ha! Portia?

BRUTUS She is dead.

CASSIUS

How scaped I killing when I crossed you so?   200

O insupportable and touching loss!

Upon what sickness?

---

192 *Exeunt . . . Titinius*] *not in* F   *Exit Lucius*] *not in* F

185 **fashion** (three syllables)
186 **I'll . . . time** I'll put up with his freaks when he knows the right time for them.
187 **jigging** frivolous (alluding to the 'light, rapid, jerky' dance called a jig, or to the ballads – often jocular or scurrilous – of that name. The poet could accompany his own little poem with some skipping dance steps.)
188 **Companion** fellow

195 **your philosophy** This is usually taken to be Stoicism, but Brutus was not in fact a Stoic ('above all the rest he loved Plato's sect best'; *Brutus*, p. 103). Classical philosophy, which he studied devotedly, widely urged superiority to life's accidents.
201 **touching** grievous, hurtful (a stronger sense than the modern one)

BRUTUS   Impatient of my absence,
  And grief that young Octavius with Mark Antony
  Have made themselves so strong – for with her death
  That tidings came – with this she fell distract,
  And, her attendants absent, swallowed fire.

CASSIUS

  And died so?

BRUTUS   Even so.

CASSIUS   O ye immortal gods!

          Enter Boy (Lucius) with wine and tapers

BRUTUS

  Speak no more of her. Give me a bowl of wine.
  In this I bury all unkindness, Cassius.

          He drinks

CASSIUS

  My heart is thirsty for that noble pledge.   210
  Fill, Lucius, till the wine o'erswell the cup.
  I cannot drink too much of Brutus' love.

          He drinks. Exit Lucius.
          Enter Titinius and Messala

BRUTUS

  Come in, Titinius. Welcome, good Messala.
  Now sit we close about this taper here,
  And call in question our necessities.

204 strong – for] This edition; strong; for F   205 came – with] This edition; came. With F
207.1 *Boy (Lucius)*] F (*Boy*), CAPELL (*Lucius*)   209.1 *He*] not in F   212.1 *He . . . Lucius*]
not in F   213 Come . . . Messala] ROWE; *as two lines, breaking after 'Titinius'* F

202–6 **Impatient . . . fire** 'This common but
  improbable story . . . is found in Plutarch
  and other ancient writers' (Kittredge).
  Many pages after the quarrel scene, in the
  final lines of *Brutus*, Plutarch relates that
  Portia, 'determining to kill herself (her
  parents and friends carefully looking to
  her to keep her from it), took hot burning
  coals and cast them into her mouth'
  (*Brutus*, p. 173). This is told as having
  happened at some unspecified time earlier, unconnected with any particular
  crisis in Brutus' affairs. In the play it
  becomes a tragic element in his sense of
  doom.
202 **Impatient of** unable to endure (the original strong sense). Regular construction

would require 'Impatience of' but, Capell
  suggested, ' "*Impatience*" and "absence"
  concurring wounded the poet's ear; he
  put up with "Impatient" and hopes his
  reader will do so.' No more may be involved, however, than a simple misreading.
204 **her death** i.e. news of her death
205 **That tidings** Like 'news', *tidings* could
  be singular or plural.
  came – with On the replacement of F's full
  stop see Commentary, 2.1.136.
212.2 **Titinius** In view of l. 191 it is odd
  that Lucilius too does not enter.
  Messala Brutus' 'great friend' (*Brutus*, p.
  172).
215 **call in question** discuss

CASSIUS (*aside*)

Portia, art thou gone?

BRUTUS (*aside to Cassius*) No more, I pray you.

Messala, I have here receivèd letters

That young Octavius and Mark Antony

Come down upon us with a mighty power,

Bending their expedition toward Philippi.   220

MESSALA

Myself have letters of the selfsame tenor.

BRUTUS With what addition?

MESSALA

That by proscription and bills of outlawry

Octavius, Antony, and Lepidus

Have put to death an hundred senators.

BRUTUS

Therein our letters do not well agree.

Mine speak of seventy senators that died

By their proscriptions, Cicero being one.

CASSIUS

Cicero one?

MESSALA   Cicero is dead,

And by that order of proscription.   230

Had you your letters from your wife, my lord?

BRUTUS No, Messala.

MESSALA

Nor nothing in your letters writ of her?

BRUTUS

Nothing, Messala.

MESSALA   That, methinks, is strange.

BRUTUS

Why ask you? Hear you aught of her in yours?

229–30 Cicero is . . . proscription] CAPELL; *as one line* F   229 Cicero is] F; Ay, Cicero is
CAPELL   230–1 proscription. | Had] F3; proscription | Had F1   235 Why . . . yours] ROWE;
as two lines, breaking after 'you' F

220 **expedition** rapid advance
  toward Philippi Brutus and Cassius are at
  Sardis (l. 28). Philippi is far across the
  Aegean Sea in Thrace, but 'Shakespeare
  altered his map, like his clock and his
  calendar, to suit his convenience' (Wilson). His sense of Aegean geography may
  in any case have been uncertain.

225–8 **an hundred . . . one** Plutarch reports
  two hundred, 'and among that number
  Cicero was one' (*Brutus*, p. 137), or three
  hundred (*Antonius*, p. 194).
230 **proscription** (four syllables)
231–45 **Had you . . . bear it so** On the probable intended deletion of this passage see
  the Introduction, pp. 78–81.

MESSALA No, my lord.

BRUTUS

Now, as you are a Roman, tell me true.

MESSALA

Then like a Roman bear the truth I tell,

For certain she is dead, and by strange manner.

BRUTUS

Why, farewell, Portia. We must die, Messala.   240

With meditating that she must die once,

I have the patience to endure it now.

MESSALA

Even so great men great losses should endure.

CASSIUS

I have as much of this in art as you,

But yet my nature could not bear it so.

BRUTUS

Well, to our work alive. What do you think

Of marching to Philippi presently?

CASSIUS

I do not think it good.

BRUTUS   Your reason?

CASSIUS   This it is:

'Tis better that the enemy seek us;

So shall he waste his means, weary his soldiers,   250

Doing himself offence, whilst we, lying still,

Are full of rest, defence, and nimbleness.

BRUTUS

Good reasons must of force give place to better.

The people 'twixt Philippi and this ground

Do stand but in a forced affection,

For they have grudged us contribution.

The enemy, marching along by them,

By them shall make a fuller number up,

Come on refreshed, new-added, and encouraged;

241 **once** some time
244 **art** mental acquirement
249–62 **'Tis better . . . our back** 'Cassius was of opinion not to try this war at one battle, . . . considering that they were the stronger in money and the weaker in men and armours. But Brutus in contrary manner did . . . desire nothing more

than to put all to the hazard of battle, as soon as might be possible, to the end he might either quickly restore his country to her former liberty, or rid him forthwith of this miserable world' (*Brutus*, p. 152).
255, 256 **affection . . . contribution** The *-tion* is disyllabic in both words.
259 **new-added** reinforced

From which advantage shall we cut him off   260
If at Philippi we do face him there,
These people at our back.
CASSIUS   Hear me, good brother –
BRUTUS
Under your pardon. You must note beside,
That we have tried the utmost of our friends;
Our legions are brim-full, our cause is ripe.
The enemy increaseth every day;
We, at the height, are ready to decline.
There is a tide in the affairs of men
Which, taken at the flood, leads on to fortune;
Omitted, all the voyage of their life   270
Is bound in shallows and in miseries.
On such a full sea are we now afloat,
And we must take the current when it serves,
Or lose our ventures.
CASSIUS   Then, with your will, go on.
We'll along ourselves and meet them at Philippi.
BRUTUS
The deep of night is crept upon our talk,
And nature must obey necessity,
Which we will niggard with a little rest.
There is no more to say.
CASSIUS   No more. Good night.
Early tomorrow will we rise, and hence.   280

260 off] ROWE (off,); off. F   274–5 Then . . . Philippi] CAPELL; *as two lines, breaking after* 'along' F

263–75 **Under your pardon . . . Philippi** Brutus' 'solemn obstinacy' (Kittredge) is introduced by patronizing courtesy (like the 'By your pardon' of 3.1.235) and once more overrules the sounder judgement of Cassius, who explains his forebodings at 5.1.74–6.

268–71 **There . . . miseries** Aphorisms about opportunities irretrievably lost abound from antiquity. Kittredge cites, from *Cato's Distichs* ii. 26 (an Elizabethan school text), Latin lines against missing the apt occasion, since Opportunity has long locks in front for catching but is bald behind. Similar adages occur in Chaucer, *Troilus and Criseyde* ii. 281–7; Fletcher, *The Custom of the Country* 2.3.63–8 and *Rollo, or, The Bloody Brother* 2.1.3–8; Chapman's *Bussy D'Ambois* 1.1.113–17; and elsewhere. Tilley lists proverbs on taking the time and tide: T283, 312, 313, 323, and 334.

274 **ventures** undertakings (particularly in the specific sense of investments in cargoes of trading voyages)

278 **Which we will niggard** which (i.e. nature) we will treat sparely

BRUTUS

Lucius!

Enter Lucius

My gown.   *Exit Lucius*

Farewell, good Messala.

Good night, Titinius. Noble, noble Cassius,

Good night, and good repose.

CASSIUS   O my dear brother,

This was an ill beginning of the night.

Never come such division 'tween our souls!

Let it not, Brutus.

Enter Lucius with the gown

BRUTUS   Everything is well.

CASSIUS

Good night, my lord.

BRUTUS   Good night, good brother.

TITINIUS *and* MESSALA

Good night, Lord Brutus.

BRUTUS   Farewell, every one.

Exeunt Cassius, Titinius, and Messala

Give me the gown. Where is thy instrument?

LUCIUS

Here in the tent.

BRUTUS   What, thou speak'st drowsily?   290

Poor knave, I blame thee not, thou art o'erwatched.

Call Claudius and some other of my men.

I'll have them sleep on cushions in my tent.

---

281 *Enter Lucius*] F *(after l. 280)*   *Exit Lucius*] *not in* F   288.1 *Cassius . . . Messala*] *not in* F
292 Claudius] Q5, ROWE;   *Claudio* F;   *so for rest of scene*

---

281 **Lucius** See Commentary, 2.1.1.
281–8 **Farewell . . . every one** In this parting Brutus completely restores himself after his intractability. For Cassius' 'O my dear brother', see Commentary, 2.1.70.
287 **my lord** Unexpectedly reverential, but a moving tribute.
289–325 **Give me . . . comes here** 'The low-pitched tone, . . . the kind courteous words, . . . create an atmosphere which by its very quietness and intimacy arouses expectation' (W. H. Clemen, *Shakespeare's Dramatic Art*, 1972, p. 57).

289 **instrument** Presumably a lute. Cassius 'hears no music' (1.2.204): Brutus' wish for it, as for reading, reveals his sensitive private nature.
291 **knave** lad (often used affectionately) **o'erwatched** tired out with being too long awake
292, 294 **Claudius . . . Varro** F names them Claudio and Varrus throughout this scene. On the change see the Introduction, p. 74. They do not appear in Plutarch.

LUCIUS Varro, and Claudius!
          Enter Varro and Claudius
VARRO Calls my lord?
BRUTUS

I pray you, sirs, lie in my tent and sleep.
It may be I shall raise you by and by
On business to my brother Cassius.

VARRO

So please you, we will stand and watch your pleasure.

BRUTUS

I will not have it so. Lie down, good sirs.   300
It may be I shall otherwise bethink me.
          Varro and Claudius lie down
Look, Lucius, here's the book I sought for so;
I put it in the pocket of my gown.

LUCIUS

I was sure your lordship did not give it me.

BRUTUS

Bear with me, good boy, I am much forgetful.
Canst thou hold up thy heavy eyes awhile,
And touch thy instrument a strain or two?

LUCIUS

Ay, my lord, an't please you.

BRUTUS   It does, my boy.
I trouble thee too much, but thou art willing.

LUCIUS It is my duty, sir.   310

BRUTUS

I should not urge thy duty past thy might.
I know young bloods look for a time of rest.

LUCIUS I have slept, my lord, already.

294 Varro] Q5, ROWE; *Varrus* F; *so for rest of scene   299 So . . . pleasure] ROWE; *as two lines,*
breaking after* 'stand' F   300 will] F2; will it F1   301.1 *Varro . . . down*] *not in* F

297 **raise you** call you up, rouse you
299 **watch your pleasure** stay awake for
   your service
302–16 **Look, . . . good to thee** 'This kind of
   natural incident, which the more "classical" of the Elizabethans would have
   regarded as beneath the dignity of
   tragedy, is . . . the genuine Shakespearean touch' (Kittredge).
302 **here's the book** 'when others slept, or
   thought what would happen the morrow

after, he fell to his book, and wrote all day
long till night' (*Brutus*, p. 105); 'He never
slept in the day time, and in the night no
longer than the time he was driven to be
alone. . . . after he had slumbered a little
after supper, he spent all the rest of the
night in dispatching of his weightiest
causes; and after he had taken order for
them, if he had any leisure left him, he
would read some book' (*Brutus*, p. 148).

BRUTUS

It was well done, and thou shalt sleep again;
I will not hold thee long. If I do live,
I will be good to thee.

    Music, and a song. Lucius falls asleep
This is a sleepy tune. O murd'rous slumber!
Layest thou thy leaden mace upon my boy,
That plays thee music? Gentle knave, good night.
I will not do thee so much wrong to wake thee.   320
If thou dost nod, thou break'st thy instrument;
I'll take it from thee; and, good boy, good night.
Let me see, let me see – is not the leaf turned down
Where I left reading? Here it is, I think.

    Enter the Ghost of Caesar
How ill this taper burns! Ha! Who comes here?
I think it is the weakness of mine eyes
That shapes this monstrous apparition.
It comes upon me. Art thou any thing?
Art thou some god, some angel, or some devil,

316.1 *Lucius . . . asleep*] not in F

316.1 *a song* By eighteenth-century
tradition 'Orpheus with his lute' (*Henry
VIII* 3.1.3–14) was sung here as 'very
appropriate' (Granville-Barker, p. 130).
As no words are given, modern directors
often content themselves with a few
strains of incidental music. F. W. Stern-
feld, *Music in Shakespearean Tragedy*
(1963), suggests as suitable to this 'scene
of dramatic importance and poignancy'
Dowland's 'Weep you no more, sad foun-
tains' (p. 81), though, as he remarks,
'any sleepy tune' will do (p. 21).
318 **leaden mace** The bailiff or sergeant
arrested offenders by touching them with
his rod of authority, *leaden* here because
of the weight of sleep. In Spenser, *The
Faerie Queene* I. iv. 44, at nightfall in the
House of Pride, 'Morpheus had with
leaden mace | Arrested all that courtly
company'.
324.1 *the Ghost of Caesar* Plutarch does not
present the apparition as Caesar's, but
Valerius Maximus' *Acta et Dicta
Memorabilia* I. viii. 8 relates that Caesar's
figure, of more than mortal stature,
haunted Cassius before the battle of

Philippi (Furness, p. 234), and tradition
naturally took it that the murdered man's
spirit was seeking retribution, as it does
very prominently in *Caesar's Revenge* (see
the Introduction, p. 26). In Plutarch, 'the
ghost that appeared unto Brutus showed
plainly that the gods were offended with
the murder of Caesar' (*Caesar*, p. 99), and
the natural inference is that it is Caesar's.
325 **How ill ... burns** The dimming, or turning blue, of lamplight was the sign of a
ghost or evil spirit; in *Richard III* 5.3.180
'The lights burn blue' as the spectres
haunt Richard. In Plutarch Brutus
'thought he heard a noise at his tent
door; and, looking towards the light of
the lamp that waxed very dim, he saw a
horrible vision' (*Caesar*, p. 100).
327–31 **this monstrous apparition ... what
thou art** The ghost is like Caesar but it
may be deceptive – 'the devil hath power
| T'assume a pleasing shape' (*Hamlet*
2.2.595–6). Brutus soon identifies it
(5.5.17–19).
monstrous abnormal, portentous (but
also 'of a wonderful greatness and dreadful look'; *Caesar*, p. 100).

That mak'st my blood cold, and my hair to stare?   330
Speak to me what thou art.

GHOST

Thy evil spirit, Brutus.

BRUTUS   Why com'st thou?

GHOST

To tell thee thou shalt see me at Philippi.

BRUTUS Well; then I shall see thee again?

GHOST Ay, at Philippi.

BRUTUS

Why, I will see thee at Philippi then.   *Exit Ghost*
Now I have taken heart thou vanishest.
Ill spirit, I would hold more talk with thee.
Boy! Lucius! Varro! Claudius! Sirs, awake!
Claudius!   340

LUCIUS The strings, my lord, are false.

BRUTUS

He thinks he still is at his instrument.
Lucius, awake!

LUCIUS My lord?

BRUTUS

Didst thou dream, Lucius, that thou so criedst out?

LUCIUS

My lord, I do not know that I did cry.

BRUTUS

Yes, that thou didst. Didst thou see anything?

LUCIUS Nothing, my lord.

BRUTUS

Sleep again, Lucius. Sirrah Claudius!
(*To Varro*) Fellow, thou, awake!

---

336 *Exit Ghost*] *not in* F   349–50 Claudius! | (*To Varro*) Fellow, thou] CAPELL (*subs.*);   *Claudio*,
Fellow, | Thou F

---

330 **stare** stand on end, as in *Tempest*
  1.2.213 – 'with hair up-staring, then like
  reeds, not hair'
332–53 **Thy evil spirit . . . my lord** 'Brutus
  boldly asked what he was, a god or a
  man. . . . The spirit answered him: "I am
  thy evil spirit, Brutus; and thou shalt see
  me by the city of Philippes." Brutus, being
  no otherwise afraid, replied again unto it:
  "Well, then I shall see thee again." The

spirit presently vanished away; and
Brutus called his men unto him, who told
him that they heard no noise, nor saw
anything at all' (*Brutus*, p. 149). *Caesar's*
account is very similar, but the spirit is
'thy ill angel' (*Caesar*, p. 100); Shakespeare catches up both phrases.
334–6 **shall see . . . will see** The *shall* is simple
  futurity; the *will* is conscious resolution.
341 **false** out of tune

VARRO   My lord?
CLAUDIUS   My lord?   350
BRUTUS

Why did you so cry out, sirs, in your sleep?
VARRO *and* CLAUDIUS

Did we, my lord?
BRUTUS   Ay. Saw you anything?
VARRO

No, my lord, I saw nothing.
CLAUDIUS   Nor I, my lord.
BRUTUS

Go and commend me to my brother Cassius.
Bid him set on his powers betimes before,
And we will follow.
VARRO *and* CLAUDIUS   It shall be done, my lord.   *Exeunt*

5.1   *Enter Octavius, Antony, and their army*
OCTAVIUS

Now, Antony, our hopes are answerèd.
You said the enemy would not come down,
But keep the hills and upper regions.
It proves not so. Their battles are at hand;
They mean to warn us at Philippi here,   5
Answering before we do demand of them.
ANTONY

Tut, I am in their bosoms, and I know
Wherefore they do it. They could be content
To visit other places, and come down

352 VARRO *and* CLAUDIUS] F (*Both.*);   *so also at l.* 356
5.1] F (*Actus Quintus*)

355 **set . . . before** advance his forces without
  delay
5.1.3 keep the hills Plutarch writes of 'the
  valley between both camps [called] the
  Philippian fields' (*Brutus*, p. 151), though
  also of Antony and Octavius as occupy-
  ing marshy seaside ground. Appian IV.
  xiii. 105 describes Philippi itself as
  crowning a precipitous hill, but clearly
  Shakespeare takes it to be on the same
  low level as the army of Antony and
  Octavius; see l. 5.
  regions (three syllables)

4 **battles** forces (*OED*, Battle, *sb.* II. 8 – 'a
  body . . . of troops in battle array'; archaic
  since *c.* 1700)
5 **warn** challenge, defy
  at Philippi Historically, the opponents
  met at Philippi early in 42 BC, but the
  battle took place only the following
  autumn.
6 **Answering . . . demand of them** taking
  the initiative that should be ours (*demand*
  means 'ask')
7 **am in their bosoms** have means of knowing their secrets

With fearful bravery, thinking by this face   10
To fasten in our thoughts that they have courage.
But 'tis not so.
          Enter a Messenger
MESSENGER   Prepare you, generals:
The enemy comes on in gallant show.
Their bloody sign of battle is hung out,
And something to be done immediately.

ANTONY

Octavius, lead your battle softly on,
Upon the left hand of the even field.

OCTAVIUS

Upon the right hand I; keep thou the left.

ANTONY

Why do you cross me in this exigent?

OCTAVIUS

I do not cross you; but I will do so.   20
          Drum, beating a march. Enter Brutus, Cassius, and
          their army, with Lucilius, Titinius, and Messala

BRUTUS They stand and would have parley.

CASSIUS

Stand fast, Titinius. We must out and talk.

OCTAVIUS

Mark Antony, shall we give sign of battle?

20.1 *Drum . . . march.*] F (*March.* [*against l. 20*] | *Drum.*)   20.2 *with Lucilius . . . Messala*] *not in* F

10 **With fearful bravery** 'In magnificent
array, but with timorous hearts'
(Kittredge). Plutarch writes of the 'bravery and rich furniture' and the 'bravery of
armour and weapon' distinguishing
Brutus' army, but far from suggesting
that this was to mask fear he describes it
as 'an encouragement unto them that by
nature are greedy of honour [which]
maketh them also fight like devils'
(*Brutus*, p. 151).
  face putting a brave face on it
14 **bloody sign of battle** 'the signal of battle
was set out . . . which was an arming
scarlet coat' (*Brutus*, p. 154); similarly
Chapman's *Caesar and Pompey*, c.1603,
3.2.97–9 – 'Hang out of my tent | My
crimson coat of arms, to give my soldiers
| That ever-sure sign of resolved-for fight'.

16 **softly** warily
17–18 **left hand . . . right hand** In Plutarch
it is Brutus who insists on leading the
right wing, 'the which men thought was
far meeter for Cassius, both because he
was the elder man, and also for that he
had the better experience' (*Brutus*, pp.
155–6). Shakespeare transfers the contention to the opposite camp, showing
Antony and Octavius as potential rivals.
19 **cross me . . . exigent** oppose me at this
critical point
20 **I do not . . . do so** I am not opposing you
but I will have it so. Kittredge notes the
'cold imperturbability' which charac-
terized the historical Augustus', i.e.
Octavius (on whom the honorary title of
'Augustus' was conferred in 27 BC).

ANTONY

No, Caesar, we will answer on their charge.

Make forth, the generals would have some words.

OCTAVIUS Stir not until the signal.

BRUTUS

Words before blows; is it so, countrymen?

OCTAVIUS

Not that we love words better, as you do.

BRUTUS

Good words are better than bad strokes, Octavius.

ANTONY

In your bad strokes, Brutus, you give good words.   30

Witness the hole you made in Caesar's heart,

Crying 'Long live! Hail, Caesar!'

CASSIUS   Antony,

The posture of your blows are yet unknown;

But, for your words, they rob the Hybla bees,

And leave them honeyless.

ANTONY Not stingless too?

BRUTUS O yes, and soundless too!

For you have stol'n their buzzing, Antony,

And very wisely threat before you sting.

ANTONY

Villains! You did not so when your vile daggers   40

Hacked one another in the sides of Caesar.

You showed your teeth like apes, and fawned like hounds,

30 words.] words F   36 too?] DELIUS; too. F   42 You . . . hounds] ROWE; *as two lines,*
breaking after 'Apes' F   teeth] F3; teethes F1

24 **answer on their charge** counter when-
     ever they attack (whether with verbal or
     armed assault)
27 **Words before blows** The phrase varies the
     proverbial tag 'Not words but deeds'
     (Tilley W820). This is the primitive prac-
     tice of exchanging insults before battle, of
     which there are many examples in
     Elizabethan drama – e.g. *1 Henry VI*
     1.3.29 ff. and 3.2.41 ff.; *3 Henry VI*
     1.4.27 ff. and 2.2.81 ff.; *Romeo* 1.1.41 ff.;
     Coriolanus 1.8.1. ff.; *Cymbeline* 4.2.71 ff.
33 **The posture . . . are** how you will strike
     your blows is (the verb attracted into the
     plural by *blows*; see Abbott 412)
     posture *OED*'s first occurrence (1605) is
     antedated by this instance.
34 **Hybla** A district in Sicily famous for

honey; in *1 Henry IV* 1.2.40 the Hostess
is praised as being sweet 'As the honey of
Hybla'.
35 **honeyless** (*OED*'s first occurrence)
37 **soundless** (*OED*'s first occurrence in this
     sense)
41 **Hacked one another** Together with the
     portrayal of hypocritical and treacherous
     malevolence (ll. 42–3) Antony recalls the
     murderers' ferocity, despite Brutus' noble
     intentions, Caesar being 'hacked and
     mangled' (*Caesar*, p. 94; similarly *Brutus*,
     p. 124).
42 **like apes** i.e. grinning with subhuman
     menace
     fawned like hounds See Commentary,
     3.1.43, for canine fawning and flattery.

And bowed like bondmen, kissing Caesar's feet;
Whilst damnèd Casca, like a cur, behind
Struck Caesar on the neck. O you flatterers!
CASSIUS
Flatterers? Now, Brutus, thank yourself!
This tongue had not offended so today
If Cassius might have ruled.
OCTAVIUS
Come, come, the cause. If arguing make us sweat,
The proof of it will turn to redder drops.   50
Look, I draw a sword against conspirators.
When think you that the sword goes up again?
Never till Caesar's three-and-thirty wounds
Be well avenged, or till another Caesar
Have added slaughter to the sword of traitors.
BRUTUS
Caesar, thou canst not die by traitors' hands
Unless thou bring'st them with thee.
OCTAVIUS   So I hope.
I was not born to die on Brutus' sword.
BRUTUS
O, if thou wert the noblest of thy strain,
Young man, thou couldst not die more honourable.   60
CASSIUS
A peevish schoolboy, worthless of such honour,
Joined with a masquer and a reveller!
ANTONY
Old Cassius still!
OCTAVIUS   Come, Antony. Away!
Defiance, traitors, hurl we in your teeth.

47–8 **This tongue ... ruled** 'The first fault he
  [Brutus] did was when he would not consent . . . that Antonius should be slain;
  and . . . thereby . . . saved . . . a strong and
  grievous enemy' (*Brutus*, pp. 127–8).
50 **proof of it** trial (in battle)
53 **three-and-thirty** In Plutarch 'three-and-
  twenty' (*Caesar*, p. 95).
54–5 **another Caesar . . . slaughter** i.e. I
  myself have fallen a further victim
59 **strain** stock, lineage
61 **peevish** silly (a common Elizabethan

sense, rather than 'irritable')
61–3 **schoolboy ... Old Cassius** On Octavius'
  youthfulness see Commentary, 3.1.296.
  Old Cassius combines a reference to
  Cassius' years with the taunt, 'The same
  scornful Cassius as ever'.
62 **masquer . . . reveller** See Commentary,
  2.1.190 and 2.2.116. The words have an
  Elizabethan flavour. Plutarch refers
  repeatedly to Antony's dissipations (e.g.
  Antonius pp. 175, 177, 183, 195, 197).

If you dare fight today, come to the field:
If not, when you have stomachs.

> *Exeunt Octavius, Antony, and their army*

CASSIUS

Why now, blow wind, swell billow, and swim bark!
The storm is up, and all is on the hazard.

BRUTUS

Ho, Lucilius! Hark, a word with you.

LUCILIUS *(standing forth)* My lord?   70

> *Brutus and Lucilius converse apart*

CASSIUS

Messala.

MESSALA *(standing forth)* What says my general?

CASSIUS   Messala,

This is my birthday; as this very day
Was Cassius born. Give me thy hand, Messala.
Be thou my witness that against my will –
As Pompey was – am I compelled to set
Upon one battle all our liberties.
You know that I held Epicurus strong,
And his opinion. Now I change my mind,
And partly credit things that do presage.

66.1 *Exeunt*] F (*Exit*)   *their*] *not in* F   67 Why . . . bark] ROWE;   *as two lines, breaking after*
'Billow' F   70, 71 *standing forth*] *Lucillius and Messala stand forth* F (*after l. 69*)   70.1 *Brutus*
. . . apart] *not in* F   71–2 Messala, | This . . . very day] POPE (*subs.*);   *as one line in* F

---

66 **stomachs** appetites (for battle)

67–8 **Why now . . . hazard** Similarly *Macbeth*
5.5.51–2 – 'Blow wind, come wrack, | At
least we'll die with harness on our back.'

68 **on the hazard** in jeopardy, a matter of
chance

72–6 **my birthday . . . liberties** Cassius
'supped . . . with a few of his friends, and
. . . looked very sadly, . . . and . . . took
[Messala] by the hand, and holding him
fast . . . told him . . . "I . . . make thee my
witness, that I am compelled against my
mind and will, as Pompey the Great was,
to jeopard the liberty of our country to the
hazard of a battle."' He then invited
Messala to supper the following night
'because it was his birthday' (*Brutus*, pp.
153–4).

72 **as this very day** For *as* used redundantly
with expressions of time see Abbott 114.
A similar usage occurs in *Measure*
5.1.73–4 – 'One Lucio, | As then the

messenger', and in the Anglican Collect
for Christmas Day – 'as at this time to be
born of a pure Virgin'.

75 **As Pompey was** With inexperienced
troops Pompey wished to avoid battle
before Pharsalus, in Thessaly, but he
yielded to their impatience and was utter-
ly defeated, 48 BC.

77–90 **You know . . . partly** Plutarch mentions that Cassius was an Epicurean
(*Caesar*, p. 92; *Brutus*, p. 149).
Epicureans held supernatural beings to
be indifferent to worldly affairs and not to
influence them. Nevertheless, before the
murder Cassius 'did softly call upon
[Pompey's image] to aid him' (*Caesar*, p.
92), and before the battle, as in l. 94, he
prayed the gods for aid (*Brutus*, p. 154).
'Certain unlucky signs', also, appeared to
him, including 'fowls of prey, that feed
upon dead carcases, . . . which began
somewhat to alter Cassius' mind from

Coming from Sardis, on our former ensigns   80
Two mighty eagles fell, and there they perched,
Gorging and feeding from our soldiers' hands,
Who to Philippi here consorted us.
This morning are they fled away and gone,
And in their steads do ravens, crows, and kites
Fly o'er our heads and downward look on us
As we were sickly prey. Their shadows seem
A canopy most fatal, under which
Our army lies, ready to give up the ghost.

MESSALA
Believe not so.

CASSIUS   I but believe it partly,   90
For I am fresh of spirit and resolved
To meet all perils very constantly.

BRUTUS
Even so, Lucilius.
            He rejoins Cassius

CASSIUS   Now, most noble Brutus,
The gods today stand friendly, that we may,
Lovers in peace, lead on our days to age!
But since the affairs of men rest still incertain,
Let's reason with the worst that may befall.
If we do lose this battle, then is this

---

80 ensigns] This edition (*conj.* W. N. Lettsom *in* Cambridge);   Ensigne F   93 *He rejoins Cassius*]
not in F   96 rest] ROWE;   rests F

Epicurus' opinions' (*Brutus*, pp. 151–2).
In Plutarch, as in the play (4.2.248–52),
Cassius counsels delay.

80–4 **Coming from Sardis . . . gone** 'When
they raised their camp, there came two
eagles that, flying with a marvellous
force, lighted upon two of the foremost
ensigns, and always followed the soldiers,
which gave them meat, and fed them,
until they came near to the city of
Philippes; and there, one day only before
the battle, they both flew away' (*Brutus*,
p. 150). Plutarch mentions this merely
incidentally, not as one of Cassius'
forebodings.

80 **former ensigns** foremost standards. F
reads 'Ensigne', but one ensign would
hardly accommodate two eagles, and in
view also of Plutarch's 'two of the former

ensigns' Lettsom's conjectured plural
need not be resisted.

83 **Who** i.e. which

85 **ravens, crows, and kites** Scavenging
birds of ill omen.

88 **fatal** deadly, of destined doom

89 **give up the ghost** The phrase was already
a commonplace (*OED*, ghost, *sb.* 1).

94 **The gods . . . stand** may the gods stand
(the subjunctive mood)

95 **Lovers** dear friends

97 **Let's reason . . . befall** Tilley W912
illustrates as proverbial, apropos this line,
'It is good to fear the worst', but the sense
is rather, 'Let us see how to counter the
worst that may happen', probably in the
sense of *Troilus* 3.2.70 – 'To fear the
worst oft cures the worse'.
reason with consider, take account of

The very last time we shall speak together.
What are you then determinèd to do?   100
BRUTUS

Even by the rule of that philosophy
By which I did blame Cato for the death
Which he did give himself – I know not how,
But I do find it cowardly and vile,
For fear of what might fall, so to prevent
The time of life – arming myself with patience
To stay the providence of some high powers
That govern us below.
CASSIUS   Then, if we lose this battle,
You are contented to be led in triumph
Thorough the streets of Rome?   110
BRUTUS

No, Cassius, no. Think not, thou noble Roman,
That ever Brutus will go bound to Rome.
He bears too great a mind. But this same day
Must end that work the Ides of March begun,
And whether we shall meet again I know not.
Therefore our everlasting farewell take.
For ever and for ever farewell, Cassius!
If we do meet again, why, we shall smile.
If not, why then this parting was well made.

111 No . . . Roman] ROWE; *as two lines, breaking after* 'no' F

101–8 **Even . . . below** In the ancient world
there were two main attitudes to suicide:
(a) a man should endure all (Socrates, in
Phaedo, 62b); (b) a man may choose his
end (Seneca, *Epistles*, lxx; *De Providentia*,
ii. 12).
102 **I did blame Cato** See Commentary,
2.1.296.
105 **fall** befall, chance
105–6 **prevent | The time** forestall the due
ending
107 **To stay . . . powers** to await the designs
of whatever gods there be
111 **No, Cassius, no** Brutus' apparent self-
contradiction does not occur in Amyot's
French version of Plutarch, where Brutus
says that when young he wrongly
blamed Cato but now he thinks him right.
The confusion originated with North. In
his version Brutus says that, when a

young man, 'I trust . . . a certain rule of
philosophy' (condemning suicide) but
now, endangered, he thinks otherwise
(*Brutus*, p. 155). 'I trust' sounds like his
present view but is the shortened past
form (= 'trusted'; Abbott 341). Even
with North's ambiguity Brutus may be
taken as saying that to kill oneself merely
to avoid uncertain dangers is wrong, but
that actual capture is not to be borne.
'Before defeat, one rises above panic fear
by "patience"; faced with defeat and dis-
grace, one maintains greatness of mind
by choosing suicide' (Brower, p. 233).
114 **the Ides of March** 'I [Brutus] gave up my
life for my country in the Ides of March,
for the which I shall live in another more
glorious world' (*Brutus*, p. 155).
116 **everlasting farewell** farewell as if for
ever (they do in fact never meet again)

CASSIUS

For ever and for ever farewell, Brutus!   120
If we do meet again we'll smile indeed.
If not, 'tis true this parting was well made.

BRUTUS

Why then, lead on. O that a man might know
The end of this day's business ere it come!
But it sufficeth that the day will end,
And then the end is known. Come, ho, away!

Exeunt

5.2   *Alarum. Enter Brutus and Messala*

BRUTUS

Ride, ride, Messala, ride, and give these bills
Unto the legions on the other side.

Loud alarum

Let them set on at once, for I perceive
But cold demeanour in Octavius' wing,
And sudden push gives them the overthrow.   5
Ride, ride, Messala! Let them all come down!

Exeunt

5.2.4 Octavius'] POPE; *Octavio's* F

5.2.0.1 *Alarum* Summons to arms by drum or trumpet, 'A technical term for offstage noises during battle sequences' (Taylor, Commentary to 3.0.33.1 of the Oxford *Henry V*, quoting Gervase Markham's *The Soldier's Accidence* (1625), as requiring all soldiers when campaigning to learn 'all the sounds or beatings of the drum' (p. 8) relating to 'a call, a march, . . . a charge, a retreat' (p. 16)).

Enter Brutus and Messala Their re-entry immediately after their *Exeunt* in scene 1 is surprising, as also is the re-entry at the start of 5.4 of those who have just left in 5.3. The rush of battle no doubt explains these sudden irruptions. Irwin Smith, in 'Their Exits and Entrances', in *Shakespeare Quarterly*, 18 (1967), 7–16 finds sixteen points in Shakespeare where characters re-enter at once after leaving, and twenty-four others at which only alarums and excursions intervene. Flavius and Marullus come in at 1.2.0 but a short time is assumed to have elapsed since they left at 1.1.75, and they re-enter merely as onlookers.

1–2 give . . . side 'Brutus, that led the right wing, sent little bills [i.e. dispatches] to the colonels and captains . . . in the which he wrote the word of the battle' (*Brutus*, p. 156). However defective in political strategy, Brutus wages war vigorously and indeed routs Octavius' forces (ll. 4–5), though his over-impetuous troops (5.3.5–8) squander their advantage (*Brutus*, p. 157).

2.1 *Loud alarum* F's *Lowd Alarum* may be an error for *Lowe Alarum*, final 'd' and 'e' being often confused in Shakespeare's writing. At 5.5.23.1 *Loud Alarums* in some copies of F was proof-corrected to *Low Alarums* (see the Introduction, pp. 82–3). Loud alarums were normally used only for special effects, and their occurrence within dialogue is exceptional. But perhaps the urgency of the situation here calls for particular emphasis.

4 Octavius' In F, '*Octavio's*'; see the Introduction, p. 74.

6 come down i.e. speed to the attack (the conspirators' troops being above their opponents)

5.3 *Alarums. Enter Cassius and Titinius*

CASSIUS

O, look, Titinius, look, the villains fly!
Myself have to mine own turned enemy.
This ensign here of mine was turning back;
I slew the coward and did take it from him.

TITINIUS

O Cassius, Brutus gave the word too early,
Who having some advantage on Octavius
Took it too eagerly. His soldiers fell to spoil,
Whilst we by Antony are all enclosed.

            Enter Pindarus

PINDARUS

Fly further off, my lord, fly further off!
Mark Antony is in your tents, my lord.   10
Fly, therefore, noble Cassius, fly far off!

CASSIUS

This hill is far enough. Look, look, Titinius —
Are those my tents where I perceive the fire?

TITINIUS

They are, my lord.

CASSIUS   Titinius, if thou lovest me,
Mount thou my horse and hide thy spurs in him,
Till he have brought thee up to yonder troops
And here again, that I may rest assured
Whether yon troops are friend or enemy.

TITINIUS

I will be here again, even with a thought.   *Exit*

5.3.1–50 **O, look ... note of him** The details closely follow Plutarch, who tells of Cassius' efforts to rally his men and save his standard, his complaint of Brutus' impetuosity, Antony's destruction of his camp, his retirement to a little hill, his poor sight, Titinius' sortie to identify a troop of riders, the way they surround him shouting and, though friends, are mistaken for enemies, Cassius' suicide with Pindarus' help, and Pindarus' disappearance.

1 **the villains fly** These are Cassius' men, unsupported by Brutus' forces and routed by Antony's (ll. 51–3 and *Brutus*, p. 157).

3 **ensign** standard-bearer; *it* in l. 4 is the standard itself. 'Perceiving his footmen to give ground, [Cassius] did what he could to keep them from flying, and took an ensign from one of the ensign-bearers that fled' (*Brutus*, p. 159). Plutarch does not say that the man was slain.

11 **far** Probably 'farther'; see Commentary, 3.2.164.

19 **with a thought** as swiftly as thought; similarly *Antony* 4.14.9–10 – 'even with a thought | The rack dislimns' – and *Tempest* 4.1.164 – 'Come, with a thought'. The idea was proverbial (Tilley, T240).

CASSIUS

Go, Pindarus, get higher on that hill;   20
My sight was ever thick. Regard Titinius,
And tell me what thou not'st about the field.
    Pindarus goes up
This day I breathèd first – time is come round,
And where I did begin, there shall I end;
My life is run his compass. (*To Pindarus*) Sirrah, what
    news?

PINDARUS (*above*) O my lord!

CASSIUS What news?

PINDARUS

Titinius is enclosèd round about
With horsemen that make to him on the spur,
Yet he spurs on. Now they are almost on him.   30
Now, Titinius! Now some light. O, he lights too!
He's ta'en! (*Shout*) And hark! They shout for joy.

CASSIUS Come down, behold no more.
                              Exit Pindarus from above
O coward that I am to live so long,
To see my best friend ta'en before my face.
    Enter Pindarus
Come hither, sirrah.
In Parthia did I take thee prisoner,
And then I swore thee, saving of thy life,
That whatsoever I did bid thee do,
Thou shouldst attempt it. Come now, keep thine oath.   40
Now be a free man, and with this good sword
That ran through Caesar's bowels, search this bosom.

5.3.22.1 *Pindarus goes up*] *not in* F   32 He's . . . joy.] POPE; *as two lines, breaking after* 'tane. *Showt.*' F   33.1 *Exit . . . above*] *not in* F   36–7 Come . . . prisoner,] POPE; *as one line* F   41 free man] F (Free-man)

21 **thick** dim
22.1 *Pindarus goes up* Pindarus has 'just enough time to exit at one of the side doors [of the stage] and climb the hidden stair to the upper stage' (Wilson). This has been disputed, with the suggestion that he may rather have mounted some kind of dais meant to represent an elevation (Saunders, p. 252), or else a stage-property rock; see Commentary, 5.5.1.
25 **compass** full circle

25 **Sirrah** See Commentary, 3.1.10.
29 **make to** make towards
37–45 **In Parthia . . . the sword** Cassius 'took Pindarus with him, one of his freed bondmen . . . since the cursed battle of the Parthians, . . . then casting his cloak over his head . . . he gave him his head to be stricken off' (*Brutus*, p. 160).
38 **swore thee** made thee swear
42 **search** probe (as one does a wound, with a surgical instrument; *OED v.* 8)

Stand not to answer. Here, take thou the hilts,
And when my face is covered, as 'tis now,
Guide thou the sword.
⌐*Pindarus stabs him*⌐
'   Caesar, thou art revenged,
Even with the sword that killed thee.   *He dies*

PINDARUS

So, I am free; yet would not so have been
Durst I have done my will. O Cassius!
Far from this country Pindarus shall run,
Where never Roman shall take note of him.   *Exit*   50
Enter Titinius, crowned with laurel, and Messala

MESSALA

It is but change, Titinius; for Octavius
Is overthrown by noble Brutus' power,
As Cassius' legions are by Antony.

TITINIUS

These tidings will well comfort Cassius.

MESSALA

Where did you leave him?

TITINIUS   All disconsolate,
With Pindarus his bondman, on this hill.

MESSALA

Is not that he that lies upon the ground?

TITINIUS

He lies not like the living. O my heart!

MESSALA

Is not that he?

TITINIUS   No, this was he, Messala,
But Cassius is no more. O setting sun,   60

45 *Pindarus stabs him*] CAMBRIDGE (*after* l. 46); *not in* F   46 *He dies*] CAPELL (*Dies*); *Kills him*
F2; *Kills himself* POPE; *Cassius falls on his sword* COLLIER 1877; *not in* F1   47 So . . . been]
ROWE; *as two lines, breaking after* 'free' F   50 *Exit*] *not in* F   50.1 *crowned with laurel*] *not in* F

43 **hilts** Made of several parts, the sword-hilt
often appears in the plural.
45–6 **Caesar . . . killed thee** '[He] slew himself
with the same sword with the which he
strake Caesar' (*Caesar*, p. 99). Caesar's
spirit, which Brutus wished to 'come by'
(2.1.170), is 'ranging for revenge'
(3.1.270) and exacting retribution.
50.1 *crowned with laurel* The wreath is
meant for Cassius; see l. 83.

51 **change** vicissitude of war, exchange of
fortunes (*OED sb. 2*)
54 **comfort** hearten
60–4 **O setting sun . . . done** In l. 109 the
time is only three o'clock and a further
fight is due before night, but the sunset
image is justified by its poetic
appropriateness. 'As the conspiracy at its
stormy beginning was set in a dramatic
background of actual tempest, so its

As in thy red rays thou dost sink to night,
So in his red blood Cassius' day is set.
The sun of Rome is set. Our day is gone;
Clouds, dews, and dangers come; our deeds are done.
Mistrust of my success hath done this deed.

MESSALA

Mistrust of good success hath done this deed.
O hateful Error, Melancholy's child,
Why dost thou show to the apt thoughts of men
The things that are not? O Error, soon conceived,
Thou never com'st unto a happy birth,   70
But kill'st the mother that engendered thee.

TITINIUS

What, Pindarus! Where art thou, Pindarus?

MESSALA

Seek him, Titinius, whilst I go to meet
The noble Brutus, thrusting this report
Into his ears. I may say 'thrusting' it;
For piercing steel, and darts envenomèd,
Shall be as welcome to the ears of Brutus
As tidings of this sight.

TITINIUS   Hie you, Messala,
And I will seek for Pindarus the while.   *Exit Messala*
Why didst thou send me forth, brave Cassius?   80

79 *Exit Messala*] *not in* F

decay and death is dramatically sym-
bolised by setting sun and growing darkness' (Hunter).

64 **Clouds, dews, and dangers** *Cloud* can
mean 'any state of obscurity or darkness'
(*OED sb.* 9), and like the other natural
images here has figurative implications.
Dews, like the 'contagion of the night
. . . the rheumy and unpurgèd air' of
2.1.266–7, suggests atmospheric
menace clearly related to nightfall
(which is also, of course, traditionally a
time of *dangers*).

65 **Mistrust . . . success** fear of my mission's
outcome (*success* means 'result', good or
bad; *good success* (l. 66) is the advantage
Brutus has gained)

67 **hateful** (a) odious (b) malignant
Error, Melancholy's child Cassius'
suicidal dejection could to the
Elizabethan mind indicate vulnerability
to 'melancholy' which, apart from the
obvious sense of depression, was regarded as a disease consequent on the
predominance of black bile, the source of
morbid irascibility and irrationality, and
giving rise to despairing delusions.

68 **apt** quickly responsive

71 **the mother . . . thee** the mind that gave
thee birth (not the 'Melancholy' of l. 67)
engendered conceived, bore (in Shakespeare's time, often used of the female
parent)

76 **darts** spears, arrows

80 **brave** noble (as frequently; e.g. l. 96)

Did I not meet thy friends, and did not they
Put on my brows this wreath of victory,
And bid me give it thee? Didst thou not hear their shouts?
Alas, thou hast misconstrued everything.
But hold thee, take this garland on thy brow –
Thy Brutus bid me give it thee, and I
Will do his bidding. Brutus, come apace,
And see how I regarded Caius Cassius.
By your leave, gods; this is a Roman's part.
Come, Cassius' sword, and find Titinius' heart.   90

> *He stabs himself and dies.*
>
> *Alarum. Enter Brutus, Messala, young Cato, Strato,*
> *Volumnius, Lucilius⌈, Labeo, and Flavius⌉*

BRUTUS

Where, where, Messala, doth his body lie?

MESSALA

Lo, yonder, and Titinius mourning it.

BRUTUS

Titinius' face is upward.

CATO   He is slain.

BRUTUS

O Julius Caesar, thou art mighty yet!

90.1 *He . . . and*] *not in* F   90.3 *Volumnius*] F (*Volumnius, and*) *Labeo, and Flavius*] WILSON
(*omitting 'Strato, Volumnius'*); *not in* F

82 **wreath of victory** Plutarch refers to Titinius as 'crowned with a garland of triumph' in token of Brutus' success but does not suggest it was sent to honour Cassius (*Brutus*, p. 161). Shakespeare may be recalling Prince Hal's honouring of the dead Hotspur by spreading over him his 'favours' (plumes? scarf?); *1 Henry IV* 5.4.96–8.

84 **misconstrued** The accent is on *con*.

89 **a Roman's part** In Plutarch he dies 'cursing himself a thousand times that he had tarried so long, and so slew himself presently' (*Brutus*, p. 161). Shakespeare allows him a grander gesture.

90.2 *young Cato* See Commentary, 5.4.4.

90.2–3 *Strato, Volumnius* Respectively, a friend of Brutus 'with whom he came first acquainted by the study of rhetoric', and 'a grave and wise philosopher that had been with Brutus from the beginning of this war' (*Brutus*, pp. 171–2, 166). Wil-

son omits them here, substituting Labeo and Flavius for whom he thinks they were doubling. F includes them but they remain silent until 5.5.16 and 50.

0.3 *Labeo, and Flavius* Respectively, Brutus' lieutenant and his captain of pioneers (*Brutus*, p. 169). F does not include them here but most editors do, since l. 108 names them. Their presence is not essential unless (with most editors) one inserts a comma in that line (F has none), so making it a command addressed to them; see Commentary, l. 108. Shakespeare clearly meant them to figure among Brutus' supporters (Flavius appears in F's direction at 5.4.0.2), though he gave neither anything to say.

94–6 O . . . entrails Again the unifying theme that Caesar's spirit is as potent after death as before, and final proof of the conspirators' misjudgement.

Thy spirit walks abroad and turns our swords
In our own proper entrails.
    Low alarums
CATO   Brave Titinius!
Look whe'er he have not crowned dead Cassius.
BRUTUS
Are yet two Romans living such as these?
The last of all the Romans, fare thee well.
It is impossible that ever Rome   100
Should breed thy fellow. – Friends, I owe more tears
To this dead man than you shall see me pay.
I shall find time, Cassius, I shall find time.
Come, therefore, and to Thasos send his body.
His funerals shall not be in our camp
Lest it discomfort us. Lucilius, come,
And come, young Cato; let us to the field.
Labeo and Flavius, set our battles on.
'Tis three o'clock; and, Romans, yet ere night
We shall try fortune in a second fight.   110
                              Exeunt, bearing off the bodies

---

97 whe'er] F (where)   have not] F *corr.* (haue not); haue F *uncorr.*   99 fare thee] F1 (far thee),
F2   101 more] F *corr.* (mo); no F *uncorr.*   104 Thasos] THEOBALD (Thassos);   *Tharsus* F
108 Labeo] HANMER (*after* F, '*Labio*')   Flavius,] F4; *Flauio* F1; *Flavius* F2   110.1 *bearing off
the bodies*] *not in* F

96 **own proper** very own
97 **whe'er** whether; see Commentary,
    1.1.61.
99–106 **The last . . . discomfort us** 'after
    [Brutus] had lamented the death of
    Cassius, calling him the last of all the
    Romans, being unpossible that Rome
    should ever breed again so noble and
    valiant a man as he, he caused his body
    to be . . . sent . . . to the city of Thassos,
    fearing lest his funerals within the camp
    should cause great disorder' (*Brutus*, pp.
    161–2).
104 **Thasos** An island near Philippi, off the
    coast of Thrace: 'Thassos' in North;
    'Tharsus' (Tarsus, in Asia Minor) in F.
105 **funerals** The plural, not infrequent in
    Elizabethan usage, echoes Plutarch; see

Commentary, ll. 99–106 ('his funerals').
106 **discomfort** dishearten (cf. l. 54)
108 **Labeo and Flavius,** As F has no comma
    l. 108 looks like a statement about these
    two, not an instruction to them. But ll.
    104, 106, and 107 establish a context of
    commands, and it seems right to insert
    the comma and have Brutus address an
    order to them. In F, '*Labio* and *Flavio*'; see
    the Introduction, p. 74.
109–10 **three o'clock . . . fight** Brutus
    'caused his army to march, being past
    three of the clock in the afternoon'
    (*Brutus*, p. 166). The play follows this,
    despite the different timing of ll. 60–2.
    The second battle of Philippi occurred
    twenty days later, but Shakespeare ig-
    nores the gap.

5.4   *Alarum. Enter⌈, fighting, soldiers of both armies; then⌉*
         Brutus, Messala, young Cato, Lucilius, and Flavius

BRUTUS

Yet, countrymen, O yet, hold up your heads!

⌈*Exit fighting, followed by Messala and Flavius*⌉

CATO

What bastard doth not? Who will go with me?

I will proclaim my name about the field –

I am the son of Marcus Cato, ho!

A foe to tyrants, and my country's friend.

I am the son of Marcus Cato, ho!

Enter more soldiers and fight

LUCILIUS

And I am Brutus, Marcus Brutus, I!

Brutus, my country's friend! Know me for Brutus!

Cato is killed

O young and noble Cato, art thou down?

Why, now thou diest as bravely as Titinius,   10

And mayst be honoured, being Cato's son.

Lucilius is captured

5.4.0.1 *fighting . . . then*] *not in* F   0.2 *young*] *not in* F   1.1 *Exit . . . Flavius*] WILSON (*subs.*);
not in F   6.1 *more*] *not in* F   7 LUCILIUS] MACMILLAN; *not in* F; *Bru.* ROWE   8.1 *Cato is killed*]
not in F   9 O] MACMILLAN; *Luc.* O F   11.1 *Lucilius is captured*] *not in* F

5.4.0.1 **fighting . . . then** This preliminary
skirmish (originated by Capell) averts the
awkwardness produced by strict ad-
herence to F's directions, by which
Brutus hastens off at 5.3.110 and immediately hastens on again here. See
Commentary, 5.2.0.1.

1.1 **Exit . . . Flavius** F has no direction, perhaps supposing Brutus to be still on stage
at ll. 7–8 (see note). But he must leave
before then, and this is the likeliest point,
brief though his appearance.

2 **What bastard doth not** i.e. which of us is
so base-born that he does not (a similar
form to that at 4.2.72–3)

4 **Marcus Cato** 'The Roman republicans . . .
had exalted Cato as the martyr of their
cause' (Kittredge). He was Portia's father
(see Commentary, 2.1.296) and his son
was Brutus' brother-in-law. In Plutarch,
'the son of M. Cato, . . . manfully fighting
and laying about him, telling aloud his

name and also his father's name, . . . at
length was beaten down amongst many
other dead bodies of his enemies whom
he had slain' (*Brutus*, p. 167).

7–8 **LUCILIUS . . . Brutus** F has no speech
heading at l. 7 (though it slightly indents
the start of the line) and no *Exit* for
Brutus after l. 1: it puts '*Luc.*' before l. 9.
Rowe and many later editors, assuming
Brutus to be still present, gave him ll.
7–8. But that it is Lucilius who assumes
his name is clear in Plutarch where, to
rescue his hard-pressed leader, he
professes to be Brutus and begs his
attackers 'to bring him to Antonius'
(*Brutus*, pp. 167–8). In *1 Henry IV*
5.3.1–21, likewise, Sir Walter Blunt im-
personates the King to protect him.

11, 14 **honoured** *OED*'s first instance as participial adjective (1601) is antedated here
and by Nashe's *Christ's Tears over
Jerusalem* (1593; McKerrow ii. 9. 1).

FIRST SOLDIER
    Yield, or thou diest.
LUCILIUS   Only I yield to die.
    ⌈*Offering money*⌉ There is so much that thou wilt kill me
        straight.
    Kill Brutus, and be honoured in his death.
FIRST SOLDIER
    We must not. A noble prisoner!
SECOND SOLDIER
    Room, ho! Tell Antony, Brutus is ta'en.
FIRST SOLDIER
    I'll tell the news.
            ⌈*Enter Antony*⌉
                        Here comes the general.
    Brutus is ta'en, Brutus is ta'en, my lord!
ANTONY Where is he?
LUCILIUS
    Safe, Antony, Brutus is safe enough.   20
    I dare assure thee that no enemy
    Shall ever take alive the noble Brutus.
    The gods defend him from so great a shame!
    When you do find him, or alive or dead,
    He will be found like Brutus, like himself.
ANTONY
    This is not Brutus, friend, but, I assure you,
    A prize no less in worth. Keep this man safe;
    Give him all kindness. I had rather have

---

12 FIRST] *not in* F; *so also at l.* 15   13 *Offering money*] *not in* F   17 the news] Q1684, POPE;
thee newes F   *Enter Antony*] *after l.* 15 F

---

12 **Only I yield** I yield only. For the trans-
position see Abbott 420.
13 ***Offering money*** Hanmer originated the
direction. The likeliest sense of the line
is Johnson's – 'I yield only . . . that I
may die; here is so much gold . . . as a
reward for speedy death'. Alternatively,
without the bribe, 'This will make you kill
me forthwith: it is Brutus you kill' (Wilson). But this requires a forced reading of
l. 13.
21–5 **I dare . . . himself** 'Lucilius . . . said:
"Antonius, I dare assure thee that no

enemy hath taken nor shall take Marcus
Brutus alive. I beseech God keep him from
that fortune. For wheresoever he be
found, alive or dead, he will be found like
himself"' (*Brutus*, p. 168).
26–9 **This is not Brutus . . . enemies**
'Antonius . . . said unto them: "My
companions, I think ye are sorry that you
have failed of your purpose . . . But, I do
assure you, you have taken a better booty
than that you followed. For, instead of an
enemy, you have brought me a friend;
. . . For I had rather have such men my

Such men my friends than enemies. Go on,
And see whe'er Brutus be alive or dead;   30
And bring us word unto Octavius' tent
How everything is chanced.   *Exeunt*

5.5   *Enter Brutus, Dardanius, Clitus, Strato, and Volumnius*

BRUTUS

Come, poor remains of friends, rest on this rock.

CLITUS

Statilius showed the torchlight, but, my lord,
He came not back. He is or ta'en or slain.

BRUTUS

Sit thee down, Clitus: slaying is the word,
It is a deed in fashion. Hark thee, Clitus.

> *He whispers*

CLITUS

What, I, my lord? No, not for all the world!

BRUTUS

Peace, then. No words.

CLITUS   I'll rather kill myself.

BRUTUS

Hark thee, Dardanius!

> *He whispers*

DARDANIUS   Shall I do such a deed?

CLITUS O Dardanius!

DARDANIUS O Clitus!   10

---

30 whe'er] F (where)
5.5.5.1, 8 *He whispers*] *not in* F

friends as this man here, than enemies."
Then he embraced Lucilius' (*Brutus*,
p. 169).

30 **whe'er** whether (as elsewhere)
5.5.0.1 *Brutus . . . Volumnius* 'Hard upon
the clattering excitement of the fight and
the flattering magnanimity of the triumphant Antony, comes . . . this little group
of beaten and exhausted men, the torch-
light flickering on their faces' (Granville-
Barker, p. 118).
Dardanius 'Dardanus, Brutus' servant'
(*Brutus*, p. 169); *Dardanius* in F.

0.1 *Clitus* 'one of his [Brutus'] men' (*Brutus*,
p. 170).
1 **this rock** A theatre property. *Henslowe's
Diary*, ed. R. A. Foakes and R. T. Rickert
(Cambridge, 1961), p. 319, records a
'rocke' in the company's inventory on 10
March 1598.
2–3 **Statilius . . . slain** Statilius, who is not
seen in the play, was sent on recon-
naissance and, if satisfied, was to 'lift up
a torch-light in the air, and then return
again with speed', but having lifted it he
was killed (*Brutus*, p. 170).

CLITUS

What ill request did Brutus make to thee?

DARDANIUS

To kill him, Clitus. Look, he meditates.

CLITUS

Now is that noble vessel full of grief,

That it runs over even at his eyes.

BRUTUS

Come hither, good Volumnius, list a word.

VOLUMNIUS

What says my lord?

BRUTUS   Why, this, Volumnius:

The ghost of Caesar hath appeared to me

Two several times by night – at Sardis once,

And this last night, here in Philippi fields.

I know my hour is come.

VOLUMNIUS   Not so, my lord.   20

BRUTUS

Nay, I am sure it is, Volumnius.

Thou seest the world, Volumnius, how it goes.

Our enemies have beat us to the pit.

        Low alarums

It is more worthy to leap in ourselves

Than tarry till they push us. Good Volumnius,

Thou know'st that we two went to school together.

Even for that our love of old, I prithee

Hold thou my sword-hilts whilst I run on it.

23.1 *Low*] F *corr.*;   *Loud* F *uncorr.*

13 **vessel full of grief** Similarly *Winter's Tale*
3.3.21–2 – 'I never saw a vessel of like
sorrow | So filled'. The Bible uses the
image of human 'vessels' of various
qualities; for example, Romans 9: 22
('vessels of wrath fitted to destruction'), 2
Timothy 2: 21 ('man . . . shall be a vessel
unto honour'), and 1 Peter 3: 7 ('giving
honour unto the wife, as unto the weaker
vessel').
17–19 **The ghost . . . last night** 'The self same
night . . . the monstrous spirit which had
appeared before . . . in the city of Sardis,
did now appear to him in the self same
shape and form' (*Brutus*, p. 165). It is
now definitely identified with Caesar; see

Commentary, 4.2.327–31.
18 **several** separate
23 **pit** pitfall (for hunted prey; with the implication of 'grave')
26 **went to school** In Plutarch Brutus
beseeches Volumnius 'for the study's
sake which brought them acquainted
together' (*Brutus*, p. 170), that is, the
philosophy they read as grown men. In
Shakespeare this touchingly becomes
their childhood friendship.
28 **sword-hilts** 'Taking his sword by the hilts
with both his hands . . . [he] ran himself
through' (*Brutus*, p. 172). On 'hilts', see
Commentary, 5.3.43; *it* is the sword itself.

VOLUMNIUS

    That's not an office for a friend, my lord.

       Alarum still

CLITUS

    Fly, fly, my lord, there is no tarrying here.   30

BRUTUS

    Farewell to you; and you; and you, Volumnius.

    Strato, thou hast been all this while asleep;

    Farewell to thee too, Strato. – Countrymen,

    My heart doth joy that yet in all my life

    I found no man but he was true to me.

    I shall have glory by this losing day

    More than Octavius and Mark Antony

    By this vile conquest shall attain unto.

    So fare you well at once, for Brutus' tongue

    Hath almost ended his life's history.   40

    Night hangs upon mine eyes; my bones would rest,

    That have but laboured to attain this hour.

       Alarum. Cry within, 'Fly, fly, fly!'

CLITUS Fly, my lord, fly!

BRUTUS Hence! I will follow.

       Exeunt Clitus, Dardanius, and Volumnius

    I prithee, Strato, stay thou by thy lord.

    Thou art a fellow of a good respect;

---

33 thee too, Strato. – Countrymen,] THEOBALD;   thee, to *Strato*, Countrymen: F   44.1 *Exeunt*
. . . *Volumnius*] *not in* F

34–8 **My heart . . . attain unto** In Plutarch, taking his friends 'by the hand, he said these words unto them with a cheerful countenance: "It rejoiceth my heart that not one of my friends hath failed me at my need, . . . I think myself happier than they that have overcome, considering that I leave a perpetual fame of our courage and manhood, the which our enemies the conquerors shall never attain unto by force nor money, . . . they, being naughty and unjust men, have slain good men, to usurp tyrannical power"' (*Brutus*, p. 171).

38 **this vile conquest** Walker (*Crit.*) proposed 'their vile conquest', which may well be correct.
    vile ignoble

41–2 **my bones . . . hour** 'Fulfilling once

again the role of sacrificer, the role he himself chose, . . . he satisfies his own conscience, political necessity, history, . . . and the inscrutable power whose name is Fate' (M. W. Proser, *The Heroic Image*, 1965, p. 50). Brutus' belief in the rightness of his cause may be assessed in the light of Plutarch's comment that Rome 'could no more abide to be governed by many lords but required one only absolute governor', so God frustrated Brutus' campaign (*Brutus*, p. 165).

42 **That have . . . hour** Possibly (a) that have reached this end only with painful toil; but more probably (b) that have toiled only that they might find the peace (and honour) of this (noble) death.

46 **respect** reputation

Thy life hath had some smatch of honour in it.
Hold then my sword, and turn away thy face,
While I do run upon it. Wilt thou, Strato?

STRATO

Give me your hand first. Fare you well, my lord.   50

BRUTUS

Farewell, good Strato. – Caesar, now be still.
I killed not thee with half so good a will.
        He runs on his sword and dies.
        Alarum. Retreat. Enter Antony, Octavius, Messala,
        Lucilius, and the army

OCTAVIUS What man is that?

MESSALA

My master's man. Strato, where is thy master?

STRATO

Free from the bondage you are in, Messala;
The conquerors can but make a fire of him.
For Brutus only overcame himself,
And no man else hath honour by his death.

LUCILIUS

So Brutus should be found. I thank thee, Brutus,
That thou hast proved Lucilius' saying true.   60

OCTAVIUS

All that served Brutus, I will entertain them.
Fellow, wilt thou bestow thy time with me?

STRATO

Ay, if Messala will prefer me to you.

OCTAVIUS Do so, good Messala.

MESSALA How died my master, Strato?

STRATO

I held the sword and he did run on it.

52.1 *He . . . and*] *not in* F

47 **smatch** Variant of 'smack', relish
(without the modern tinge of disparagement).

51–2 **Caesar . . . will** Caesar's spirit is now
appeased by his killer's death as, supposedly, are outraged ghosts.

52.2 *Retreat* A trumpet call for troops to
cease pursuit.

54–68 *MESSALA . . . master* In Plutarch,
Messala, 'that had been Brutus' great
friend, became afterwards Octavius

Caesar's friend' and introduced to him
Strato, 'that did the last service to my
Brutus', the 'service' being esteemed
highly honourable (*Brutus*, p. 172).

54 **My master's man** In Plutarch, a fellow-
student of rhetoric (*Brutus*, pp. 171–2).

57 **only** alone

60 **Lucilius' saying** See 5.4.21–5.

61 **entertain them** receive them into my service

63 **prefer** recommend

MESSALA

Octavius, then take him to follow thee,
That did the latest service to my master.

ANTONY

This was the noblest Roman of them all.
All the conspirators save only he   70
Did that they did in envy of great Caesar.
He only, in a general honest thought
And common good to all, made one of them.
His life was gentle, and the elements
So mixed in him that Nature might stand up
And say to all the world 'This was a man!'

OCTAVIUS

According to his virtue let us use him,

72 He only,] Q1691 ; He, onely F

69–76 **This . . . a man** For this climactic
tribute Shakespeare takes words occur-
ring much earlier in Plutarch, in the
aftermath of Caesar's murder: 'Antonius
spake it openly . . . that he thought that
of all them that had slain Caesar there
was none but Brutus only that was
moved to do it as thinking the act commendable of itself; but that all the other
conspirators did conspire his death for
some private malice or envy' (*Brutus*,
p. 140): also, from the opening
paragraphs of *Brutus*, 'he was rightly
made and framed unto virtue. So that his
very enemies, . . . if there were any noble
attempt done in all this conspiracy, they
refer it wholly unto Brutus' (*Brutus*,
p. 102). Of Cassius Plutarch observes that
it was thought 'he made war . . . more to
have absolute power and authority than
to defend the liberty of his country', and
of the others, save Brutus, that 'the end
and hope of their victory was to be lords
of their country; and . . . of the Empire of
Rome' (*Brutus*, p. 139). Shakespeare
offers Antony's tribute as the
predominant judgement on Brutus and
his fellows. Along with other details (e.g.
5.4.26–9) it evinces generosity in
Antony and helps to redeem his ruthlessness in 4.1.

72–3 **in a general honest thought . . . to all**
with honourable intentions for the public
good

74 **gentle** noble, chivalric: 'gentle and con-

stant, in attempting of great things'
(*Brutus*, p. 102).

74–6 **the elements . . . a man** The elements
(air, fire, earth, water), tempered together
within the body, constituted the
'humours' (blood, choler, melancholy,
phlegm) which made up the 'temperament'. In Brutus they were perfectly
balanced. These lines may have prompted Jonson's *Cynthia's Revels* 2.3.123–30,
in 1600 – 'A creature of a most perfect
and divine temper. One, in whom the
humours and elements are peaceably
met, . . . so composed and ordered, as it is
clear, Nature . . . did more than make a
man, when she made him'; also Drayton's *The Barons' Wars* iii. 40 (1603
revision) – 'He was a man . . . | In whom
so mixed the elements all lay | That none
to one could sov'reignty impute; | . . . | He
of a temper was so absolute | As that it
seemed, when Nature him began, | She
meant to show all that might be in man'.

77–82 **According . . . this happy day** Some
productions make Octavius speak this
arrogantly, stressing '*my* tent' (against
the metre) and making a different exit
from Antony's. But however ungenial his
nature generally, to do so distorts the
intention here, where a Roman magnanimity fitting the end of Brutus is common to all. And even in *Antony and
Cleopatra* Octavius' closing words over his
dead opponents are exemplary.

With all respect and rites of burial.
Within my tent his bones tonight shall lie,
Most like a soldier, ordered honourably.   80
So call the field to rest, and let's away
To part the glories of this happy day.   *Exeunt*

82 *Exeunt*] F (*Exeunt omnes.*)

80 **ordered honourably** with all honourable
observance. 'Antonius having found
Brutus' body, he caused it to be wrapped
up in one of the richest coat-armours he
had' (*Brutus*, p. 172). Shakespeare transfers the idea to Octavius so that both men
may conclude nobly.
82 **part** share out
82 *Exeunt* It is an odd reflection on
Elizabethan dramatic taste that after the
sober and magnanimous gravity of this
last scene, as Thomas Platter reports (see
the Introduction, p. 1), 'they danced
together admirably and exceedingly
gracefully'. The effect (which he, and
presumably the audience, approved) may
have been to console the spirit after the
agitations of the plot.

PASSAGES FROM NORTH'S PLUTARCH

DETAILED passages quoted in the Commentary show how closely, in delivering his individual version, Shakespeare followed his source. The following extended passages exemplify the skill with which North writes narrative, and also illustrate in larger compass the same fidelity on Shakespeare's part to North's tenor and expression, along with the creative originality which even in virtual paraphrase can fully revitalize its material.

CAESAR

He was chosen Consul the fourth time, and went into Spain to make war with the sons of Pompey; who were yet but very young, but had notwithstanding raised a marvellous great army together, and showed to have had manhood and courage worthy to command such an army, insomuch as they put Caesar himself in great danger of his life. The greatest battle that was fought between them in all this war was by the city of Munda. . . . He won this battle on the very feast day of the Bacchanalians, in the which men say that Pompey the Great went out of Rome, about four years before, to begin this civil war. For his sons, the younger scaped from the battle; but, within few days after, Diddius brought the head of the elder.

This was the last war that Caesar made. But the triumph he made into Rome for the same did as much offend the Romans, and more, than anything that ever he had done before; because he had not overcome captains that were strangers, nor barbarous kings, but had destroyed the sons of the noblest man in Rome, whom fortune had overthrown. And, because he had plucked up his race by the roots, men did not think it meet for him to triumph so for the calamities of his country, rejoicing at a thing for the which he had but one excuse to allege in his defence unto the gods and men – that he was compelled to do that he did. And the rather they thought it not meet, because he had never before sent letters nor messengers unto the commonwealth at Rome, for any victory that he had ever won in all the civil wars, but did always for shame refuse the glory of it.

This notwithstanding, the Romans inclining to Caesar's prosperity, and taking the bit in the mouth, supposing that, to be ruled by one man alone, it would be a good mean for them to take breath a little after so many troubles and miseries as they had abidden in these civil wars, they chose him perpetual Dictator. This was a plain tyranny. For to this absolute power of Dictator they added this, never to be afraid to be deposed. Cicero propounded before the Senate that they should give him such honours as were meet for a man. Howbeit others afterwards added too honours beyond all reason. For, men striving who should most honour him, they made him hateful and troublesome to themselves that most favoured him, by reason of the unmeasurable greatness and honours which they gave him. Thereupon, it is reported that even they that most hated him were no less favourers and furtherers of his honours than they that most flattered him; because they might have greater occasions to rise, and that it might appear they had just cause and colour to attempt that they did against him.

And now for himself, after he had ended his civil wars, he did so honourably behave himself that there was no fault to be found in him; and therefore, methinks, amongst other honours they gave him, he rightly deserved this – that they should build him a Temple of Clemency, to thank him for his courtesy he had used unto them in his victory. For he pardoned many of them that had borne arms against him, and, furthermore, did prefer some of them to honour and office in the commonwealth; as, amongst others, Cassius and Brutus, both the which were made Praetors. And, where Pompey's images had been thrown down, he caused them to be set up again. Whereupon Cicero said then that Caesar setting up Pompey's images again he made his own to stand the surer. And when some of his friends did counsel him to have a guard for the safety of his person, and some also did offer themselves to serve him, he would never consent to it, but said, it was better to die once than always to be afraid of death.

But to win himself the love and good will of the people, as the honourablest guard and best safety he could have, he made common feasts again and general distribution of corn. Furthermore, to gratify the soldiers also, he replenished many cities again with inhabitants, which before had been destroyed, and placed them there that had no place to repair unto; of the which the noblest and chiefest cities were these two, Carthage and Corinth; and it chanced also that, like as aforetime they had been both taken and destroyed together, even so were they both set afoot again, and replenished with people, at one self time. . . .

Furthermore, Caesar being born to attempt all great enterprises and having an ambitious desire besides to covet great honours, the prosperous good success he had of his former conquests bred no desire in him quietly to enjoy the fruits of his labours, but rather gave him hope of things to come, still kindling more and more in him thoughts of greater enterprises and desire of new glory, as if that which he had present were stale and nothing worth. This humour of his was no other but an emulation with himself as with another man, and a certain contention to overcome the things he prepared to attempt.

(*Caesar*, pp. 76–9)

BRUTUS

But for Brutus, his friends and countrymen, both by divers procurements and sundry rumours of the city and by many bills also, did openly call and procure him to do that he did. For, under the image of his ancestor Junius Brutus, that drave the kings out of Rome, they wrote: 'Oh that it pleased the gods thou wert now alive, Brutus.' And again: 'That thou wert here among us now.' His tribunal, or chair, where he gave audience during the time he was Praetor, was full of such bills: 'Brutus, thou art asleep, and art not Brutus indeed.'

And of all this Caesar's flatterers were the cause; who beside many other exceeding and unspeakable honours they daily devised for him, in the night-time they did put diadems upon the heads of his images, supposing thereby to allure the common people to call him King, instead of Dictator. Howbeit it turned to the contrary, as we have written more at large in Julius Caesar's *Life*.

Now when Cassius felt his friends and did stir them up against Caesar, they all agreed and promised to take part with him, so Brutus were the chief of their conspiracy. For they told him that so high an enterprise and attempt as that did not so much require men of manhood and courage to draw their swords, as it stood them upon to have a man of such estimation as Brutus, to make every man boldly think that by his only presence the fact were holy and just: if he took not this course, then that they should go to it with fainter hearts; and when they had done it they should be more fearful, because every man would think that Brutus would not have refused to have made one with them, if the cause had been good and honest. Therefore Cassius, considering this matter with himself, did first of all speak to Brutus since they grew strange together for the suit they had for the Praetorship. So when he was reconciled to him again, and that they had embraced one another, Cassius asked him if he were determined to be in the Senate-house the first day of the month of March, because he heard say that Caesar's friends should move the council that day that Caesar should be called King by the Senate. Brutus answered him, he would not be there.

'But if we be sent for,' said Cassius, 'how then?'

'For myself then,' said Brutus, 'I mean not to hold my peace, but to withstand it, and rather die than lose my liberty.'

Cassius being bold, and taking hold of this word,

'Why,' quoth he, 'what Roman is he alive that will suffer thee to die for the liberty? What, knowest thou not that thou art Brutus? Thinkest thou that they be cobblers, tapsters, or suchlike base mechanical people, that write these bills and scrolls which are found daily in thy Praetor's chair, and not the noblest men and best citizens that do it? No, be thou well assured, that of other Praetors they look for gifts, common distributions amongst the people, and for common plays, and to see fencers fight at the sharp, to show the people pastime. But at thy hands they specially require, as a due debt unto them, the taking away of the tyranny, being fully bent to suffer any extremity for thy sake, so that thou wilt show thyself to be the man thou art taken for, and that they hope thou art.'

Thereupon he kissed Brutus, and embraced him: and so, each taking leave of other, they went both to speak with their friends about it.

Now amongst Pompey's friends there was one called Caius Ligarius, who had been accused unto Caesar for taking part with Pompey, and Caesar discharged him. But Ligarius thanked not Caesar so much for his discharge, as he was offended with him for that he was brought in danger by his tyrannical power. And therefore in his heart he was alway his mortal enemy, and was besides very familiar with Brutus, who went to see him being sick in his bed, and said unto him:

'O Ligarius, in what a time art thou sick!'

Ligarius rising up in his bed and taking him by the right hand, said unto him:

'Brutus,' said he, 'if thou hast any great enterprise in hand worthy of thyself, I am whole.'

(*Brutus*, pp. 110–13)

BRUTUS AND PORTIA

Now Brutus (who knew very well that for his sake all the noblest, valiantest, and most courageous men of Rome did venture their lives) weighing with himself the greatness of the danger, when he was out of his house he did so frame and fashion his countenance and looks that no man could discern he had anything to trouble his mind. But when night came that he was in his own house, then he was clean changed. For, either care did wake him against his will when he would have slept, or else oftentimes of himself he fell into such deep thoughts of this enterprise, casting in his mind all the dangers that might happen, that his wife, lying by him, found that there was some marvellous great matter that troubled his mind, not being wont to be in that taking, and that he could not well determine with himself. His wife Portia ... was the daughter of Cato, whom Brutus married being his cousin, not a maiden, but a young widow ...

This young lady being excellently well seen in philosophy, loving her husband well, and being of a noble courage, as she was also wise – because she would not ask her husband what he ailed before she had made some proof by herself – she took a little razor such as barbers occupy to pare men's nails, and, causing her maids and women to go out of her chamber, gave herself a great gash withal in her thigh, that she was straight all of a gore-blood; and, incontinently after, a vehement fever took her, by reason of the pain of her wound. Then perceiving her husband was marvellously out of quiet and that he could take no rest, even in her greatest pain of all she spake in this sort unto him:

'I being, O Brutus,' said she, 'the daughter of Cato, was married unto thee, not to be thy bedfellow and companion in bed and at board only, like a harlot, but to be partaker also with thee of thy good and evil fortune. Now for thyself, I can find no cause of fault in thee touching our match. But for my part, how may I show my duty towards thee and how much I would do for thy sake, if I cannot constantly bear a secret mischance or grief with thee, which requireth secrecy and fidelity? I confess that a woman's wit commonly is too weak to keep a secret safely. But yet, Brutus, good education and the company of virtuous men have some power to reform the defect of nature. And for myself, I have this benefit moreover: that I am the daughter of Cato and wife of Brutus. This notwithstanding, I did not trust to any of these things before, until that now I have found by experience that no pain nor grief whatsoever can overcome me.'

With those words she showed him her wound on her thigh and told him what she had done to prove herself. Brutus was amazed to hear what she said unto him, and, lifting up his hands to heaven, he besought the gods to give him the grace he might bring his enterprise to so good pass, that he might be found a husband worthy of so noble a wife as Portia. So he then did comfort her the best he could.

(*Brutus*, pp. 116–18)

ANTONY

. . . it is reported that Caesar answered one that did accuse Antonius and Dolabella unto him for some matter of conspiracy:

'Tush,' said he, 'they be not those fat fellows and fine combed men that I fear; but I mistrust rather these pale and lean men,' – meaning by [this] Brutus and Cassius, who afterwards conspired his death and slew him.

Antonius unwares afterwards gave Caesar's enemies just occasion and colour to do as they did; as you shall hear. The Romans by chance celebrated the feast called *Lupercalia*, and Caesar, being apparelled in his triumphing robe, was set in the Tribune where they use to make their orations to the people, and from thence did behold the sport of the runners. The manner of this running was this. On that day there are many young men of noble house, and those specially that be chief officers for that year, who, running naked up and down the city anointed with the oil of olive, for pleasure do strike them they meet in their way with white leather thongs they have in their hands. Antonius being one among the rest that was to run, leaving the ancient ceremonies and old customs of that solemnity, he ran to the tribune where Caesar was set, and carried a laurel crown in his hand, having a royal band or diadem wreathed about it, which in old time was the ancient mark and token of a king. When he was come to Caesar, he made his fellow-runners with him lift him up, and so he did put this laurel crown upon his head, signifying thereby that he deserved to be king. But Caesar, making as though he refused it, turned away his head. The people were so rejoiced at it that they all clapped their hands for joy. Antonius again did put it on his head. Caesar again refused it; and thus they were striving off and on a great while together. As oft as Antonius did put this laurel crown unto him, a few of his followers rejoiced at it; and as oft also as Caesar refused it, all the people together clapped their hands. And this was a wonderful thing, that they suffered all things subjects should do by commandment of their kings, and yet they could not abide the name of a king, detesting it as the utter destruction of their liberty. Caesar in a rage rose out of his seat and, plucking down the collar of his gown from his neck, he showed it naked, bidding any man strike off his head that would.

This laurel crown was afterwards put upon the head of one of Caesar's statues or images, the which one of the Tribunes plucked off. The people liked his doing therein so well that they waited on him home to his house with great clapping of hands. Howbeit Caesar did turn them out of their offices for it.

This was a good encouragement for Brutus and Cassius to conspire his death, who fell into a consort with their trustiest friends to execute their enterprise, but yet stood doubtful whether they should make Antonius privy to it or not. All the rest liked of it, saving Trebonius only. He told them that, when they rode to meet Caesar at his return out of Spain, Antonius and he always keeping company and lying together by the way, he felt his mind afar off; but Antonius, finding his meaning, would hearken no more unto it; and yet notwithstanding never made Caesar acquainted with this talk, but had faithfully kept it to himself. After that they consulted whether they should kill Antonius with Caesar. But Brutus would in no wise consent to it, saying that venturing on such an enterprise as that, for the maintenance of law and justice, it ought to be clear from all villainy. Yet they, fearing Antonius' power and the authority of his office, appointed certain of the conspiracy, that, when Caesar were gone into the Senate, and while others should execute their enterprise, they should keep Antonius in a talk out of the Senate-house.

Even as they had devised these matters, so were they executed; and Caesar was slain in the midst of the Senate. Antonius, being put in a fear withal, cast a slave's gown upon him and hid himself. But afterwards, when it was told him that the murderers slew no man else and that they went only into the Capitol, he sent his son unto them for a pledge and bade them boldly come down upon his word. The selfsame day he did bid Cassius to supper, and Lepidus also bade Brutus. The next morning the Senate was assembled; and Antonius himself preferred a law that all things past should be forgotten, and that they should appoint provinces unto Cassius and Brutus; the which the Senate confirmed; and further ordained that they should cancel none of Caesar's laws. Thus went Antonius out of the Senate more praised and better esteemed than ever man was, because it seemed to every man that he had cut off all occasion of civil wars, and that he had showed himself a marvellous wise governor of the commonwealth, for the appeasing of these matters of so great weight and importance.

But now the opinion he conceived of himself after he had a little felt the good will of the people towards him, hoping thereby to make himself the chiefest man if he might overcome Brutus, did easily make him alter his first mind. And therefore when Caesar's body was brought to the place where it should be buried, he made a funeral oration in commendation of Caesar, according to the ancient custom of praising noblemen at their funerals. When he saw that the people were very glad and desirous also to hear Caesar spoken of and his praises uttered, he mingled his oration with lamentable words, and by amplifying of matters did greatly move their hearts and affections unto pity and compassion. In fine, to conclude his oration, he unfolded before the whole assembly the bloody garments of the dead, thrust through in many places with their swords, and called the malefactors cruel and cursed murderers. With these words he put the people into such a fury that they presently took Caesar's body and burnt it in the market-place with such tables and forms as they could get together. Then, when the fire was kindled, they took firebrands, and ran to the murderers' houses to set them a-fire and to make them come out to fight. Brutus therefore and his accomplices, for safety of their persons, were driven to fly the city.

(Antonius, pp. 186–9)

BEFORE PHILIPPI

The Romans called the valley between both camps, the Philippian fields; and there were never seen two so great armies of the Romans, one before the other, ready to fight. In truth, Brutus' army was inferior to Octavius Caesar's in number of men. But, for bravery and rich furniture, Brutus' army far excelled Caesar's. For the most part of their armours were silver and gilt, which Brutus had bountifully given them, although in all other things he taught his captains to live in order without excess. But, for the bravery of armour and weapon which soldiers should carry in their hands or otherwise wear upon their backs, he thought that it was an encouragement unto them that by nature are greedy of honour, and that it maketh them also fight like devils, that love to get and be afraid to lose; because they fight to keep their armour and weapon, as also their goods and lands.

Now when they came to muster their armies, Octavius Caesar took the muster of his army within the trenches of his camp, and gave his men only a little corn, and five silver drachmas to every man to sacrifice to the gods and to pray for victory. But Brutus, scorning this misery and niggardliness, first of all mustered his army and did purify it in the fields, according to the manner of the Romans. And then he gave unto every band a number of wethers to sacrifice, and fifty silver drachmas to every soldier. So that Brutus' and Cassius' soldiers were better pleased, and more courageously bent to fight at the day of battle, than their enemies' soldiers were.

Notwithstanding, being busily occupied about the ceremonies of this purification, it is reported that there chanced certain unlucky signs unto Cassius. For one of his sergeants that carried the rods before him brought him the garland of flowers turned backwards, the which he should have worn on his head in the time of sacrificing. Moreover it is reported also that another time before, in certain sports and triumph where they carried an image of Cassius' victory of clean gold, it fell by chance, the man stumbling that carried it. And yet further, there were seen a marvellous number of fowls of prey, that feed upon dead carcases. And beehives also were found, where bees were gathered together in a certain place within the trenches of the camp; the which place the soothsayers thought good to shut out of the precinct of the camp, for to take away the superstitious fear and mistrust men would have of it; the which began somewhat to alter Cassius' mind from Epicurus' opinions, and had put the soldiers also in a marvellous fear.

Thereupon Cassius was of opinion not to try this war at one battle, but rather to delay time and to draw it out in length, considering that they were the stronger in money and the weaker in men and armours. But Brutus in contrary manner did alway before, and at that time also, desire nothing more than to put all to the hazard of battle, as soon as might be possible, to the end he might either quickly restore his country to her former liberty, or rid him forthwith of this miserable world, being still troubled in following and maintaining of such great armies together.

(*Brutus*, pp. 151–2)

THE DEATH OF CASSIUS

... The vaward and the midst of Brutus' battle had already put all their enemies to flight that withstood them, with great slaughter; so that Brutus had conquered all on his side, and Cassius had lost all on the other side. For nothing undid them but that Brutus went not to help Cassius, thinking he had overcome them, as himself had done; and Cassius on the other side tarried not for Brutus, thinking he had been overthrown, as himself was. And, to prove that the victory fell on Brutus' side, Messala confirmeth it, that they won three eagles and divers other ensigns of their enemies, and their enemies won never a one of theirs.

Now Brutus returning from the chase after he had slain and sacked Caesar's men, he wondered much that he could not see Cassius' tent standing up high as it was wont, neither the other tents of his camp standing as they were before, because all the whole camp had been spoiled and the tents thrown down, at the first coming in of the enemies. But they that were about Brutus, whose sight served them better, told him that they saw a great glistering of harness and a number of silvered targets, that went and came into Cassius' camp and were not, as they took it, the armours nor the number of men that they had left there to guard the camp; and yet that they saw not such a number of dead bodies, and great overthrow, as there should have been if so many legions had been slain.

This made Brutus at the first mistrust that which had happened. So he appointed a number of men to keep the camp of his enemy which he had taken, and caused his men to be sent for that yet followed the chase, and gathered them together, thinking to lead them to aid Cassius, who was in this state as you shall hear. First of all he was marvellous angry to see how Brutus' men ran to give charge upon their enemies and tarried not for the word of the battle nor commandment to give charge; and it grieved him beside that, after he had overcome them, his men fell straight to spoil and were not careful to compass in the rest of the enemies behind. But with tarrying too long also, more than through the valiantness or foresight of the captains his enemies, Cassius found himself compassed in with the right wing of his enemies' army. Whereupon his horsemen brake immediately, and fled for life towards the sea. Furthermore, perceiving his footmen to give ground, he did what he could to keep them from flying, and took an ensign from one of the ensign-bearers that fled, and stuck it fast at his feet; although with much ado he could scant keep his own guard together. So Cassius himself was at length compelled to fly, with a few about him, unto a little hill from whence they might easily see what was done in all the plain; howbeit Cassius himself saw nothing, for his sight was very bad, saving that he saw, and yet with much ado, how the enemies spoiled his camp before his eyes. He saw also a great troop of horsemen whom Brutus sent to aid him, and thought that they were his enemies that followed him. But yet he sent Titinnius, one of them that was with him, to go and know what they were. Brutus' horsemen saw him coming afar off, whom when they knew that he was one of Cassius' chiefest friends, they shouted out for joy; and they that were familiarly acquainted with him lighted from their horses, and went and embraced him. The rest compassed him in round about a-horseback, with songs of victory and great rushing of their harness, so that they made all the field ring again for joy.

But this marred all. For Cassius thinking indeed that Titinnius was taken of the enemies, he then spake these words:

'Desiring too much to live, I have lived to see one of my best friends taken, for my sake, before my face.'

After that, he got into a tent where nobody was, and took Pindarus with him, one of his freed bondmen, whom he reserved ever for such a pinch, since the cursed battle of the Parthians where Crassus was slain, though he notwithstanding scaped from that overthrow. But then casting his cloak over his head and holding out his bare neck unto Pindarus, he gave him his head to be stricken off. So the head was found severed from the body. But after that time Pindarus was never seen more. Whereupon, some took occasion to say that he had slain his master without his commandment.

By and by they knew the horsemen that came towards them, and might see Titinnius crowned with a garland of triumph, who came before with great speed unto Cassius. But when he perceived, by the cries and tears of his friends which tormented themselves, the misfortune that had chanced to his captain Cassius by mistaking, he drew out his sword, cursing himself a thousand times that he had tarried so long, and so slew himself presently in the field. Brutus in the meantime came forward still, and understood also that Cassius had been overthrown. But he knew nothing of his death, till he came very near to his camp. So when he was come thither, after he had lamented the death of Cassius, calling him the last of all the Romans, being unpossible that Rome should ever breed again so noble and valiant a man as he, he caused his body to be buried and sent it to the city of Thassos, fearing lest his funerals within the camp should cause great disorder.

(*Brutus*, pp. 158–62)

THE DEATH OF BRUTUS

Brutus thought that there was no great number of men slain in battle; and, to know the truth of it, there was one called Statilius that promised to go through his enemies, for otherwise it was impossible to go see their camp, and from thence, if all were well, that he would lift up a torch-light in the air, and then return again with speed to him. The torch-light was lift up as he had promised, for Statilius went thither. Now Brutus seeing Statilius tarry long after that, and that he came not again, he said:

'If Statilius be alive, he will come again.'

But his evil fortune was such that as he came back he lighted in his enemies' hands and was slain.

Now, the night being far spent, Brutus as he sat bowed towards Clitus one of his men and told him somewhat in his ear, the other answered him not, but fell a-weeping. Thereupon he proved Dardanus, and said somewhat also to him. At length he came to Volumnius himself, and, speaking to him in Greek, prayed him, for the study's sake which brought them acquainted together, that he would help him to put his hand to his sword, to thrust it in him to kill him. Volumnius denied his request, and so did many others. And, amongst the rest, one of them said, there was no tarrying for them there, but that they must needs fly. Then Brutus rising up:

'We must fly indeed,' said he, 'but it must be with our hands not with our feet.'

Then, taking every man by the hand, he said these words unto them with a cheerful countenance:

'It rejoiceth my heart that not one of my friends hath failed me at my need, and I do not complain of my fortune, but only for my country's sake. For, as for me, I think myself happier than they that have overcome, considering that I leave a perpetual fame of our courage and manhood, the which our enemies the conquerors shall never attain unto by force nor money, neither can let their posterity to say that they, being naughty and unjust men, have slain good men, to usurp tyrannical power not pertaining to them.'

Having said so, he prayed every man to shift for themselves. And then he went a little aside with two or three only, among the which Strato was one, with whom he came first acquainted by the study of rhetoric. He came as near to him as he could, and, taking his sword by the hilts with both hands and falling down upon the point of it, ran himself through. Others say that not he, but Strato, at his request, held the sword in his hand, and turned his head aside, and that Brutus fell down upon it; and so ran himself through, and died presently.

Messala, that had been Brutus' great friend, became afterwards Octavius Caesar's friend. So, shortly after, Caesar being at good leisure, he brought Strato, Brutus' friend, unto him and weeping said:

'Caesar, behold, here is he that did the last service to my Brutus.'

Caesar welcomed him at that time, and afterwards he did him as faithful service in all his affairs as any Grecian else he had about him.

(*Brutus*, pp. 170–2)

THE ENTRY DIRECTION AT 4.2.0

It is not easy to reconcile the Folio's entry direction with the details of the text. (For Wilson's interesting reorganization of it, see the Collation.) Having written it Shakespeare may somewhat have changed his plan as the text evolved. The Folio prescribes a beating drum, then the joint entrance of Brutus and Lucilius and the army, to be met by Titinius and Pindarus from another direction. In the text, Brutus orders a marching army to halt (whether he or Lucilius is heading it is not specified); Lucilius (a new character but evidently involved in the march as a leading officer) relays the order; Brutus greets him as (it seems) newly met and enquires after Cassius; Lucilius, having evidently come from Cassius, announces his approach and introduces his emissary Pindarus bringing greetings; and after Pindarus has delivered a vaguely tactful opinion Lucilius himself proves the actual source of information.

Cassius then enters and Brutus soon invites him into his tent, appointing Lucilius, Lucius, and Titinius to ensure their privacy (the latter two having been speechless and remaining so; Titinius, like Lucilius, has not been seen before). From l. 53 onwards the scene becomes the interior of Brutus' tent, and then it needs furniture – probably a table (for the reception of Lucius' '*tapers*' at l. 207.1 and for the wine-drinking) and certainly seats at l. 214 (these might well also be used earlier, during the long scene of dissension).

Various questions arise. If, as in the Folio, Brutus and Lucilius enter together and jointly order their troops to halt, why does Brutus then accost Lucilius as if he is newly met (l. 3)? If he is newly met, has he joined Brutus so recently that Brutus has had no time to greet him and to seek his information (which would, of course, be useless delivered off-stage)? If Lucilius has arrived separately and only at the moment of entry, does Brutus enter with one body of men and order them to halt, Lucilius with another, likewise ordering them to halt, and Cassius later with a third, similarly – which would intolerably strain the players' resources? If Lucilius has come from Cassius, as clearly he has, why bring in Pindarus too, to deliver no more than a discreet platitude? And is the scene laid at Brutus' tent from the outset? If so, what is Brutus doing marching towards it with his men? And does Titinius enter at the beginning, as in the Folio, or with Cassius, as Dover Wilson held?

Some of these questions are unimportant. Where Titinius enters is immaterial; he is only a bystander. Others occur only to the logistically minded, a category which probably did not include Shakespeare or who-ever prepared the Globe's production; they suggest an over-earnestly realistic sense, of the 'How-Many-Children-Had-Lady-Macbeth?' kind. The stage is not a real campaign ground; a stage army is not a real army. A producer may fix things in various effective ways. In fact, the Folio direction works well enough for practical purposes, and no one in the audience will be sceptical. Brutus and Lucilius may in fact enter together in joint command, and then deal with the question of where Cassius is, without causing worry as to how Lucilius, just arrived from Cassius, comes to be jointly leading Brutus' army, or why the hardly necessary Pindarus is escorted not by Lucilius but by the almost unnecessary Titinius, when Lucilius himself can furnish all the information needed. Some of the uncertainty may arise from Shakespeare's initial imprecision about the new supporters of Brutus and Cassius introduced from this point onwards; Lucilius, Titinius, and Pindarus are picked somewhat at random from Plutarch and not yet firmly defined. (See the Commentary at 4.2.50–2.)

But whence does Brutus emerge? Until l. 53 the scene need not actually be his tent, but naturally it will be thought of as in its vicinity, or before it. Hearing the drum, Brutus steps forth and utters his command. Whether he addresses his own troops or Lucilius' is a non-question; Lucilius proves to be one of Brutus' officers and Brutus has every reason to take the initiative in issuing orders. What is harder to envisage on the Globe's stage is how the exterior – or the vicinity – of Brutus' tent became the interior at l. 53, with a table and chairs. To set these behind the traverse of the inner stage would mean playing much of the quarrel scene and its after-math at some distance from the audience, an arrangement which seems unlikely. Did attendants discreetly smuggle the furniture on during the bustle of the departing army at l. 52.1? The modern stage will have the scene at Brutus' tent from the start and can manage the change from exterior to interior easily: how it was effected at the Globe presents an interesting problem.

INDEX

THIS is a selective guide to points in the Introduction and Commentary of more than routine note. Biblical illustrations are grouped together; so are proverbial parallels. Citations from other Shakespeare texts are not listed, nor are those from other works unless their significance is striking. References to the Introduction confine themselves to the main areas of interest. An asterisk indicates that the note supplements information given in *OED*.

Women's Writing 1778–1838

WILLIAM BECKFORD	Vathek
JAMES BOSWELL	Life of Johnson
FRANCES BURNEY	Camilla
	Cecilia
	Evelina
	The Wanderer
LORD CHESTERFIELD	Lord Chesterfield's Letters
JOHN CLELAND	Memoirs of a Woman of Pleasure
DANIEL DEFOE	A Journal of the Plague Year
	Moll Flanders
	Robinson Crusoe
	Roxana
HENRY FIELDING	Joseph Andrews and Shamela
	A Journey from This World to the Next and
	The Journal of a Voyage to Lisbon
	Tom Jones
WILLIAM GODWIN	Caleb Williams
OLIVER GOLDSMITH	The Vicar of Wakefield
MARY HAYS	Memoirs of Emma Courtney
ELIZABETH HAYWOOD	The History of Miss Betsy Thoughtless
ELIZABETH INCHBALD	A Simple Story
SAMUEL JOHNSON	The History of Rasselas
	The Major Works
CHARLOTTE LENNOX	The Female Quixote
MATTHEW LEWIS	Journal of a West India Proprietor
	The Monk
HENRY MACKENZIE	The Man of Feeling
ALEXANDER POPE	Selected Poetry

JANE AUSTEN	**Emma**
	Persuasion
	Pride and Prejudice
	Sense and Sensibility
MRS BEETON	**Book of Household Management**
ANNE BRONTË	**The Tenant of Wildfell Hall**
CHARLOTTE BRONTË	**Jane Eyre**
EMILY BRONTË	**Wuthering Heights**
WILKIE COLLINS	**The Moonstone**
	The Woman in White
JOSEPH CONRAD	**Heart of Darkness and Other Tales**
	Nostromo
CHARLES DARWIN	**The Origin of Species**
CHARLES DICKENS	**Bleak House**
	David Copperfield
	Great Expectations
	Hard Times
GEORGE ELIOT	**Middlemarch**
	The Mill on the Floss
ELIZABETH GASKELL	**Cranford**
THOMAS HARDY	**Jude the Obscure**
	Tess of the d'Urbervilles
WALTER SCOTT	**Ivanhoe**
MARY SHELLEY	**Frankenstein**
ROBERT LOUIS STEVENSON	**Treasure Island**
BRAM STOKER	**Dracula**
WILLIAM MAKEPEACE THACKERAY	**Vanity Fair**
OSCAR WILDE	**The Picture of Dorian Gray**

HONORÉ DE BALZAC	**Père Goriot**
CHARLES BAUDELAIRE	**The Flowers of Evil**
DENIS DIDEROT	**Jacques the Fatalist**
ALEXANDRE DUMAS (PÈRE)	**The Count of Monte Cristo** **The Three Musketeers**
GUSTAVE FLAUBERT	**Madame Bovary**
VICTOR HUGO	**Notre-Dame de Paris**
J.-K. HUYSMANS	**Against Nature**
PIERRE CHODERLOS DE LACLOS	**Les Liaisons dangereuses**
GUY DE MAUPASSANT	**Bel-Ami** **Pierre et Jean**
MOLIÈRE	**Don Juan and Other Plays** **The Misanthrope, Tartuffe, and Other Plays**
JEAN RACINE	**Britannicus, Phaedra, and Athaliah**
ARTHUR RIMBAUD	**Collected Poems**
EDMOND ROSTAND	**Cyrano de Bergerac**
JEAN-JACQUES ROUSSEAU	**Confessions**
MARQUIS DE SADE	**The Misfortunes of Virtue and Other Early Tales**
STENDHAL	**The Red and the Black** **The Charterhouse of Parma**
PAUL VERLAINE	**Selected Poems**
JULES VERNE	**Twenty Thousand Leagues under the Seas**
VOLTAIRE	**Candide and Other Stories**
ÉMILE ZOLA	**L'Assommoir** **La Bête humaine**

Women's Writing 1778–1838

JAMES BOSWELL   **Life of Johnson**

FRANCES BURNEY **Cecilia**
Evelina

JOHN CLELAND **Memoirs of a Woman of Pleasure**

DANIEL DEFOE **A Journal of the Plague Year**
Moll Flanders
Robinson Crusoe

HENRY FIELDING **Joseph Andrews and Shamela**
Tom Jones

WILLIAM GODWIN **Caleb Williams**

OLIVER GOLDSMITH **The Vicar of Wakefield**

ELIZABETH INCHBALD **A Simple Story**

SAMUEL JOHNSON **The History of Rasselas**

ANN RADCLIFFE **The Italian**
The Mysteries of Udolpho

SAMUEL RICHARDSON **Pamela**

TOBIAS SMOLLETT **The Adventures of Roderick Random**
The Expedition of Humphry Clinker

LAURENCE STERNE **The Life and Opinions of Tristram**
Shandy, Gentleman
A Sentimental Journey

JONATHAN SWIFT **Gulliver's Travels**
A Tale of a Tub and Other Works

HORACE WALPOLE **The Castle of Otranto**

MARY WOLLSTONECRAFT **Mary and The Wrongs of Woman**
A Vindication of the Rights of Woman

The
Oxford
World's
Classics
Website

www.worldsclassics.co.uk

- Information about new titles
- Explore the full range of Oxford World's Classics
- Links to other literary sites and the main OUP webpage
- Imaginative competitions, with bookish prizes
- Peruse the Oxford World's Classics Magazine
- Articles by editors
- Extracts from Introductions
- A forum for discussion and feedback on the series
- Special information for teachers and lecturers

www.worldsclassics.co.uk